THE REVELATION
OF GOD

Yves Congar OP

THE REVELATION OF GOD

Translated by A. Manson and L. C. Sheppard

231.74

HERDER AND HERDER

This book together with *Faith and Spiritual Life* was first published as *Les Voies du Dieu Vivant* in 1962 by Les Éditions du Cerf, Paris.

1968
Darton, Longman & Todd Ltd, 64 Chiswick High Road, London W4.
Herder and Herder, 232 Madison Avenue, New York 10016

232 35657 2

Library of Congress Catalog Card Number 68-29093

CONTENTS

PRINCIPAL ABBREVIATIONS

AAS	*Acta Apostolicae Sedis* (Rome, from 1909)
CIC	Codex Iuris Canonici (1918)
CSEL	*Corpus Scriptorum Ecclesiasticorum Latinorum* (Vienna, from 1866)
DACL	*Dictionnaire d'Archéologie chrétienne et de Liturgie*, ed. Cabrol and Leclercq (15 vols., 1907–53)
Denz. Bann.	H. Denziger, *Enchiridion Symbolorum et Definitionum*, etc., 28th edition, after that of C. Bannwart and others, Freiburg, 1952
Dict. Bibl.	*Dictionnaire de la Bible*, ed. Vigouroux (5 vols., 1895–1912)
Dict. Sp.	*Dictionnaire de Spiritualité*, ed. M. Villier and others (from 1937)
DTC	*Dictionnaire de Théologie Catholique*, ed. Vacant, Mangenot and Amann (15 vols., 1903–50)
Doc. cath.	*La Documentation catholique*, Paris
EC	*Enciclopedia Cattolica* (12 vols., 1949–54)
EL	*Ephemerides Liturgicae* (Rome, from 1887)
JTS	*Journal of Theological Studies*
Lay People	Congar, *Lay People in the Church*, London and Westminster, Md., 1957, translated by Donald Attwater
L. Th. K.	*Lexikon für Theologie und Kirche*, ed. Burchberger, (10 vols., 1930–38)
Mansi	J. D. Mansi, *Sacrorum Conciliorum Nova et Amplissima Collectio* (31 vols., Florence, 1759–98)
NRT	*Nouvelle Revue Théologique*
PG	*Patrologia Graeca*, ed. J. P. Migne (162 vols., Paris, 1857–66)
PL	*Patrologia Latina*, ibid. (221 vols., 1844–64)
QLP	*Questions Liturgiques et Paroissiales* (Louvain)
Rech. S.R.	*Recherches de Science Religieuse* (Paris, from 1911)
R. Bibl.	*Revue Biblique* (Paris, from 1892)

RHPR	*Revue d'Histoire et de Philosophie religieuses* (Paris, from 1950)
RSPT	*Revue des Sciences Philosophiques et Théologiques* (Paris, from 1953)
Rev. S.R.	*Revue des Sciences Religieuses* (Strasbourg, from 1925)
RTP	*Revue Théologique et Philosophique*
Sum. Theol.	St Thomas Aquinas, *Summa Theologica*
TWB z. NT	*Theologisches Wörterbuch zum Neuen Testament* (ed. Kittel from 1933)
Vie Int.	*La Vie Intellectuelle*
Vie Sp.	*La Vie Spirituelle*
ZKT	*Zeitschrift für katholische Theologie* (Vienna, from 1947)

PART ONE

The Holy Scriptures

CHAPTER ONE

What can we find in the Scriptures?[1]

'FOR WHATEVER WAS WRITTEN IN FORMER days was written for our instruction that by steadfastness and by the encouragement of the Scriptures we might have hope' (Rm 15:4). This passage is an invitation to read the Scriptures, an invitation that has been made in every age. The early Christian generations were great readers of the Scriptures; they formed the principal element of the first part of the Mass and still today the introit, epistle and gospel come from the same source, not counting the sermon which in former days was essentially a commentary on the Scripture readings. They were also read at home, and many Christians carried a copy of the Gospels around with them. The Church's whole tradition is one of a life lived in close touch with the Scriptures. The Fathers and early theologians were so saturated with them that their writings, St Bernard's for example, are literally held together by quotations from the Bible. Christian families in the past hallowed their evenings, and Sundays in particular, by reading the Scriptures together. I can hardly recommend Restif de la Brétonne as an author, but this generally pornographic author of the mid-eighteenth century, in his book *La Vie de mon Père*, on the history of his family, describes what amounts to the life of a saint. His father, superbly human and Christian, every evening after supper used to gather together his whole family, including the farm labourers and, before reading

[1] A talk given on Radio Luxembourg 14 December 1947; published in *Vie Sp.*, October 1949, pp. 225–31.

three or four chapters of the Scriptures to them, in a phrase that sums up the spirit of family worship, would say: 'We must recollect ourselves, children: the Holy Spirit is about to speak'. Similar evidence is available in more recent times; there is, for example, that other admirable record to be found in the *Mémoires et Récits* by Frédéric Mistral, in which we learn what is the real nature of the poetic gift.

The present period is noteworthy for the genuine biblical renewal that is taking place. On all sides, in almost every country, fresh translations or commentaries are being published. Catholics everywhere are rediscovering the Bible. Small groups and communities gather round to study it, rather in the same way as they meet together in the Eucharist. We shall see later that this relationship is well grounded and traditional. Conferences and books on the Bible, provided they are written in plain language, are now meeting with real success, and this is not just a matter of fashion.

What is happening? What do people seek? What can we find in the Holy Scriptures?

Could it be profound ideas, ideas of the kind we are sure to find in Pascal's *Pensées*? It may be so, but it is to be feared that more often than not we shall be disappointed, either because we find nothing of the kind, but only platitudes or long narratives, or because the idea is buried in a tangle of obscure words that one feels powerless to elucidate, or else, if we do come across something fine, it is foreign to our ideas and presupposes an outlook with which we have nothing in common.

Shall we find in Scripture revelations about an unknown world, secrets about the remote past near the times when things began, about the hidden future, or about wars to come and the end of the world? In a sense this is true; there are such things in Scripture, but not at a level that we can grasp them or at which we expect them. The Bible speaks to us about the origin of things, but not as a scientist would, not on the level of a scientific or historical description: it speaks of it 'from God's point of view', to connect everything with God, and to show the meaning that it all possesses in relation to God. It speaks to us of the future and of the end of the world, but not in order to tell us beforehand what historians will later explain to us with admirable hindsight—the details and the sequence of events, how in fact they occurred. It speaks of them to make us realise that all things exist in a relationship with God, that nothing evades his power, and how, in the end, he will bring all things under his sovereignty and that because his sovereignty is a sovereignty of love, this means that they will be incorporated in the purpose of his grace and goodness.

What we should look for in the Scriptures is an interpretation of things—of all things visible and invisible, an interpretation of human life and history 'from God's point of view'.

In a sense, the Old Testament is a history of the Jewish people, but it is not their history in the way that the *Annals* of Tacitus, for example, are a history of the Roman people. The Old Testament is the history of Israel as the people 'of God', from 'God's point of view'. There are, of course, books that discuss what things are 'in themselves'. If you wish to find out how the earth was made and how it evolved do not turn to the Bible, but to geology or palaeontology. It is not the Bible's purpose to tell us what things are 'in themselves' (that is the domain of the sciences), but what they are, what they become, what man is and what he becomes, 'in their relationship with God and according to the relationship they have with God'.

What the Bible reveals to us, and what we find in it alone, is something we cannot learn from prehistory, history or philosophy; it is God's plan for man. It is a plan that has been in operation from the beginning but whose development is not yet complete.

This plan, with whose unfolding Scripture is filled, follows the progress of the people of God. God's will is to communicate himself to man, to bring man into fellowship with himself, to incorporate man even into the mystery of his own life, that unique life which is one and yet common to three Persons. This is why, on the first page of Genesis, man is described as being made in God's image. This is why in the last page of the last book, the 'Apocalypse' in which the 'revelation' of God's plan is completed, we are shown the wedding feast of the Lamb; the wedding feast, the espousals, that is the realisation of this mystery of one and the same life led by several persons and shared by them. It is that mystery of communion which was proclaimed, prepared and begun by the covenant of the Old Testament, concluded by the ministry of Moses, but promised to Abraham. It was a covenant consummated in the blood of Jesus, the new and final covenant that will have no successor. For when we have received, in the Son of God, the status of the children of God, co-heirs of the Father's patrimony, what more can we want or imagine? We are now definitively established in the realm of the new and final covenant. The seeds have been sown in us, we possess what St Paul calls the pledge. God's plan, as it is revealed to us by the Scriptures, includes a measure of promise; it awaits its final completion. Christian faith, therefore, essentially includes hope. Belief in Jesus Christ meant committing, staking one's life on the words of a man who has promised to make us live an everlasting life and, at the last, to raise us up for an immortal life.

This suggests, perhaps, one of the major difficulties in all the study of Scripture. It is a thickly planted forest in which not only are we in danger of losing ourselves but in which we may not see the wood for the trees. Scripture is the progressive revelation of God's plan for man and the world. The parts only become intelligible when the whole has been understood because they have no meaning if they are not seen as stages or applications of a plan which alone makes the whole process comprehensible. The great difficulty in a real understanding of the Bible springs from the fact that it needs a synthesis at the outset. What we lack are the keys which, revealing to us the meaning of the whole, show us at the same time the meaning of the parts and even of the details.

But it is also true that one of the most certain results of assiduous study of the Scriptures is consolation. The Books of Maccabees bear witness to this as does St Paul, as do the Fathers and every genuine believer. Our own personal experience also bears witness to it. When we read the Scriptures we are no longer alone. We have the unshakable certainty that someone is thinking of us, that someone is seeking us, that someone is by our side. We are encouraged and given new strength, as we should be by the presence of a friend.

Man does not live by bread alone, but by every word that issues from the mouth of God. Scripture, together with the Blessed Sacrament, is the bread of life come down from heaven. And if God, to unite us to himself, acts through the sacraments of the Church, he acts also, and no less effectively, in the sacrament of his Word. And do we not find both in the Mass? In its two parts is it not there precisely that is distributed the fullness of the sacrament of one and the other? In the Scriptures as in the Eucharist we really find the bread of life, that bread on which they must feed who are called to live, beyond this world, an everlasting life.

CHAPTER TWO

The Old Testament as a Witness to Christ[1]

DELACHAUX AND NIESTLÉ, WHO HAVE PUB-
lished a number of works of real value in the sphere of Protestant
theology, have now issued the first volume of a French translation
of an important book.[2] This is a commentary on the writings of the
Old Testament by the Swiss Protestant theologian W. Vischer,
with the title *Das Christuszeugnis des Alten Testaments*, the testimony of the Old Testament about Christ.

I have personally read this commentary in German, in its entirety. I find it remarkable, though I am not of course unaware of
its limitation and defects. Reading it has been of great benefit to
me, spiritually and theologically. Others who have done so will, I
am sure, agree with me. What then did I find in Vischer and what
can we expect from him?

To him I owe a better understanding of the fact that God's purpose, manifested throughout the Bible, follows a law of promise
and fulfilment, of seed ripening, and that it belongs to the realm
of what the Fathers rightly called 'mystery' or 'sacrament'. What
on a final analysis Vischer is seeking in the Old Testament is exactly what the Fathers called the *sacramenta Veteris Testamenti* and
the title of his book might be translated as 'The mystery of Christ
in the Old Testament'. It is not surprising, therefore, that from his
own studies, or from Luther who was a student of the Fathers, he
should find himself in harmony with patristic exegesis, even in

[1] Published in *La Vie Intellectuelle*, October 1949, pp. 335-43.
[2] *La loi ou les cinq livres de Moïse*, Neuchâtel and Paris, 1949.

8

matters of detail. It is certainly no accident that God's workman-
ship, like the Bible itself, moves from a genesis to an apocalypse,
from a seed to the unfolding of everything that was implicit in that
seed. It is the carrying out of a plan and this plan, wholly directed
to Christ as its centre and to our communion with God in Christ
as its conclusion, is what is really expressed by everything which
brings it to our notice and begins to set it in motion, starting with
the creation and continuing throughout the Old Testament. It
is this real meaning that Vischer is seeking; he is well informed,
often illuminating, and he makes use of the most relevant studies.
Later on, I shall add the requisite criticism, but for the moment
the need is to indicate what positions have been regained that pro-
mote a thorough and basically traditional understanding of the
Word of God. These are expressed in a series of admirable phrases.
Vischer has the poetic gift, the gift of perceiving and expressing
penetratingly the meaning and underlying harmony of things.

I am thinking of the idea of *pars pro toto* used with reference to
the choice of Israel, of Abraham and of the Promised Land, and
that will certainly be used later for the idea of the 'Remnant'. It is
bound up with the essential system of promise and fulfilment; the
promise is made first to a single person or to a small group and
afterwards it is extended to all men. I am thinking here of the idea
of 'history as promise', or of the related idea of 'prophecy', applied
in conformity with the divisions of the Jewish Bible, to the Books
of Joshua, Judges, Samuel and Kings. From the biblical point of
view the fulfilment is wholly involved and present in the beginning. Vischer is most illuminating on what the Bible means by the
'fulfilment' of the Law. This does not consist in adding new rules
to old ones, in some fresh and more rigorous obligation, but in
bringing out the unalloyed and total content of what God first intended. This is most important with regard to the meaning of
Scripture and to our understanding of it. We realise in fact that
the promise and the seed of things, their beginning and first statement, only gains their real meaning in their final completion.
This is exactly what the Fathers meant by 'sacrament' or 'mystery'. As an application of this idea Vischer refers to the canticle of
Hannah, Samuel's mother, which, far from explaining the Magni-
ficat to which it is related in literary form, is simply its prefigurement and needs it for its own explanation. But it is really Vischer's

book as a whole, with its main theme running through it, that illustrates this fundamental principle.

Objections may, of course, be raised against this method; some critics have not refrained from describing Vischer's work as poetry and exegetical romance.

I fail to understand how any Doctors in Israel can remain so apart from a Scriptural practice which has in its favour, or at least in favour of the principle upon which it is based, the testimony of almost the entire course of tradition. I can understand still less the animosity that moves some exegetes to attack every symptom of what they call the spiritual or symbolic sense while at the same time to all intents and purposes they bring back under different names[3] the substance of what they have repeatedly assailed in others.

Personally I consider that the customary categories of 'literal sense' and 'spiritual sense' are inadequate to express the special nature of the written Word of God. The Bible is a unique reality and categories that are valid for other writings can only be applied to it analogically. Just as the sacraments cannot be explained by the categories of instrumental cause and sign, or the body of Christ by those of biological or social body, so the Bible, whose primary author is the Holy Spirit, cannot be adequately understood by rules of interpretation exactly similar to those used for ordinary writings. The only adequate authority for the interpretation of the Bible is the tradition of the Church which is a principle of knowledge similar to that which presided over its composition. In my view, for example, the real meaning of the passover lamb in Exodus is Christ in the mystery of his own passover, because this is the meaning originally intended in Exodus by the Holy Spirit. But this meaning can only be perceived by the aid of the kind of knowledge that corresponds to it, and this is the tradition of the Church. It is natural that a Christian and a Jew will not interpret the same text in the same way,[4] nor will a Catholic and a non-

[3] 'Density of the literal sense' (Fr Spicq) 'plenary sense' (J. Coppens, *NRT*, Jan. 1949, especially pp. 30f, 33).

[4] Cf. St Irenaeus, *Adv. Haer*, 4, 26, 1, 'When the law is read by Jews, even in our time, it is like a myth, for they lack the interpretation of any of it. . . . But when it is read by Christians it is the treasure hidden in a field, revealed now and explained by Christ's cross.' Irenaeus was not Origen; he is reacting against the excesses of Gnosticism.

Catholic Christian. As an example we might take Lk 1:28, which we translate as 'full of grace'.

Does this mean that since the Bible is a divine book, no human method of studying documents is relevant to it? Not in the least. First of all, if we consider its composition, it is a collection of human writings, written by men who thought out their work and expressed it in the same way as any author would do. Thus there is in the Bible, considered as a document, an area in which philologists, historians and critics may freely practise their craft. In addition, sacred history, directly concerned with the 'mysteries', did not take place in some lofty clime foreign to this world; it occurred in places and periods which belong to history, in a series of facts which really happened and are fully historical events. Human composition, history, both belong to the very substance of God's intention and his word. It is by no means fortuitous that, in the Bible and in the history of Israel, the texts of the one and the history of the other should acquire their full meaning, *a meaning intended from the outset by God* through their relationship to Christ, to his passion and resurrection and to the everlasting life of all men in him. In like manner, it is not fortuitous that the text of the Bible and this history should in themselves be entirely human— real documents and real history.

Two things follow from this. The first is that it is always possible to treat the Bible as an ordinary document and to regard the history of Israel as a history *like any other*. In one sense this is legitimate, because such in fact is the case. And in this way we can obtain real knowledge about them, valid at its own level and in its own order. But that level and that order are both inadequate in relation to what God really effected in Israel and expressed in the Bible. So the complete meaning both of the document and the history is missed. The second result is that we cannot obtain this complete meaning if we do not study the history and the texts in which it was providentially given. Only in the Apocalypse does the full meaning of Genesis become apparent, only in the Marriage of the Lamb can we really understand what was meant by 'Let us make man in our image'. The messianic ideas of Israel and the song of the Suffering Servant become intelligible only in Jesus. This is illustrated by a profound remark made by Maurice Blondel about tradition: 'It will arrive at Alpha only when it has reached

Omega.' However, under the system of signs and of development by stages in which we live, the Spirit must be perceived within the letter and the content of Omega in the stammering but significant expressions which successively lead up to it from Alpha. This means that in order to grasp the meaning of the Old Testament, which is the mystery of Christ,[5] we cannot dispense with a close literal study of its text, using all the resources of philology, archaeology etc., and an accurate survey of its history, with the same resources, and with an historical method as critical as possible.

Vischer has been blamed for the fact that in his concern to find Christ, his death and resurrection, everywhere, he telescopes the stages of development and the strictly historical aspect of development is, so to say, flattened out or levelled down. It is in fact possible to see Christ (who constitutes their ultimate meaning) in Ex 12 or in David so vividly that the real historical character of these things becomes obscured. Such criticism, which applies only to a limited extent to Vischer, is certainly fully deserved by those forms of allegorical exegesis which entirely ignore history and the literal meaning.[6] On the other hand, biblical scholars who seek the Word of God in its fullness in the Bible, and therefore include the messianic or Christological meaning of the Old Testament, but, *for this very reason*, try to be as serious philologists and historians as possible, search in and through history, in the stages of its real concrete development, for the revelation and therefore for the meaning of God's purpose to which the Bible testifies.

[5] Cf. Lk 24:27; Jn 1:45; 5:46; 1 Cor 10:4 and 11, etc.

[6] It is true that there has not always been sufficient emphasis on the gulf that divides typology from allegory—whatever the terms used. Between the type and the antitype there is a real historical correspondence, related to the event or the institution. Between the allegory and its application the correspondence only exists in certain points arbitrarily selected to represent events or institutions of different kinds. A 'typical' reality presupposes a purposive happening in history which is developed and fulfilled by stages; it is first just mentioned or hinted at, and then becomes more definite and fulfilled; unlike any allegory a 'typical' event is related to the central meaning of the Bible, directed wholly to Christ, to his death and resurrection, to the extension of his passover mystery to all believers so that they may have everlasting life. The allegorical method is a product of the mind, introducing, more or less arbitrarily, accidental relationships with the events, and it is the enemy of real typology which it drags into its own discredit. It is an imaginative product of the human mind that is sometimes justified and sound. Typology allows us to enter into the working of God's plan as this is manifested throughout the Bible.

With an outlook of this kind, the historical stages (and ultimately, including the literary structure, the historical circumstances that determined the vocabulary or the composition of a given book) become the means for understanding God's plan which is centred in Christ and is completed by our everlasting life in him.[7]

No book is faultless. Vischer's is certainly not perfect. In general, it seems to me calculated to help Christians towards an understanding of the inner meaning of the Bible, in a way substantially in conformity with the tradition of the Church which the author, gladly, as I know, has so often rediscovered. It is a Protestant book, and its Protestantism, coloured by Barth, becomes evident here and there: for example, in a somewhat unilateral eschatology in an idea of God and his word that is only relevant to the here and now, in the omission, to some degree, of all communication between God and man, in an emphasis on the dialectic of transcendence to the exclusion of immanence.[8] In my view, these are grave criticisms. A Catholic would have avoided unilateralism of this kind, but quote for me a Catholic commentary which gives me what Vischer has given, which opens to me in this way the understanding of the Bible as the mystery of Christ. The commentary on Genesis by Chaine, interesting and profitable in many respects, falls short on this precise point. In so many spheres it is our lot to have to advance with the help of books whose imperfections compensate each other, to develop only 'dialectically',

---

[7] This is the method followed, for example, by Fr Féret in the biblical conferences he gives either to priests, in the 'Journées sacerdotales de Saint-Jacques', or to the Institut Catholique in Paris, or to the Groupe évangélique.

[8] It would take an article to explain these remarks. Here are two examples which may illustrate what I am trying to say.

  i. The way in which Vischer comments on Gn 1:27: 'Let us make man in our image'. Instead of seeing this as the foundation for the whole process of God's communication with man which fills the Bible and constitutes its unity, he emphasises the aspect of separation, of God's transcendence; not the fact of being *in the image of God*, but that of *being created*.

  ii. With reference to Gn 13 and 15 on the alliance with Abraham, Vischer only develops the theme, in itself true and profound, that what is impossible for man is possible for God; Abraham believed in God's promise beyond all human probability, and Isaac was born through God's power alone. In other words he emphasises what Barth and Kierkegaard would emphasise. He says no word on the aspect of God's gift or God's communication to man.

through successive approaches, in situations one of which contains what the other lacks. A study that is perfect from the philological or historical point of view is lacking in the mystical understanding of things. We are given, for example, an excellent translation of Haggai and Zechariah, and yet the reference to Christ is inadequate precisely where it seems imperative.[9] All we can do, therefore, is to hope for the perfect commentary; to hope, for example, that the 'Jerusalem Bible' now in process of publication by the 'Éditions du Cerf' will one day appear in a volume that will allow more space for the typological and messianic aspect of the Bible which gives it its 'true' meaning.

Perfection is plenitude, and plenitude will not be reached in this world. We can but strive after it.

This summary description of the work of W. Vischer is obviously quite insufficient for any proper treatment of so complex a subject as that of the meaning and the 'senses' of Scripture. It might, however, claim the patronage of the *Doctor communis*. St Thomas, in fact, admitted that 'since the mind of a prophet is an imperfect instrument, even true prophets do not know everything which the Holy Spirit has in view, either through the words they use or the actions they perform' (IIa–IIae, qu. 173, art. 4c). More-

[9] At this point I should like to state more clearly, with examples, my criticism of this great undertaking from which the public, avid for the word of God, rightly expects so much. I am sorry that its authors, e.g. M. Gelin, to whom we owe an excellent book on *Les idées maîtresses de l'A. T.*, seem content to confine themselves, as far as possible, to an immediately historical situation. Antecedents to a text are readily given, but not what these texts foretell. Messianic and Christological implications are thus not clearly revealed.

Examples: Nothing on Hg 2:1–10—so important for the understanding of God's plan. Nothing on the messianic character of the promise to Zerubbabel (Hg 2:20–3). On Zc 3–8 the historical foreground is exclusively considered (Zerubbabel and Joshua son of Jehozadak) and the messianic background neglected; there is one slight note to say that 'seed' is a name for the Messiah, and another, well-balanced but so cautious as to risk being passed unobserved. Nothing on the messianic character of Zc 13:7, not even a reference to Mt 26:31. On 'the house opened to the house of David . . . for sin and for uncleanness' (13:1) references are given to earlier texts (Isaiah and Ezekiel), but not to Jn 7:38 and 4:14. With reference to Zc 12:10, a note says: 'The great anonymous dead person mentioned here, is considered to be the Servant of Yahweh of Isaiah 53'—and that is all.

The 'public' expects something else, or rather that and something else besides; a whole dimension, like that of Vischer's, is lacking.

over, it is possible that what St Thomas said about the literal sense and its uniqueness may have been interpreted too rigidly. I have suggested elsewhere that his *sensus litteralis* might be translated not as 'literal', but as 'literary' sense (cf. *Festgabe J. Lortz*, Wiesbaden 1958, vol. 2, pp. 91f.

The preceding article, written in 1949, contained a criticism of one of the early sections of the Jerusalem Bible which was the work of Fr Albert Gelin. He died prematurely on 7th February 1960. Neither in what I thought, nor in what I wrote, was there any question of his scientific competence, which I greatly respected. My criticism was concerned with some quite definite points in the treatment of the biblical text. Since that time a constant and careful study of the Jerusalem Bible,[10] completed in 1955, has convinced me of its immense value. I have expressed my appreciation in the *Le Mystère du Temple*, Paris, Éditions du Cerf, 1958, pp. 10–11.

[10] English version of the Jerusalem Bible was published in 1966 by Darton, Longman & Todd London, and Doubleday, U.S.A.

CHAPTER THREE

The Bible and the Word of God[1]

THIS SUBJECT IS GOVERNED BY AN HYPOTHESIS which, to the believer, is a basic certainty, that of an action on the part of God to communicate himself to men in order that they might enter into communion with him. On God's part it was the will to draw men into communion with him. I shall consider two themes in sequence: 'The Bible and the Word of God' and 'The Bible or the Word of God and the Church'.

THE BIBLE AND THE WORD OF GOD

The Bible is a book, a document. That book is the Word of God because men have spoken and written from a certain impulse or under a certain inspiration, some divine force, in the way a poet is stirred by the power within him, and this is why the document has God for its author. God is the author of this book. He moved the writer to write this or that, and to do so in this or that way.

I should like to situate what I have to say in the context of a very general idea; things exist in their own nature. Independently of us, the world objectively exists and its content is immensely rich. The products of art, for example, have a distinctive reality. But they speak to us in different ways according to our powers of appreciation. A poem or symphony or a great work of literature has a material nature. We may tackle them with a dictionary or a

---

[1] Shorthand notes of two lectures given in London at the Centre of Our Lady of Walsingham on 20 and 21 October 1956.

grammar which will only give us an understanding of the external reality of a document. There is a story, told by Péguy, of Tharaud's examination for his degree. The examiner gave Tharaud a copy of *Le Bourgeois Gentilhomme* to read, and then said sharply, 'Explain it'. 'There was nothing to explain,' remarks Péguy 'it only had to be read and it explained itself . . .'. A poet draws the words from the depths of his being. Something happens to him. Words acquire shape and he speaks. Péguy himself is a perfect example of this. Music is very similar. Leopold II said, 'Music is the most expensive way of making a noise so far discovered'. A musician would think otherwise. Wherein lies the difference? It is the power of inner perception. The former merely perceives the external nature of things; the latter hears the beat of the spirit of poetry or music which is a living reality. In proportion to my power of poetic or musical appreciation, these things speak to me in a different way.

Whatever the writing, whatever the work of art, there are two ways of approaching it:

1. With the help of the dictionary alone. The result is not negligible; it yields authentic knowledge.

2. With a power of inner perception which means that the spirit of the work of art, of Mozart or Molière, has become a living reality in one's own existence.

These remarks may be literally applied to the Bible. The Bible may be approached in two stages, in two degrees of depth. First, there is the technical approach; that of history, by dictionary methods which in this case are very complicated (Hebrew or Greek, and also the customs of peoples vastly different from ourselves; history; geography also—for things exist in space as well as in time). Secondly, there is the approach made by a man who has within himself the spirit in which the Bible was written. This is a religious quality, and since the Bible was written by the Spirit of God, it can really be approached in depth only by a man who has the Spirit of God living within him.

This means that there are two stages in reading the Bible, two kinds of attention which may be called scientific or literary and religious attention.

1. *Here is a document. What information can the enquiring mind obtain from it?* A Hebrew scholar like Alfred Loisy or Dupont-

Sommer, from this point of view, would have an advantage over an unlearned unbeliever. But a believer cannot consider himself dispensed from this initial approach to the text. What are we faced with? We possess a book, guaranteed by God, for which God is responsible, but written by men whose names we know—or do not know, for many of its contents are anonymous. In civilisation there are a number of things whose author is unknown. Many of those we find most useful bring us into touch with their anonymous creators. Social life always involves a multitude of unknown persons.

In the case of the Bible God is its primary guarantor. The impulse to write it came from the Holy Spirit, but it was actually written by men, known or unknown, not placed between heaven and earth but firmly established on this earth, men of a definite race, born on a definite date, following a definite trade (Amos the herdsman and gatherer of sycamore fruit, belonging to a quite definite period of the eighth century B.C.).

God is the author of the Bible, but considered as a human book, it was written by men. It is something incorporated in the flux of human events; it is a part of history; it has its geography; time and place determine it. This being so, what it records is not intelligible apart from its context. Great things transcend their historical context, and yet the best way of coming into contact with the eternal is not to evade the concrete conditions of our work, but to live with intensity the particular task assigned. It is always the concrete problem that must be faced. This applies equally to great literary or musical works; they form an answer to a concrete problem. When this is become an authentic living experience, the absolute is reached, but within the concrete circumstances.

The composition of the books that form this unique volume extends over thirteen centuries; equal, in French history, from Merovingian to modern times. It is a book written during the course of historical events. This history of Israel was as full of happenings and as difficult as that of any other nation; during its thirteen centuries there were as many wars and as many invasions. Consider a book written during the Merovingian period and another produced in the age of Napoleon. There will be a considerable difference between them. The language will have evolved. In a good translation experts will make this evolution plain. The language of the second part of Isaiah or of Maccabees is not the same as that of Judges. In the former the style is flowing, tinged with emotion, and perhaps more superficial: in the latter it is simpler and more rugged.

Many translations do not express this difference between the books of the Bible. It has been one of the boons of the Jerusalem Bible to give each book its own characteristics, not to make the translation of so early a book as Joshua as limpid as the second part of Isaiah or Maccabees.

All this is a matter of date. It belongs to the historical facts of a certain period.

In addition, the Bible contains every kind of *literary form*, and these differ considerably in nature.

What is meant by 'literary form'? History, as now written, is one of these forms; it gives a photographic account of past events. Another form is that of the *Pensées* of Pascal. There is also the short story, a novel or even the fable. All these constitute literary forms each having its own rules. The rules according to which history, for example, is written are not the same as those for writing a short story.

In the Bible there are historical books that conceive history practically as we do—the Books of Kings and Samuel. They are history based on documents. It also contains other literary forms —the Pentateuch, the Song of Songs, the Psalms. Some are in the form of a story; in these the truth does not lie in the facts described, but in the lesson that emerges, as in La Fontaine's Fables—such as Jonah, Judith, Esther. Critics have shown that the Babylonian setting of Esther is full of imaginary situations which do not correspond with what we learn from authentic documents. The aim of the book is to declare that God will deliver his people. It is a piece of fiction written for the sake of its lesson; God, and no one else, is the deliverer of his people.

The study of the various literary forms provides the answer to almost all the difficulties we encounter in reading the Bible. These are, in fact, often the result of asking for something from a given literary form which its nature does not equip it to give: a short story is not intended to yield historical truth. To take another example: in the Semitic world a 'form' of history existed, very different from ours, which was made up of genealogical trees. History became genealogy; an explanation of a given characteristic is found by attributing it to some ancestor. Genesis culminates in the twelve sons of Jacob and the blessings given them, prophetic blessings that explain the future destiny of the twelve tribes. We may think also of the apocalyptic literary form that has its own metaphorical structure which we have come to understand. If the Apocalypse of St John is analysed it will be found that some of the objects and some of the scenes described in it cannot be reconstructed in the world of fact. It would be impossible to produce a model of the heavenly Jerusalem from the details it provides. We find such metaphors strange, but unless we grasp the literary form the book remains unintelligible.

Not everyone, of course, can make a personal study of such matters. We need books that will explain them, just as we need dictionaries and grammars as helps towards ordinary understanding of a biblical text. It is a very serious difficulty, because our civilisation becomes increasingly alien to that of the ancient world. Ours is a technical civilisation. Even in the Middle Ages symbols were still eloquent. They have no meaning for us, and, in fact, demand an effort and almost a special training if they are to be understood. This constitutes a very grave difficulty with regard to the Bible and also for the liturgy which is permeated with the Bible. Nevertheless, a real understanding of the liturgy is of service to us; like an understanding of ancient monuments such as cathedrals, it introduces us into the ancient world of symbols.

2. *A more inward relationship.* We now come to an attitude of mind and to helps towards understanding that are not grammatical, but religious, to an attitude of the soul. *It is the relationship that results from the soul's search for God and the personal answer which he gives in his Word.*

The first approach to the Bible is from below, with the aid of history, philology and archaeology. This presupposes considerable labour on our part and for which teaching is required.

There is another approach, this time from above, from our inner resources that may be summed up as *seeking for God*. A genuine approach to the Bible from this deeper level requires us to have its spirit within us, to seek God is to be anxious to find him, to obey him and be faithful to him. It means having the same disposition as in prayer—that God's will be done. To seek God is not to wander about aimlessly. In one place only can God be found—in his will and its demands, in that inner willingness to do his will which has its perfect expression in the Lord's Prayer. If God is sought in this way and obeyed, it is he who is the master, not we. We may sincerely pray for this, but if it is to happen our life must be cleansed by suffering, by the cross, by frustration, because so long as we feel safely successful, and 'lead our own lives', we are asserting ourselves. We have to be reduced to nothingness in order that we may become really obedient to God. Léon Bloy remarks, 'There are spaces in our poor heart which do not yet exist; it needs suffering for them to come into being.' I consider that this is also true: the attitude of obedience to God only comes into existence when we have experienced the cross in one form or another. This is the existentialist theme of Kierkegaard: 'Faith consists in a deepening of existence'. By following this direction we spark off a light within ourselves. This is a fact, and a fact of personal experience, moments in prayer when the mind sees a light, when we perceive the object in its integrity and depth, with a profounder vision than that of many philosophers. It is a light of this kind which enables us to read the Bible with fresh and deeper understanding. When we approach it in this way its text seems to be lit up from within. I have often met simple and unlearned persons who threw a light upon some biblical character or some passage, an application that was exactly right, with the irresistible force of an utterance that issues from the depths of life, from a certain quality of existence.

In the initial approach to the Bible with the help of a grammar—I am not speaking disparagingly as it is most necessary and useful—the word of God confronted me as something external to myself. I tried to illuminate it with the beams of biblical grammar, but it remained an external reality. I knew it as I might know Mozart or Molière when I try to understand them simply by means of literary or musical techniques.

But when I approach the Bible with the inner resources of a profound Christian awareness, the word of God no longer confronts me as an object to be analysed and dissected. It is a living arrow that pierces my heart. This expression is, in fact, scriptural: the world of God is a sharp sword which penetrates to the joints and the marrow. It overthrows routine and persists in asking uncomfortable questions. It is a flame, a flame that consumes, with an urgent living warmth. The word of God thus ceases to be an object, *a thing*. I see it as something alive, a person, drawing me to it with the force of a living being. It utters a word to me personally, not as an echo from the past, but as a voice speaking now. I do not say that this always happens, but when the Bible is read with prayerful reverence I am quite sure that it happens on occasion. From time to time I encounter words in the Bible which I do not simply *read*, but which *speak* to me. They well up within me with the force of living speech. They 'come' to me, sustain me and are wholly satisfying. The experience is what St John of the Cross calls a 'substantial word', that is, not merely something addressed to my ears, but a life-containing cord, a word that brings with it the reality it expresses. All of us have experienced during prayer, especially in times of trial, a kind of inner assurance which fills the mind with peaceful strength and certainty. In St Paul's life there were those difficulties which he calls the sting of the flesh, a phrase whose meaning will always be debatable. When he murmured and asked God to deliver him from it, God replied, 'My grace is sufficient for thee, for strength is made perfect in weakness.' The words: 'My grace is sufficient for thee', as used by St Paul, express not only something he inwardly heard and understood, but also a living 'substantial' word, making what they say really exist. The moment he felt the impact of the words: 'My grace is sufficient for thee, I love thee as thou art', he knew they were true, that the strength of that grace within him really was enough. Another example: we read in the Bible that God said to Abraham, 'Walk in my presence and be perfect.' This remark was not a mere edict; it was an experience that produced the power to walk in God's presence, an energising gladness that made it possible.

We experience the same sort of thing in our own lives.

Another example: St Margaret Mary endured great interior trials, doubting everything. Her physical condition was probably responsible for this. Then she heard our Lord saying to her, 'A child that is loved as I love thee cannot perish.' This gave her an inner certainty, a kind of joy, a light which, though not removing the difficulty, made it completely insignificant. The difficulty remained but it was transcended.

Reading the Scriptures with reverence, seeking God in them, being willing to obey him, from time to time we come across words that we do not only read, but which speak to us. A phrase kindles into burning life and pervades our whole being with its reality.

When we read the Bible, therefore, there is this second degree of depth to be reached; we have to discover a word that is addressed personally to us. One phrase can give meaning to a whole life. At a given moment a word is spoken, a real Word of God. The Bible now confronts me as something actually speaking to me. This is not just a matter of feeling. There is, of course, the danger that we may mistake our own impressions for divine visitations. All great things can be faked; doctors report that they meet with stigmatics in their clinics. Nevertheless, authentically great things do exist. The criterion is the general quality of life, a quality that depends upon humility, obedience, a willingness to accept the cross, a genuine search for God, an attempt to discover his will.

These two stages in the reading of the Bible are not contradictory. The ideal would be to assemble into a unity our knowledge of the biblical environment, a good translation, an explanation of the literary forms and of the human situations in which the books were written, and to ensure reverential reading, and, if possible, to check one stage by the other.

THE BIBLE AS THE WORD OF GOD AND THE CHURCH

The problem of the relationship between the Bible and the Church is frequently discussed in countries where the tradition is mainly Protestant. It came to a head as the result of the Reformation. It was often put in the form: 'Is the Church founded on the Bible, or is the Bible founded on the Church?' 'Is the Church to be judged by the Bible, or does the Church judge the Bible?'

Protestants assert, 'It is the Church that is founded on the Bible, therefore it is the Bible that judges the Church. It is the word of God that judges the Church.' French Calvinists are particularly anxious to reduce the whole problem to these terms. The Church is judged by the word of God, that is by the written text of the Bible.

It was thus that the question was set out in the sixteenth century.

But it is precisely this way of putting it that we cannot accept. Sometimes one simply has to say: you have not asked the right question. In this matter there are two incorrect ways of putting the question; the first is the Protestant way; the second is the one which the Protestants attribute to us, though we are not obliged to accept it. This latter position has an historical explanation, and it is interesting to note how it arose. It originated quite naturally, in the fourteenth and fifteen centuries, for two reasons:

1. During the Middle Ages there was an immense increase in the authority of the Church. By that I mean the authority of the hierarchy, papal authority of a judicial kind. It was the period when canon law took possession of the life of the Church; the popes were the canon lawyers. As ecclesiastical authority grew, even Catholic theologians sometimes asserted that the authority of the Church is superior to that of Scripture. The consequence was that the Reformers, Calvin for example, were the victims of a mis-statement of the problem by those Catholic theologians of the fourteenth and fifteenth centuries.

2. It is an important fact that it was only in the fourteenth century that the problem could have been expressed in these terms: this was due to the invention of the printing press and to the widespread diffusion of copies of the Bible. In earlier periods when the Bible was a rarity and costly (it was as expensive as a horse), it was a luxury. Also, most people could not read, and for the laity, the question of reading the Bible hardly arose. The laity gained contact with the word of God through the Church, through preaching, through the statues of the cathedrals, through all the activities of a Christian society itself permeated by the Bible. During this period the question did not arise. The Bible as a book was not available. When culture developed among the laity (the end of the twelfth, thirteenth and fourteenth centuries) a literate middle class came into being, with an enquiring mind. Secular civilisation was beginning. By the end of the fifteenth century a great number could read. Books became more accessible and cost less than manuscripts. Laymen began to read and study the Bible. They did so somewhat apart from the clergy and inevitably in a critical spirit. This led the Church to intervene and to forbid the reading of Scripture by the

laity. Every time a heretical movement, based on the Bible, sprang up, the Church erected fresh barricades. (Cf. an historical account of this in *Laypeople in the Church*.) Thus, threatened by the Reformation, ecclesiastical authority declared: 'I forbid you to read the Bible, except under the following conditions.' As always these conditions were swept away by life. Gradually this attitude was relaxed and a position was reached when, with certain precautions, by requiring Catholic editions with explanatory notes, the reading of the Bible was not only allowed, but positively encouraged.

To return to the position taken up by the Reformers: it is unacceptable. It was the result of a doctrine which may be schematised in this way:

God   the Scriptures   Each individual believer   the Church

The Church is constituted by believers, and these are simply individuals gathered together in obedience to the word of God which each has heard or read. This is the logic of congregationalism. The doctrine attributed to us by the Reformers could be schematised in this way:

God   the Church (hierarchy)   Scripture

In fact, however, this direct line of dependency, God, the Church, Scripture, does not express the truth. God is over all, and there are what may be called two equal and complementary emanations from him: his Word and the Church. In short we have this scheme:

God
Scripture   the Church

It is this position that I shall try to explain in the two following propositions: (1) The Bible cannot do without the Church. (2) The Church cannot do without the Bible.

1. *The Bible cannot do without the Church*

a. Without the Church it would not exist—*as a Bible*.

b. Without the Church it could not be authentically understood as the word of God.

B

(a) The word 'Bible' is deceptive. We can buy it in a bookshop in one volume, like a novel or dictionary, and this deceives us into thinking of it as a single work existing within the boundaries imposed by its subject matter. This is not so. What, in fact, is the structure of the Bible? It is composed of forty-six different writings that make up the Old Testament, and twenty-seven that make up the New. Why should it contain these books and not others? And on what principle were other seemingly relevant works excluded?

For many other Jewish or Christian religious works exist: we call them the apocrypha. More of them have been discovered at Qumrân. Why have such works not been included in 'the Bible'?

A selection was made, a number of these writings were declared to be 'inspired'; others, even though deeply religious, like Pascal's *Pensées* or the *Imitation of Christ*, have been declared by the Church not to be inspired, at least not in the dogmatic sense of 'inspiration'. In the New Testament we find the writings of the apostles. But other Christian writings were in existence, composed even before the death of the apostles. There is the epistle of Clement, written before St John's gospel, and while St John was still alive, but it is not included in the New Testament. Choice has intervened: a collection was formed out of the works then in existence, and only those selected were declared to be inspired by God.

Who made this choice and how was it made? The first stage occurred in the Synagogue before Christ came. Certain books were accepted for reading in the Synagogue; its worship consisted of the reading of a passage, a commentary on it, together with chants and psalms. It is recorded that Jesus unfolded the roll of the Book of Isaiah and read a passage from it. In the period before Christ the people of God had recognised certain books as inspired by God and therefore able to sustain them with his word. What amounted to a normative list was formed, a canon of Scripture comprising the books of the Old Testament. When St Paul says, 'It is written . . .', he is always referring to some book of the Old Testament that formed a part of the canon of Scripture used in the Synagogue.

The Church took over this canon which the Synagogue, that is, the people of God under the Old Covenant, had selected. But she was confronted also by a Christian literature, and this included not only St Paul's letters and the apostolic writings which are our present gospels, but other works also; for example, what are called the gospels of the Infancy that supply detailed information about the childhood of Jesus in which miraculous features abound; The *Gospel of Nicodemus*, the complete text of which was recently discovered in Abyssinia, that describes all the circumstances of our Lord's burial; or, again, the *Gospel of Peter* or *Thomas*. Many such exist, and others may yet be found. Why did the Church not include them in the canon? The constant factor is the ability of the people of God to perceive that certain books can provide sustenance for their life as that people, and therefore to decide what books shall be used in its public worship. At first, indeed, there was some uncertainty. Some books, for example, the Apocalypse of St John, were rejected by certain local churches. Some early Christian writings, like *The Shepherd of Hermas* were used for a time in worship and later rejected. Such uncertainty did not last for long. Towards the end of the third century a position was reached which for all intents and purposes corresponds to our present canon of Scripture.

There are two points to note:

(i) This recognition was made instinctively, under God's guidance, by the people of God, the body of believers in union with their pastors.

(ii) There were, however, some interventions on the part of authority. The first that we have information about are Roman: the *Canon of Muratori*, dating from the middle of the second century; it is a Roman list that includes one or two books that were later dropped; and then the Gelasianum or decree of Pope Gelasius (end of the fifth century) which in reality goes back to the Roman council of 382. The important thing to remember is that there were two factors at work: firstly, an activity on the part of the Church as a whole, and secondly, hierarchical decisions made from time to time, the authority being in actual fact the pastor of the Church of Rome.

The word 'Church' is the key word here. In modern writing the word is most often equated with the hierarchy. There is truth in this; the hierarchy is a principal part of the Church, but it is not the whole Church. How often we come across a question and answer like the following: What view should we take of the theory of polygenesis? *Answer*: The Church has come to no decision about it, and that means that no decree has been issued from Rome.

But the Church is also you and I. We are the Church. Pius XII said to the laity, 'You are the Church'. England is not simply the government and the bureaucracy, it is all Englishmen. Similarly the Church does not mean the bishops only, but all Christians who belong to the Body of Jesus Christ. The Church is the world of the baptised of all believers who are quickened by the spirit of God.

The Church is an *organic* body. It is an organism whose members have different functions. A heap of severed branches does not form a tree; a tree consists of wood 'organised' into a tree. A body does not consist simply of a given quantity of chemicals, not even if these are endowed with life: it is constructed according to a definite order, with arms, legs, head, stature, eyes, ears and containing a nervous system, loins, lungs, etc. In a body, the whole, every part of it, is alive. But each part has a life that befits its function; some are more essential than others. If I lose a foot I can still go on living, but not if my head is cut off. In the same way, the Church is an organic living body, with different functions. All believers are endowed with a life that enables them to live as Christians, but there are functions whose purpose is to direct and lead them, to decide, when controversies arise, what is the meaning of the word of God. This is the work of the magisterium.

'Unity without multitude is tyranny: multitude without unity is anarchy'[2] A body is neither tyranny or anarchy. The same is true of the Church. And this explains why we can see the recognition of the inspired writings taking place in the Church, quickened in its entirety by the Spirit of God, the same spirit who 'spoke through the prophets' and inspired the apostles. But within this Church a teaching authority exists, aided by God, whose function is to 'define', and so construct a normative law.

We have, therefore, the answer to our question (who made the selection?) and this answer also tells us how it is that apart from the Church no 'Bible' exists, because there is no means of differentiating between the *Ascension of Moses* and Genesis, or between

[2] The exact quotation is: 'Multitude which does not reduce to unity is confusion; unity which does not depend on multitude is tyranny'.

St Mark and the apocryphal *Gospel of Nicodemus*. The Bible, as Bible, exists only in the Church.

(b) *The Bible, if it is to be authentically understood as the word of God, needs the Church.* This is true in two ways that correspond to the distinction (not separation!) that we made between the aspects of the Church as a living body and as an hierarchical power of discernment.

The Bible can only be understood in communion with this body as a whole. Scripture is intelligible only in communion with the vast fellowship of those living from the life of God, in continuity and communion with everything God has given in order to make himself known.

We will begin with Jn 14:11–13, a part of the passage assigned for our meditation today. The Father is first mentioned. He is in heaven, and heaven is what transcends this world. He is mysterious and absolutely first author of all things; he remains hidden, like a spring of water. The spring is hidden. But he has made himself known through the Son and in the Son. So Ignatius of Antioch remarks, 'There is only one God, the Father, manifested by Jesus Christ his Son who is his Word come forth out of silence', and St Paul speaks of the 'gospel and preaching of Jesus Christ, according to the revelation of the mystery which kept secret for long ages, but is now disclosed' (Rm 16:25–6). The Father, then, is hidden, like a spring, like silence, but made known in Jesus Christ and through him: 'Philip, who has seen me has seen the Father. . . .' But how is Jesus Christ to be known? There is only one way of getting to know the Father, and that is to reach him through the Son. There is only one way of getting to know Jesus Christ, and that is to reach him through the apostolic testimony. (On this cf. Fr Féret *Connaissance chrétienne de Dieu*, Éditions du Cerf, Paris). But I shall study not only the apostles but also all those in whom the Holy Spirit has worked and who have been living members of Jesus Christ. Only the Body of Jesus Christ in its totality understands the word of God. The only power that can adequately and accurately understand God's gift is the whole Church, quickened by the Spirit of God. It is through communion in the knowledge of these Christians that I shall enrich my knowledge of Jesus Christ, and therefore, of the Father: in communion with

St Augustine, the Fathers, St Thomas. Gradually, through this mighty fellowship we learn to know Jesus Christ. In communion with the apostles and the Fathers of the Church, all of whom were saints (intellectual geniuses, but geniuses of holiness also) we come to know the meaning of the gospel, and hence of Jesus Christ, and hence of the Father.

If now I consider the Church in its more restricted sense as a hierarchy, I am dealing with the authority of the bishops in union with the pope (that is, the teaching Church). As a body, they are assisted by the Holy Spirit to guard the deposit of faith throughout its history and development. The hierarchy does not pass judgement on the deposit received from the apostles: it is subject to it. But it does pass judgement on human interpretations of it. May I here quote St Francis de Sales: 'It is not Scripture that requires to be regulated or lit up from outside, as Beza thinks we hold. It is the glosses that we make, the conclusions we draw, the way we understand and interpret it; our conjectures and interpretations, and similar adventures of man's brain that will not stay quiet, but is always undertaking fresh discoveries. Still less do we desire a judge between God and ourselves, as his letter would seem to infer; it is between a man such as Calvin, Beza, Luther and another such as Echius, Fisher and More; for we do not enquire whether God understands the Scriptures better than we do, but whether Calvin understands them better than St Augustine or St Cyprian (Controv., part III, Chap. III, art. i).

In reality the Church does not pass judgement on the Scriptures; she is not above them. But the Church, quickened by God's Spirit, does judge of the way believers understand and interpret them. She has within her the same Spirit as the writers of the Scriptures had. She is no stranger to the Scriptures. The Church and the Scriptures are like two children of the same parents; twins both issued from that Spirit of God who lives in the Church.

2. *The Church cannot do without the Bible*

The Church cannot do without the Bible. In a sense, she could. There was a time when the Church was integrally constituted and yet the Bible had not come into existence. Before the first pages of the New Testament were written the Church existed. Jesus himself wrote nothing and the Church was perfect. She existed for twenty or thirty years without any of the books of the New Testament and for sixty more years before it was completed. This shows that she can exist without the Bible and that the Protestant position is invalid. The 'rule of faith' is not the written text as such; it is that which the apostles delivered. Tradition: what the apostles bequeathed and handed on, the deposit, the treasure, the inheritance, which was completely constituted when the apostle St John died, and which is enough for the Church to live on until the end. The Church lives from this tradition, and she could exist without written documents.

But the divine economy of salvation does, in fact, include such writings. The Bible has been given to us all, not to be buried but as the source of life. God's Providence includes a written work of God, the Bible, the Old and New Testaments. All we have to do is to show reverence for this plan, to respect this work of God's will and to try to understand its meaning.

Why did God provide a normative text, the Bible? Imagine, for a moment, that it did not exist. Strictly speaking, the Church could exist, but as time went on things would become problematic and doubtful. We might wonder whether what was transmitted to us really did conform to the original. The function of Scripture is to provide a standard of God's thought to which we can refer in order to see what is in conformity with apostolic thought. With the Bible we have always an element of reference, a standard measure to which we can refer in order to verify whether the word is in genuine conformity with the original deposit. In fact without it we could not prove to heretics that the word of the Church is in conformity with the gospels. Without it our minds would have some measure of doubt.

In order to consolidate your thoughts I should like to conclude with a brief sketch of the relations between Scripture, the written word of God, and Tradition.

It is not an easy problem partly because the word 'tradition' includes several things which need to be distinguished. We must distinguish between the formation of the deposit of revealed truths which was completed at the death of the last apostle, and the understanding of that deposit progressively acquired by the Church, quickened by the Spirit, during the course of time.

The Catholic position is that the deposit which forms the inheritance received by the Church from the apostles, and which provides her endless source of life, is not formed from the *text* of the Bible alone; it also involves a certain number of non-written traditions. But when we try to find out exactly what these traditions are, we are faced with very few points indeed. Examples quoted are: the institution of Sunday as the Lord's day; the baptism of newly-born infants; the rite of mingling a little water with the eucharistic wine. There are very few of them.[3] Observe that when the pope declared the Assumption of Mary to be dogma he did not say that this was a non-written tradition, orally transmitted. It was the result of the Christian mind, gradually becoming aware of the real content of revelation.

Indeed, there has been a gradual unfolding of the content of what the People of God received from him, as the source of their life. Often it is this which is meant by Tradition. For my part, I prefer to speak of 'non-written traditions' (with a small t and in the plural) when referring to what I have described, and to reserve the name Tradition (in the singular and with a capital T) for the living transmission, the explanatory conservation of the original treasure (of. Jn 14:26; 16:12–14).

Protestants would follow us thus far only with some reserve. At least they would put an exclusive emphasis on the fact that this Tradition is entirely relative to the apostolic text, which provides the only norm. Among Protestants the tendency is always—clearly evident in the works of Oscar Cullman—to sever the history of the Church from its divine origins. They are not sympathetic to the idea of the incarnation's being continued. They also tend to regard the initial divine deposit, the treasure from which the Church must live, exclusively as a document. The truth is, however, that what was given to the Church for her sustenance, was not so much a document as the actual substance of the realities of the Christian life. Consider, for example, the Eucharist: it really is not just a matter of a few verses (hardly more than twenty to thirty) that mention it in the different books of the New Testament: it is the real existence of the Eucharist, its celebration from the time of that Upper Room through the period recorded in the Acts and on to the Mass we know. Dwell for a few moments on this fact:

[3] On this see my book, *La Tradition et les traditions*, I. *Essai historique* (Paris, Fayard), 1960. (Eng. trans.)

you will see how the Church, *through living the eucharistic mystery*, whose *reality* has never ceased to be present and active in her, vivifying and intimate, may understand more than what may ultimately result from an exegetical study of the text. And similarly with other matters, the Blessed Virgin Mary, the priesthood, monastic life, and so on.

What position does the Bible hold with respect to Tradition understood in this way? It is a question of non-written traditions, at the same level as the constitution of the deposit of revelation, we should say that Scripture and the traditions are distinct. And yet Scripture and the traditions together form the deposit transmitted to the Church as the source of her life; and certainly nothing prevents our saying that in this deposit the Bible holds the first, by far the first, place. If we understand Tradition in its secondary sense, that is, the living transmission and gradual penetration of the deposit, then Scripture is its richest resource. Tradition and Scripture should never be set up against each other. Scripture forms the major part of what the Church transmits, and from which she lives by assimilating its content. We have seen that it is not possible to understand it completely and authentically unless it is received in and from that Tradition.

CHAPTER FOUR

The Bible, the Book of Reconciliation among Christians?[1]

YOU ARE AWARE THAT A TEXT MAY ACQUIRE A different meaning according to the punctuation given to it. This is a fact of interest for your own biblical studies, for if we knew the intonation which Jesus gave to some of his sayings we might be able to translate them differently. For example, the well-known words at the marriage at Cana: 'My hour is not yet come', might be punctuated and translated thus: 'Has my hour not come?'

Similarly, the title of this chapter could be an affirmation: The Bible (*is*) the book of reconciliation among Christians. Actually, I have put a question mark: Is it, in fact, that book?

Certainly the Bible is meant to be such a book, a book that makes for unity. Historically, however, we find that in the sixteenth century it was on the interpretation of the Bible that Christians came to be divided. The Reformers had received the Bible from the Church of the Middle Ages, but they interpreted it differently. Thus the facts indicate two aspects with which I shall deal successively in my conference this evening.

We can begin by accepting the fact that the Bible *is* the book of reconciliation among Christians, and that it contains an astonishing power to achieve this. Then we shall note that it is also the book that divides, and we shall make an effort to understand what

[1] Notes taken at a conference given during a 'Semaine Biblique' at Montpellier, 3 November 1960.

34

was at stake, what really was the difficulty that came between the Reformers and ourselves concerning this book. Finally, I think I can show you that factors now exist which will enable this difficulty to be overcome. We shall thus conclude in hope.

I am fully aware of the delicate nature of what I am to say to you tonight, especially because I am speaking not just anywhere in France, but *here*, in Montpellier, and am not evading the problematic aspect of this subject, and, ultimately, the encounter between Protestants and Catholics which it must involve. I hope that what governs my words will be what has governed my life; it is much more pleasant to be honest than diplomatic, and much easier. I trust that what I shall say tonight will be earnestly and completely honest.

I should like to say that for me this conference is more than a conference, it is a kind of celebration, a religious act, and if I might do so without presumption, I would apply to myself the words of the Lord Jesus, 'With desire have I desired to eat this Passover with you'. This gentle and profound saying is the perfect expression of that kind of nostalgia which animates every worker for Christian union, every ecumenical Christian, Catholic or Protestant—the nostalgia to eat the Lord's Passover together, to form one family.

We cannot celebrate the Lord's Supper together. But although we may not take part in the Eucharist together, we can share a Passover of sincerity and truth—to adopt a phrase of St Paul—for the bread of life (according to Jn 6) has itself two forms: there is the supreme, sacramental form, the Eucharist, but there is also the preliminary or preparatory way of sharing the bread of life in the form of the word of God and of faith. If we begin with a unity of mind and heart in the sphere of truth, in the sphere of the word and of the act of faith, in the realm of the Bible, we have already taken a decisive step and, if God wills, may be making ready for the celebration of the Lord's Supper in common.

The first thing to note is the immense, positive contribution made by the present position of biblical studies. We live in a period when the 'grace' of the Bible is being truly diffused. We are also living in a time of ecumenical 'grace'. I am certain that when, about the year 2000, historians write the history of the present period, they will say that, as regards religion, the twentieth century was the century of the ecumenical movement, and that this great movement irresistible as a tide, and, like a tide, denoting the all compelling influence of a planet, that is the Holy Spirit. They will say that this movement in which Christians sought to come together again in the visible body of Christ, a movement quickened by the Spirit of God, was the specific Christian reality of the twentieth century. At the same time they will also record the beginning, the early stages, the growth, and expansion of a powerful biblical movement, particularly in the Catholic Church. The Bible has again begun to draw men. It is often possible to speak about the Bible to audiences for whom an ordinary mission would no longer appeal. The Bible draws men. This is apparent also in the material fact of the publication and the success of works on the Bible. Publishers are very conscious of this; even non-Christian publishers are anxious to have a translation of the Bible. It has become financially worthwhile.

If you agree, we will keep to France. Other countries show similar results, but if we confine ourselves to France and to the Catholic Church, then, in the last ten years we have had four French Catholic translations of the Bible:

1. The old translation by Crampon, now revised.
2. The Bible entitled 'The Bible of Cardinal Liénart'.
3. The Maredsous Bible.
4. And lastly, the Bible de Jérusalem.

The Bible de Jérusalem is the most accomplished of them all. It has been isued in four or even five different forms: the books of the Bible have been published separately; as a single large volume; in pocket form; in the 'édition du Club Français du Livre'; and lastly in a *de luxe* edition. Now if of these five editions I select only the pocket form, I was told only yesterday that 250,000 copies have been sold. We may estimate, therefore, that more than a million copies of a complete French translation of Holy Scripture have in the course of a few years been purchased by the public. This is not only a monumental literary and even commercial fact; it is also a spiritual fact, and I would call it, in the strict sense, a pastoral fact of the greatest importance. For believers who read their Bible ask their priests questions which their parents, forty years previously, would not have asked the clergy of their day: they ask for information, explanation and a sound initiation; they ask that the forms of worship shall be determined by the Bible. Among student bodies and in many parishes there is a new way of singing the Psalms which is changing the religious mentality of a whole generation. It is clear that these men who sing glory 'to God who is, who was, and who is to come', are in process of acquiring a kind of Christian manhood, a quality marking them as religious men which differs considerably from that of men who were brought up in the 'devotions' that were formerly so predominant.

This fact particularly impresses me because I have made some personal study of it. I began by studying the matter in *Les origines de la France contemporaire*, by Taine; I followed it up by a personal enquiry. I was deeply impressed by the fact that Catholic France in the seventeenth and eighteenth centuries was genuinedly biblical. The Bible was read in family prayers. But in the nineteenth century, when France was endeavouring to revive her religious fervour after the torment of the Revolution and the wars of the empire, devotions were the central interest: pilgrimages, devotions to the Sacred Heart, the Holy Family, our Lady. Preaching, the pastoral ministry, was profoundly affected in the same way.

I believe that now, in our civilisation, which has other difficulties than those of the nineteenth century, when a superhuman effort is demanded from the priesthood, we are beginning to bring answers drawn from much deeper sources. Whenever we return to Scripture we get the feeling that we are drinking from the headwater. The experience is like that of a man who in mid-summer crosses a desert. He becomes dehydrated. Not only his throat, but his whole body is thirsty. And then he finds water. . . . At this moment we are rediscovering the Source.

I have described the impressive literary fact. I might also mention the substantial change, the substantial improvement of biblical teaching in the seminaries that has taken place during the past fifteen or twenty years as the result of the formation of competent instructors. In short, among Catholics, there is now, unquestionably, a full-scale biblical renewal.

Among Protestants this renewal did not require to be so striking because during the nineteenth century, especially in Germany,

Protestants had published a very great number of biblical studies. A remark by Péguy is to the point, 'A Catholic is a man who has read from the time of his grandfather, a Protestant for three hundred years, a Jew for two thousand. . . .' It is, however, also true that these same Protestants—chiefly in Germany—spread abroad numerous errors and aberrations. The Bible was not only studied, it was dissected, destructively criticised, and its content often reduced to thin air. It was at this time when so much was being made doubtful, that the Catholic Church firmly sustained the truths which she knew were certain, and by doing so she saved for *all* Christians, Protestants included, the essential affirmations of the apostolic faith.

That period is over, and we have now entered an era in which, on the whole, Protestant exegetes produce commentaries of the greatest significance from which we ourselves derive immense benefit, while they in turn are reading ours. Today, among biblical students and specialists there is not only an interchange of views but a kind of intellectual republic is being steadily created, within which a consensus, an agreement as to results, already substantially deep and broad, is being established and developed. Protestant exegesis, formerly very disturbing to us has now become, with few exceptions, soundly balanced.

We are indeed beginning to eat the same bread and to eat it at the same table with the same ceremonies.

Scripture cannot be approached, that word of God cannot be heard without a Christian reality coming into existence among us.

Allow me to read you some words of Luther; they were written in 1539: 'The word of God cannot exist without a people of God, nor can there be a people of God without the word of God. Who apart from God's people would preach it, or listen to it?'[2]

The word of God creates belief and belief is the initial Christian activity, the initial common element that can weld together a community of believers, a parish, a group of Christians. It is the word of God which creates the people of God. That it does so becomes evident if we consider the inspired history of the origins of the Church. The Acts of the Apostles are a kind of exemplar, an abiding 'type' which the Church in every age must imitate if it is to

[2] *Von Konziliis und Kirchen*, Weimar, 50, 629.

remain authentic. In the Acts the progress of the word is parallel with, and equivalent to, the progress of the Church; or, inversely, the progress of the Church is parallel with, and equivalent to, the progress of the word.[3]

God's people are formed by God's word. This was clearly understood by Diocletian, the persecutor of the Church; he commanded Christians to hand over not only the sacred vessels, but also the Holy Scriptures (A.D. 303).

I might also quote the opinions of the Fathers,[4] and of the theologians and ecclesiastics of the Middle Ages. Medieval Christians attached great importance to the word of God as the means of presenting to believers the unique reality of Jesus Christ. Many of them in fact went so far as to say, 'Preach in any country for thirty years, without celebrating Mass, and you will still have Christians: but if you are content with celebrating Mass and never preach, you will have none'.[5]

The word of God brings into existence a people of God. Therefore if we separated Christians, Protestants and Catholics, are in process of mutual sustenance, in a more active and novel way, from the word of God, it is probable that this word, to the extent in which it is received unanimously, will tend to raise up a unanimous people and so pave the way for that reconciliation between Christians, that rediscovery, which must be achieved in time. Instead of being the enemies we thought we were, we are in reality, brothers; we have the same Lord, we are called to eat the same bread, to bear the same witness. I therefore consider that the fact that Holy Scripture is coming to be read in communities that are otherwise separated in a spirit of increasing agreement without imposed uniformity, of harmony without spineless tolerance, provides a pointer and effects a move towards that other great project of God's Spirit, the coming together and perhaps one day the reunion of the Christian people.

The Bible is our book of reconciliation because for us it is the book whose authority cannot be questioned. All of us want to obey the word of God. And the present movement of biblical re-

---

[3] Ac 6:7 (with the note in the *Bible de Jérusalem*), 12, 24, etc.

[4] St Augustine, 'Praedicaverunt (Apostoli) verbum veritatis et genuerunt ecclesias' (*En. in Ps*, 44:23; *PL*, 36, 508).

[5] E.g. Humbert of Romans, St Bernardine of Siena, John Eck, etc.

discovery or renewal which we are witnessing is extremely encouraging and fills us with hope.

Nevertheless I ended my title with a question mark, because a problem does exist and a difficult one. So that I may discuss it frankly I will begin by reading you a few lines of one of my Orthodox friends: Paul Evdokimov: 'Catholics, Protestants and Orthodox are all gathered round the Bible. The Bible when shut, unites us; as soon as we open its pages, the open Bible divides us. We read it differently; we find different truths in it.'[6]

The Bible reverenced from afar undoubtedly unites us, but the Bible opened and read, the Bible interpreted, divides us, for we do not read it in the same way. What is the reason for this? Is there one Bible that is Protestant and another that is Catholic? Must it not be *the same* Bible?

I would reply: it is the same and not the same; there is only one Bible; there is only one text of the Bible. As regards the New Testament, it is completely the same; as regards the old Testament, the Catholic Church considers a few books to be inspired which Protestants do not. But in relation to the Old Testament as a whole this does not amount to much. However important this fact may be it remains true that in its material content it is practically the same Bible.

Is the difference due to translation? This could be true only if the translation was tendentious. And nowadays this would, I think, not be very likely. A really tendentious translation would gain little credit, simply on account of that intellectual republic of which I have spoken; the mutual control it entails would soon ensure that the tendentious translation was criticised and denounced as such.

In that case, what is the issue? Wherein does the difference lie?

Catholic Bibles always contain notes, not to twist the text, but to explain it. The Bible is an objectively difficult book and its contents are not always clear. It is a difficult book because its truth is the result of its totality; there is always a danger of exploiting one verse to the detriment of another, which in relation with others would have been a balancing factor. Catholics and Protestants have fundamentally the same Bible, but in the way it is

[6] 'La Bible dans la piété Orthodoxe' in *Irénikon*, 1950, pp. 377–86.

edited there are very real differences; and Catholics naturally read a Catholic edition.

Then, with regard to the Bible as a whole, both sides do not read the same passages, or at least not with the same interest. Both sides, for example, have St Paul's epistles in their entirety. Catholics find themselves very much at home in the epistles of the Captivity, for example, Ephesians, whereas Protestants are very much at home in those epistles which Catholics tend to find somewhat obscure, for example, Romans and Galatians. When Luther read St Paul his main interest lay obviously in his interpretation of the special themes of Romans; and of Galatians he said, 'It is my Catherine', that was the name of his wife.

We, perhaps, would start from the gospel of St John; there we would find Catholicism as the religion of God's presence, of eternal life as a present fact. We are less attracted to the dialectic 'sin-grace' which permeates the Protestant outlook.

I came across the following phrase written in 1930 by a Protestant writer: 'Just as in the sixteenth century we rediscovered the epistle to the Romans, so now we must rediscover the epistle to the Ephesians'.[7] This is very true.

But it does not exhaust the matter. The Bible may be interpreted in a number of ways; it does not exhibit in a completely obvious or invincible way the meaning of some of its most important passages. A Dutch Protestant has written: 'Was not the motto of the Reformation *Scripture only*? To this I should object that the diversity of Churches contradicts the motto.'[8]

Our task is to see whether Scripture carries its evidence on its face and declares its meaning irresistibly. Apparently it does not, for Protestants, Orthodox and Catholics do not all discover exactly the same thing in it and even within the Protestant Churches there are points of interpretation upon which not all agree.

It is possible to interpret texts, and most important texts, differently. This means that the text itself is not self-sufficient, and that its meaning is, as it were, beyond it.

As regards the Old Testament the meaning of its text is outside

[7] Superintendent W. Zöllner, *Die Kirche im Neuen Testment in ihrer Bedeutung für die Gegenwart*, Berlin, 1930, p. 13.
[8] J. N. Bakhuizen Van den Buink 'La Tradition dans l'Église primitive et au XVIe siècle' in *RHPR*, 36 (1956, pp. 271–81).

it—it is revealed in the reality of Jesus Christ. For both Old and New Testaments the only eyes able to read them truly are those of the whole Church that believes, prays and bears witness, especially in its worship. The Church is bound to come into the problem, or, to put it in another way, the meaning of the Scriptures is given within the Christian communities. This is the Catholic thesis, and moreover it is the traditional thesis of the Fathers of the Church, the thesis of the seven, eight or nine centuries during which the Church was undivided. The thesis of that undivided Church was that outside the Church the Scriptures cannot really exist.

Ultimately there are three great realities: Scripture, the Church, Tradition. The Catholic genius, or rather the traditional genius, the genius of the Church of the Fathers, the genius of that un-divided Church, consisted in never separating, never setting any of these three realities against each other. For they are co-inherent and inseparable. Herein lies the main reason why the Catholic Church in the nineteenth century was so strongly opposed to the activity of the Bible societies that propagated the sacred text in every language, without any explanation of it.[9] It did not suffice because the Bible alone does not suffice. God's word only becomes completely meaningful when it is preached by the ministers of the Church. The Bible societies are now working much more ration-ally than once they did. The Church also has to some extent relaxed the severity she first showed towards them.

This then is the Catholic position, the traditional position of the Church. It is obviously not identical with the Protestant position. Protestants know better than I that according to their doctrine Scripture is interpreted directly by a believer as a result of the activity of the Holy Spirit within him; this is called 'the internal testimony of the Holy Spirit'. Sometimes an over-naïve position is attributed to them, a position which, as a principle, they do not hold—that of wholly 'free enquiry'. That is, a man may interpret Scripture personally, according to his own understanding of it. This is inaccurate; a Protestant is bound by the sacred text, and and he affirms that he does not read it simply by his own appre-ciation and unaided; the presence and activity of the Spirit of God within him is his assistance. This thesis entails a very great

[9] Cf. the author's note 'Bibliques (Sociétés) 'in *Catholicisme*, Vol. 2, col. 26–9.

and very sacred element of truth. God does speak to us in his word.

It is obvious, however, and confirmed by history, that this thesis runs a considerable risk of individualism and fragmentation. The fact is that Protestants have no common interpretation of the Bible, and indeed if there is no authority beyond and above my personal understanding, who could reprove and put the brake on my wayward interpretations? Could I not always reply—and with complete sincerity—in the way that Munzer or Carlstadt replied to Luther: I have on my side the internal testimony of the Holy Spirit? Something more is needed. Something beyond and above myself. If the Holy Spirit is considered purely as within myself and personal to me, then it cannot be said that he is given precisely as a *criterion* with the power to sustain all believers in a common unity of belief.

Recently, however, among Protestants themselves, the thesis of the interior testimony of the Holy Spirit has been developed in ways that seem to me very substantial and which I am glad to record.

I quote here two passages that indicate present tendencies. The first is by a man who died prematurely, Théo Preiss, formerly professor in the Faculty of Protestant Theology in Montpellier: 'There is a whole field of enquiry needing attention concerning the testimony which the Holy Spirit gives to the Church. This work is the more urgent because we have not yet entirely unlearnt our Protestant individualism. Although the Holy Spirit grants every believer the certainty that Christian testimony is truly the word of God and that he is saved in Jesus Christ, nevertheless this testimony and certainty are bestowed and renewed only if he lives in the communion of the Church. It is something which we all experience that the Spirit only enables us to realise the truth of some brief passage of Scripture at any given moment and that we have to go on to discover the others and in fact be constantly rediscovering them afresh. Theology, it follows, is the product of all members of the Body of Christ.'[10]

It is in the communion with all men in the Church that I shall reach the truth, the plenary meaning of Scripture. In other words, the thesis of the internal testimony of the Holy Spirit is not false,

[10] 'Le Témoignage intérieur du Saint-Esprit' (*Cahiers théolog.*, 13), Neuchâtel et Paris, 1946, p. 36, n. 2.

but it must be understood as being given in the Church, in the Christian community and not in a purely personal and individualistic way.

The second passage is more recent; I have taken it from an article in the weekly review *Réforme*, 2 February 1957, published under the initials R.M.A.: 'Protestants in their turn must agree that Rome is right when she affirms that Scripture is the book of the Church and can only be really understood from within the people of God. We have to relearn the value of communal reading of the Scripture; it is within the family brought into being by scriptural revelation that the sacred writings can be properly understood.'

If the 'internal testimony of the Holy Spirit' is understood to mean a communal reality within the community of believers, and also within the total communion of the Church as it exists throughout the course of time, we have come fairly close to what Catholics call Tradition. For, in its doctrinal aspect, we regard Tradition as essentially the 'reading' of Scripture in the Church, in communion with the Fathers of the Church, a communion obviously supervised, regulated, promoted by the responsible authorities of the Christian community, those whom the Holy Spirit has established as shepherds of the Christian flock (cf. Ac 20:28).

What, then, will our conclusion be? Is the Bible the book of Christian reconciliation, or not? There are difficulties; difficulties I have not tried to tone down, but which, I believe, are worth trying to overcome. There is hope that they may be surmounted.

I should like to conclude by mentioning something, which, in my life as a priest, apostle and Friar Preacher, is to me a matter of great joy, and which I think is largely explained by the problem which has moved us to meet together this evening. I have, during the last twenty years, been greatly impressed by the fact that our time is characterised by the reappearance of what I may be allowed to call the living substance of a Christian man. Our churches are still full of heathens who go to Mass. By that I mean people who observe God's laws, the laws of worship but in their marrow lack the qualities of Christian manhood. At the same time, we are witnessing, in much of the behaviour of present-day youth, in young families, in members of Catholic Action, the reconstitution of the living tissue of *a Christian man*.

Now the biblical renewal about which we have been speaking accounts for much of this, and it is proceeding to reconstitute, beyond Protestant man, beyond Catholic man, the face and living fibres of Christian man.

We should find in it fresh grounds for understanding, for I have often noticed that we, Protestants and Catholics, are estranged on grounds of feeling. Protestants often shudder at something without examining its content. As a concrete and expressive example, I will take that of devotion to the Sacred Heart; it is the object of a whole literature, religious outlook and a vocabulary of its own; it involves holy pictures and statues and the services of the month of June. Confronted by all this a Protestant undoubtedly draws back into his shell. But if it were explained to him in biblical terms, terms that are adequate to the doctrine, he would realise that this devotion to the Sacred Heart is simply an expression of the central reality of evangelical Christianity. For it denotes no other thing than that love for men which is in the heart of God. If we could show him that it is the doctrine of the mercy of Jesus Christ he would accept it. In this way we should have regained, for a reality which we share, an attitude of mind and a mode of feeling that are in harmony with it. This shows how greatly important it is for us to regain our stature as Christian men, formed from the same Christian sources, those sources that have such a wonderful power to produce virility and mature manhood. For the Bible creates adult Christians.

These sacred Scriptures are coming to play an absolutely decisive part in the reconstitution of the fibres of Christian men. Here also, somewhat like Israel after the schism, after the exile, re-establishing the unity of the twelve tribes in the orbit of the single temple, we are beginning to rediscover ourselves, and I look forward to the time when there will be a single table, not only of the word, but of the bread and wine.

PART TWO

The Mysteries of God:
Father, Son and Holy Spirit

CHAPTER FIVE

Mercy: God's Supreme Attribute[1]

'A MAN WHO UNDERTAKES TO PRAISE GOD',
observes St Augustine, 'and yet will not exalt his mercy above all
else, had better keep silent.'[2] There is no motive for prayer more
authentic, none more surely answered than an appeal to God's
mercy in view of the wretchedness of man. The relationship
which religion implies receives here its perfect expression: on our
side, nothingness and absolute need; on God's the utmost regality
and divine power.

The revelation of God's mercy is inseparable from that of his
holiness and his transcendent majesty. Whenever, in Scripture,
he is revealed as 'the Holy', at an infinite distance from us,
supremely above all things, he is at the same time revealed as near
us, turning towards us, communicating with us through a gift.
From all the passages that illustrate this we shall select two only,
those great verses in Exodus (33:18–34:10), that record the two
encounters, or rather, the two stages of the single encounter
between Moses and God on Sinai.

To begin with Moses comes to Sinai after he had killed an
Egyptian soldier who was ill-treating one of his fellow Hebrews.
The killing had been seen and he was obliged to hide, in fact to
leave the country, and, as we should say, go underground. He
found shelter in the Sinai peninsula, where he married. It was
during this time, while he was looking after his father-in-law's
sheep, that he had the vision of the burning bush, in consequence

[1] Published in *Vie Sp.*, April 1962, p. 380–95.
[2] 'Taceat laudes tuas qui miserationes tuas non considerat quae tibi ed
medullis meis confitentur'. Conf., 6, 7, 12 (*PL*, 32, 725).

of which he received God's call to deliver his people from Egypt. Moses replied to God, 'Very good: I will go to the children of Israel and say to them, "The God of your fathers has sent me to you!" But if they ask what his name is, what shall I tell them?' Then God said to Moses, 'I am who I am' (3:13–14).

The revelation of the burning bush is first of all a revelation of God in his supreme power, in the transcendency of his life above and beyond all human estimate and foresight. From the midst of the bush God said, 'Do not come near: take off your shoes.' God is the Eternal, he who abides while all else comes to be and passes away. God is the mysterious One, his name cannot be uttered, cannot be communicated. He is the Living God whom we meet and know in his overriding initiatives, who makes himself known in his deeds. But now a note of graciousness or mercy is added to the affirmation of transcendent holiness. God, who holds Moses at a distance, speaks to him and calls him, turns towards his people, has pity on them, takes the first step towards their deliverance. Who will he be? The answer will become evident first of all in a fact: He will be the God-who-will-bring-his-people-out-of-Egypt.

But this revelation of God's mystery needed deepening through the experience of sin, or of its consequences. This was, in fact, the development we can observe throughout the course of this revelation in the Old Testament. David only reached the heart of his understanding of God after he had sinned. The people themselves only came to realise that their God was their redeemer after they had been reduced to misery and captivity as a result of their sins. In fact they were really able to grasp it fully only when God himself became the suffering servant, foretold by the Isaiah of the exile, when in Jesus Christ he formed the new alliance with his people (Is 42:6): an alliance maintained and renewed for *sinners*, therefore a redemption! Of course the people of Israel did not have to wait for the exile in order to experience sin, nor Yahweh-God have to wait for Isaiah in order to reveal his mystery more completely with that experience as his starting point. It is all too clear that precisely when the alliance was being contracted between God and his people on Sinai it was being violated and broken at the very foot of the mountain by the disloyalty of those who asked for a 'god who walks before them', such as the other nations had, and who were amusing themselves before the statue of a young bull made for them by Aaron (Ex 32).

After this event, had God been holiness and nothing else, he could not have remained among his people nor led them: 'If I came up into the midst of thee in a moment I should consume thee' (33:5). But he willed to be gracious. The dialogue he held with Moses' soul emboldened Moses to ask, 'Allow me to see thy glory!' He had been told the mysterious name and now he sought deeper knowledge. His petition was granted, at least so far as it could be granted to a man without involving his death. But when Yahweh passed before him, not allowing himself to be really seen but sensed, Moses cried, 'Yahweh, Yahweh, God, merciful and gracious, long-suffering and abundant in goodness and truth . . .' (34:6). This is the second revelation of his name and nature that God made. He is not only the Eternal, not only the One who does not tell his name, the Mysterious One, or he who will be revealed as the Living God through the progress of his actions for his people. Not only all this, but now he is revealed as the Merciful.

This revelation remained vivid in Israel's memory: the text itself is literally reproduced at least six or eight times.[3] When David had satisfied his vanity by having a census taken of the people he had to choose between three punishments, a famine of seven years, a seven-month flight from his enemies, or a three-day plague. He chose the plague, and said, 'Let us fall into the hand of the Lord, for his mercies are great, and let me not fall into the hand of man' (2 K 24:14).

The Fathers were not mistaken in their explanation of the etymology of *misericordia*: it is the feeling of a heart that pities and has compassion for the evil endured by another.[4] Thus it is initially an emotion and even a 'passion' in the original sense of the word, that is, in some internal change effected in us as the result of an external disturbance. For this reason the Stoics rejected mercy as a weakness and therefore an evil. In the present case the external cause is human distress in every form, that is, want of any kind or

---

[3] Ps 86:15; 103:8; 145:8; Jl 2:13; Ne 9:17; Jon 4:2, cf. Nb 14:18; Na 1:3.

[4] St Augustine, 'De moribus Ecclesiae cathol', 27, 53: 'Quis ignoret ex eo appellatam esse misericordiam, quod miserum cor faciat condolentis alieno malo?', *PL* 32, 1333. Cf. St Thomas Ia, qu. 21, art. 3; *In Joan.*, c. 2, lect. 1, n. 3.

some deprivation suffered by another man which is an obstacle to happiness. The sight of it moves us to do something to allay the distress, to mitigate the deprivation, to satisfy the want.[5]

Christianity has been acutely aware of the extent of human distress, not only in its external or material forms that are so immediately affecting, but in its inner and more radical reality; ignorance, sin, inability to do good, to bring concord amid disagreement, to maintain a hold on life or existence which evades our grasp. Distress, in fact an ontological distress, has seemed to it synonymous with the human condition, the cause of man's essential dissatisfaction, of that sense of being lost which modern writers have rediscovered and analysed under the name of anguish.[6] But the anguish of the moderns does not expect salvation and does not not look to God to provide a saviour.

In all ages mercy has been considered as being essentially a royal attribute. Paganism praised its presence in princes, not so much by the name of ἔλεος mercy with a tinge of pity, as of φιλανθρωπία, humanitas, and χρηστότης, benignitas, two words which the Stoics preferred to mercy and which St Paul attributed in combination to God (Tt 3:4). To these we should add the Latin pietas, which, in Christian usage, is closely connected with mercy.[7] Humanitas, a strictly human emotion consisting of sensitivity and kindliness, is a word not much used by Christians: it seemed too human. Benignitas was more favourably regarded and in the Bible it often denotes kindly benevolence that is ready to help, and is used as a synonym for mercy.[8]

A mere official has to apply the law rigidly: he cannot pardon,

[5] Cf. St Thomas Ia, qu. 21, art. 3 and 4; IIa–IIae, quo. 30, art. 1 sol. et ad 2; art. 2 and 3.

[6] Cf. H. Urs von Balthasar, Le chrétien et l'angoisse, Paris, 1954.

[7] Cf. R. Bultmann, art. ἔλεος in TWB z. NT, vol. II, pp. 474–83. H. Petre, 'Caritas. Étude sur le vocabulaire latin de la charité chrétienne' (Spicil. Lovan., 22), Louvain, 1948 (on 'Humanitas-Philanthrôpia', pp. 200–21). H. I. Bell, 'Philanthrôpia in the Papyri of the Roman Period' in Hommages à J. Bidez et F. Cumont, Brussels, 1948, pp. 31–57; C. Spicq, 'La Philanthropie hellenistique, vertu divine et royale' in Studia Theolog., 12 (1958) pp. 169–91. L. R. Stachowlak, 'Chrestoes. Ihre biblisch-theologische Entwicklung u. Eigenart' (Studia Friburg., N.F., 7), 1957 (with appendix on 'Philanthr.' 8n Hellenism and St Paul). Pietas: so Gregory defined mercy; 'qui pietate ad proximum permovetur' (Moral., 20, 32, 63. Pl 76, 175).

[8] Cf. C. Spicq, op. cit., p. 385.

for his work is to secure respect for the law, for the social order. But a king can, since he is bound only by the common good and not by the letter of the law.[9] This is why ecclesiastics often urged emperors or kings to imitate God, whose image and vicar they were; to imitate God particularly in his clemency.[10] Bossuet who in his day held such a lofty opinion of the king's person, felt obliged to stress that one attribute of supreme authority is its dispensing power. This was an idea he cherished:

I have learnt from St Augustine that pure love, liberal love, in other words real love, has about it something great and noble which can only exist in a plenteous and kingly heart. Why is there such a thing as a kingly heart? It is that it may forestall all other hearts in regal kindness. Do you wish to know, this great man asked, what genuine affection is? 'It is, he said, that which comes down, not that which climbs up: that which proceeds from mercy and not that which springs from misery; that which issues from an inexhaustible source, not that which is squeezed out by its own need.' (cf. *De cat. rud.* 11. 7). Thus the natural seat of affection, tenderness and mercy is a kingly heart. And since God is the one true sovereign, it follows that the heart of God is infinite in extent, always ready to forestall all other hearts, and more desirous to give from abundant mercy, than others are to ask from their abundant distress.[11]

St Thomas asks whether mercy is the greatest virtue.[12] It all depends, he answers. Considered exclusively in itself, it is indeed the greatest virtue. But considered as existing in a given subject, then *for that subject*, it is only the greatest virtue if he has no

[9] John of Wales (end of 13th c.): 'Moyses lapidabat ut judex, Christus indulget ut rex' (*In Johan*, VII, *inter opera Bonaventurae*, Lyon, 1668, vol 2, p. 381) cf. St Thomas Ia, art 25, qu. 3 ad 3; IIa IIae, quo 67, art, 4 end of corpus.

[10] For example St Leo, Serm. 40, 5 and 47, 3 (*PL* 54, 271 and 279); The bishops of Syria Prima to the emperor Leo I:Mansi, *Concil. Coll.*, 7, 547.

[11] Sermon for the Annunciation, 25 March 1662 (ed. Lebarcq, vol. 4, 1892, p. 187). Cf. Sermon for Christmas, 1656, at Metz, Introd. (Lebarcq, vol. 2, pp. 99–100); Sermon for the Conception of the Virgin Mary, 8 December 1656 (idem, p. 248).

[12] IIa–IIae, qu. 30, art. 4. There is no parallel to this in the works of St Thomas.

superior; if he is not the highest being, if there is someone above him, then, for him and in him, the highest virtue is that which unites him to that superior. For a created being, for man, this is charity. That is why, St Thomas adds, the apostle Paul writes: 'Put on therefore . . . bowels of mercy (Latin: *viscera misericordiae*), kindness . . . and above all, charity' (Col 3:12-14). Ultimately, mercy is supreme when one is in a supreme position, when one has no need to seek anything for oneself, and has only to give and, through sheer liberality and kindliness, to communicate good things to beings who are in need. This is in fact the way in which St Thomas considers God's mercy.[13] Mercy, in this sense, is exactly what Nygren has described in his account of *agape*, or love in its source, love as a gift, love as sheer offering. This love which is *God's love*, that is in the way it exists in God, with God as its subject, is communicated to us by the Holy Spirit (Rm 5:5): so that we are enabled to love as God loves, our love entering into and flowing with the stream of his; enabled to become living transmitters of that love whose source is and remains in God alone, to love authentically 'from love of him', that is in the way that he loves and with the self-same love that is his. Nygren errs, however, in failing to perceive, or in holding that it is contrary to the spirit of Christianity, even when he encounters it in the texts of the New Testament, that this love is also *a love of God for his own sake*, a love *of him* which obviously has no element of that mercy which our love for all others who inevitably lack something or suffer from some evil, must contain.

Mercy has fundamentally something royal about it. It does not necessarily presuppose that its subject is exempt from every kind of evil, but it does imply that he has not been swamped by evil, that he has overcome it and is free to relieve the distress of others, that for them he is a source of giving and compassion.

Mercy is eminently a quality of God. St Irenaeus writes: 'To exercise mercy is God's own function',[14] and St Catherine of Siena heard God say, 'I can be recognised by mercy'.[15] But what form does mercy take in God and how does it exist in him?

---

[13] Ia, qu. 21, art. 5 and the parallels quoted in the editions of his works.
[14] *Epideixis* or *Demonstration of the Apostolic Preaching* n. 60 (*Patrol. Orient.*, 12, p. 785).
[15] *Dialogue* c. 166 (transl. Hurtaud, vol. 2, p. 322).

Clearly it is not in a *passio*; he does not undergo an emotional shock and feel sad at the sight of our distress.[16] It is true that Scripture speaks in such terms, but its expressions must be understood, and always understood, in the light of the analogy. Mercy exists only in God's *will*, as a disposition of that will, as an activity of giving, at least if we are thinking of God in his divinity alone. But we know that in Jesus Christ God has attached a manhood to himself, and that he has even revealed the inner secrets of his mystery in that manhood: 'Philip, he who has seen me, has seen the Father'.[17]

It is precisely God's 'humanity' and benignity that Jesus Christ revealed (Tt 3:4). In him God took a human heart and human sensitivity; he was touched, had compassion and suffered; 'he became merciful and faithful high priest. . . . For from the fact that he suffered, being tempted, he is able to help those that are tempted.'[18]

It is quite easy and very moving to follow, in the gospels, the abundant signs of the emotion and feeling of mercy which God experienced in the heart and sensitivity of Jesus. He understood his mission to be a mission of mercy (Lk 4:17–21; Mt 10:8; 18:12–14; Mk 2:17; Lk 19:10). He set himself to heal distress of every kind. He described himself with incomparable gentleness as the Good Shepherd (Jn 10:1–18): 'Come unto me all ye who labour and are heavy laden and I will give you rest ... for I am meek and humble of heart' (Mt 11:28–30). And he said, 'I have compassion on the multitude', not only because it was a flock without a shepherd (Mt 9:36; Mk 6:34), but also because it had nothing to eat, and seemed unlikely to get anything (Mt 15:22; Mk 8:2). He told the parables of mercy (Lk 15). He wept when Lazarus died (Jn 11:33 and 35), and at the thought of the coming destruction of Jerusalem (Lk 13:34–5; 19:41). He was moved by the grief of the widow of Nain (Lk 7:13), by the centurion's faith (Mt 8:10) and by that of

[16] Cf. St Gregory, *Moral.*, 'Cum miseriae nostrae subvenit, misericors vocatur, quamvis miseris subveniat, et cor miserum numquam habeat' (*PL* 76, 175): cf. St Thomas; *In Psalm* 24, 11–1 (ed. Vivas, vol. 18, p. 365): Ia, qu. 21, art. 3. IIa–IIae, quo. 30, art. 2, ad. 1.

[17] Jn 14:9, cf. '*Dum visibilitur Deum cognoscimus*. Méditation théologique', in *La Maison Dieu*, n. 59 (1959), pp. 132–61: re-published in this volume.

[18] Cf. M. Festugière, 'Misère et Misèricorde', Maredsous and Paris, Gabalda, 1913

the Canaanite woman (15:28). He forgave the adulterous woman (Jn 8:11). At the supreme moment of his life he opened eternal life to the thief crucified by his side (Mt 27:44; Mk 15:32; Lk 23:39–43). He himself experienced the full horror of the death that awaited him: 'My soul is sorrowful, even unto death' (Mt 26:38).

In this way, throughout the gospel, God's love, the Father's *agape*[19] is revealed to us, in the working out of his plan of salvation (in line with the nature of the 'mystery' which, like the gospel, combines both revelation and achievement in a single process) in the human heart of the incarnate Word.[20] Our own hearts can be moved only by a limited amount of distress, and more often by distress we personally dread than by that which is intrinsically more serious. Our compassion is limited by our knowledge, by the very restrictions of our power to love and be generous. The saints, who shared in the love of the heart of Jesus, loved more deeply and more widely. They had, said the Curé d'Ars, a heart of universal fluidity. We may recall the compassion of St Dominic: 'My God, my God what will become of sinners?' or of St Vincent de Paul, open to all the spiritual and bodily distress of his time. But Christ received from God grace, knowledge and love co-extensive with his mission as universal saviour and his dignity as God made man, with no other boundary, therefore, than the created world itself.

Christians have come increasingly to realise that God's absolutely creative and initiating love was made manifest and now acts in Jesus Christ. Especially from the fourth century, a favourite theme of the Fathers was the *agape* of God as shown in the *philanthropia* of the saviour of mankind in his love for men. This theme became more contemporary as the empire widened; it provided Christians with a category that impressively suggested the universality of salvation. The Greek Fathers, in their catecheses, outbid each other in their attempt to express this idea, and it was soon depicted in the apses of the basilicas, in the mosaics of Christ as

[19] *Agape*, an attribute of God, that is of the Father: 2 Co 13:13; Rm 5:5 and 8; Ep 1:5; Jude 1–2; 1 Jn 3:1; 4, 7, 9 and 16.
[20] *God's* mercy made manifest *in Jesus Christ*: Rm 15:9; Ep 2:45; 1 P 1:3; Lk 1:50 and 72; and cf. R. Bultmann, *loc. cit*, re-published in this volume, p. 480. On the human heart of God, H. Urs Von Balthasar, *Le Coeur du Monde*, Paris, 1956.

Lord of History, with arms extended over the redeemed world.[21]
The worship of the saviour-lover-of-man is still very real in the
East, and it is a natural development that in the modern period the
liturgical feast of the Sacred Heart should have been incorporated
in this ancient cultus and its terminology.[22]

The work of God's mercy may be considered to begin with
creation, if, with St Thomas, we accept 'distress' in its widest
meaning as a need that is utterly radical or non-being,[23] and
mercy as that sheer liberality and good nature which bestows
being upon that which does not possess it or where it does not yet
exist. But it is above all the forgiveness of sin that St Thomas, in
harmony with Catholic tradition, regards as the supreme manifestation of the divine mercy. The liturgy, which so often invokes
God as '*Omnipotens et misericors Deus*', Almighty and merciful
God, contains this petition: 'O God who declarest thy almighty

[21] Cf. G. Downey, 'Philanthropia in Religion and Statecraft in the
IVth century after Christ' in *Historia* 4 (1955), pp. 198–208. H. Bolkes-
tein, 'Humanitas bei Laktantius, christlich oder Orientalisch?' in *Pisciculi*
. . . *Festgabe F. J. Dolger*, Munster, 1939, pp. 62–5; J. Lécuyer 'Théologie de l'initiation chrétienne d'après les Pères', in *Maison-Dieu*, no. 58
(1959) pp. 5–26. In the nineteenth century and at the beginning of the
twentieth, apostolic and missionary zeal was combined with a very
definite devotion to the Sacred Heart. It would be interesting to discover
what image of redemptive love our modern alertness to missionary effort
finds apt. It would seem that there has been a return to more strictly
biblical categories, God's plan, etc.

Humanitas was not unknown to the pagan world, but in the Christian
empire it became a guiding principle in politics and law, cf. Maschi
'Humanitas come motivo giuridico', in *Annali Triestini*, 18 (1949)
'Humanitas Romana e Caritas cristana come motivi giuridici' in *Jus*, I
(1950), p. 266s; S. Riccobono, Humanitas, in *Il Circolo giuridico*, 1950;
B. Biondi, '*Humanitas* nelle leggi degli Imperatori Romano-Christiani',
in *Miscellanea Giovanni Galbiati*. Milan, 1951, vol. 2, pp. 81–94.

[22] Cf. J. Schweigl, 'Ker Kult des φιλανθρωπος', vom 11–15. 'Jahr-
hundert' in *Gregorianum*, 22 (1941), pp. 497–502. 'De cultu liturgico
*Dulcissimi Domini et Dei et Salvatoris Nostri Jesu Christi, Amatoris
hominum* in ritu Byzantino,' *ibid.*, 23 (1942), pp. 255, 265 (introduction
to the feast of the Sacred Heart, under this title, in the Roman edition of
Liturgicon, 1942).

[23] Cf. St Thomas, Ia, qu. 21, art. 3 and 4. *In Ephes.*, c. 2, lect. 2,
'quando amor causat bonitatem in dilecto, tunc est amor procedens ex
misericordia'. Now St Thomas never tires of repeating: 'amor Dei est
creans et infundens bonitatem in rebus', *Contra Gentes*, III, 150; Ia, qu.
20, art. 2, cf. M. A. Ciappi, *De divina misericordia ut prima causa operum
Dei*, Rome, 1935.

C

power most chiefly in showing mercy and pity' *Deus qui omni-potentiam tuam parcendo et miserando manifestas.*[24] This forgive-ness of sins is an act of divine omnipotence. God alone can achieve it. For when we forgive all we can do is to annul resentment, retributive justice, anger and punishment involved in our personal feelings about the matter. We cannot eradicate the fault itself, in as much as it exists as sin in the other person's conscience. Only God can do this, for he alone can penetrate into that recess where the will is free; only God and Christ as God's instrument, through his knowledge and love, through his purpose and his deeds as the activating principle of our salvation.[25]

This sense that it is by forgiveness that God makes his omni-potence and even his nature most manifest is expressed by St Ambrose in a somewhat startling passage: *Cur homo?* Why was man (created)?

> 'Let us give thanks to God for having completed a work after which he could rest. He made the heavens, but I do not read that he then rested; he made the earth, but I do not read that he rested; he made the sun, the moon and the seas, but I do not read that he rested. And then I read that he made man, and after that, he rested, *there now being someone whose sins he could forgive.*'[26]

This hymn to the divine mercy has never ceased among Christian teachers. It is repeated by St Thomas in his commentary on the verse of the psalm *Miserere*: 'Tibi soli peccavi'. (Ps 51:6; Vulg. 50). It is a difficult verse and its interpretation is still under

---

[24] Collect for the tenth Sunday after Pentecost: from the seventh century Gelasian Sacramentary (cf. Bruylants *Oraisons du Missel romain*, No. 418) St Thomas frequently quotes this prayer: Ia, qu. 25, art. 3, ad, 3; IIa–IIae, qu. 30, art. 4, cf. this prayer for the dead: 'Deus cui pro-prium est misereri semper et parcere' (Bruylants, No. 207).

[25] Cf. IIIa, qu. 16, art. 11, ad. 2. Christ is the causal Principle, the *aitios* of salvation, Heb 5:9; cf. *archè* (Col 1:18) *archègos*; Ac 3:15; 5:31, *prodromos* (Heb 6:20).

[26] 'In Hexaemeron', 6:10 (*PL* 14, 272), 'Gratias ergo Domino Deo nostro qui huiusmodi opus fecit in quo requiesceret. Fecit caelum, non lego quod requieverit; fecit terram, non lego quod requieverit: fecit solem, lunam et stellas, nec lego quod requieverit: sed lego quod fecerit hominem et tunc requievit, habens cui peccata dimitteret.'

discussion.[27] Some exegetes even regard this psalm not as a peni-
tential lament by David but as a petition by Israel against the
Babylonians. Israel was chastised by exile although it had not
sinned against Babylon, but against God. . . . For St Thomas,
however, as for the Fathers in general, the psalm is David's and
expresses, as a result of the prophet Nathan's accusation, the realisation of the gravity of his sin; he had stolen Uriah's wife, and to
conceal his theft had arranged Uriah's death. How could he then
say, 'Against thee only, have I sinned'? Was he not guilty of a
grave injury against Uriah?[28]

Historically, indeed, according to the account given in the
Bible, David realised at once the wrong he had done and realised
its full significance: 'I have sinned against *Yahweh*' (2 K 12:13).
Every sin is a sin against God and has a theological character. If it
is to be forgiven, in its true nature as a sin, God only can
be the pardoner, as we noted above. And yet can we forget
that this wrong-doing wrought the gravest injury against
Uriah?

St Thomas, in his commentary on the psalter, at the end of his
life (the winter of 1272–1273) gives two explanations of 'Against
thee only have I sinned'.[29] It could be held that since David was
the king he was responsible for his actions, not to Uriah his
servant but to God's judgement. This conclusion follows from a

---

[27] Even its translation has recently been questioned by I. Zolli, *Il
Salmo*, 51, 6 . . . , in *Biblica*, 1941, pp. 198–200. He suggests that it should
be translated: 'In thy sight, all my actions are sinful'.

[28] Cf. in the commentaries, for example by E. Pannier-H. Renard (*The
Bible* of Pirot-Clamer, vol. 5, Paris, 1950, p. 299) the different suggestions
put forward.

[29] *Expos. in Ps* 50 (ed. Vivès, vol. 18, p. 544), '*Tibi soli peccavi. Sed
numquid non peccavit contra Uriam, quem occidit? Sic. Sed dicit: Tibi
soli*, id est Deo, quia ipse non est obnoxius famulo suo, sed sententiae
Dei. Cum enim peccat dominus qui est super servum, non peccat servo,
sed Deo: *Sap.* VI, 4: *Potestas vobis data est a Deo et virtus ab Altissimo,
qui interrogabit opera tua et cogitationes scrutabitur.* Vel, *Tibi soli*, id est
per comparationem ad justum; et sic, Tibi soli peccavi, quia solus est sine
peccato. Et similiter Christus omnino fuit sine peccato. *Tibi* ergo *soli
peccavi*, contemnendo judicium tuum. Item contempsi te testem; *quia
malum coram te feci*, vidente et praesente feci.'

The first explanation is taken from the Gloss, as is evident from, for
example, Ia–IIae, qu. 96, art. 5, ad 3. Cf. *Opera Nicolai Lyrani*, Basle,
1506, vol. 3, 157 E). The Gloss of Peter Lombard (*PL* 191, 486); and
earlier, Cassiodorus, *In Ps.* (*PL* 70, 361).

principle accepted in the ancient idea of kingship. Or it could also be argued that *Tibi soli* means that I have offended thee only, because thou alone art completely just and sinless and the witness of my deeds; against thee alone, that is, thou art the one criterion.

These explanations were somewhat artificial. Shortly before, however, or maybe shortly after, St Thomas suggested another based on the fact of the supremacy of mercy in God. In the passage we are about to quote one has a feeling that St Thomas is setting forth his own position with regard to a rigid interpretation of St Anselm's teaching on the incarnation as the necessary means of reparation to God for the sin of mankind. The thesis envisages the question exclusively from the point of view of justice. It asks whether there could have been any other way of delivering mankind than Christ's Passion. St Thomas, in agreement with St Augustine, gives an affirmative answer, and then meets the objections raised by the argument from justice:

> God's justice, the justice which would seem to demand satisfaction for sin from the human race, itself depends upon his will. For if he had decreed that men should be delivered from sin without any satisfaction, he would not have acted against justice. A human judge cannot, if he is to observe justice, dismiss a crime without punishment; he is under an obligation to punish wrong done to others, to an individual, to the community or its head. But God has no superior; he is supreme, and the common good of the universe. Therefore if he forgives sin, which is culpable because it has been committed against his own person, he is injuring no one; in the same way as a man who forgives a wrong done to him, acts mercifully and not unjustly. We have an example of this when David begged for God's mercy and exclaimed, 'Only against thee have I sinned', words that imply 'Thou art able to forgive me without injustice'.[30]

If sin is considered as a failure to observe the rights of God—and that is the deepest aspect of every sin—then God can make a total and unconditional remission not of the punishment only, but of the offence itself, because God is God, unique and supreme, with no superior to respect or protect. It was because he felt that his offence was primarily a sin against God and because he was

[30] IIIa, qu. 46, art. 2, ad 3: cf. IIa IIae, qu. 67, art. 4.

terribly anxious to regain God's friendship that David could say:
It is against thee that I have sinned. It is thy forgiveness that I
implore.

When we use words like these we imply that such forgiveness
involves God in some form of what we hardly dare call renunciation or sacrifice? It is difficult to find other words to express
what is most certainly real. Sin obviously cannot detract from
God's essence, but it can impoverish his reign, his glory; it can
diminish the area covered by his bounty and his grace. *Therefore,
to forgive and to forgive absolutely*, as God can, does imply that
he foregoes some element which belongs to him as the supreme
ruler of all things. Christian tradition has not failed to observe
this; it has often contemplated this open conflict between justice
and mercy, and depicted it as the two arms or hands of God, or as
his two daughters.[31] This same tradition has been concerned to
show that justice and mercy are not divorced in the works of
God.[32] In fact, their necessary co-existence should never be forgotten. Spiritual life should certainly be based on an intense conviction of God's mercy, but it is equally certain that this should
not serve as a pretext for taking an easy line with regard to the
demands made by his justice. St Thomas connects presumption
of this kind with the sin against the Holy Ghost.[33]

Would it be too anthropomorphic to speak of God making a
sacrifice? And yet how else can we denote the renunciation involved when he forgoes just restitution and completely forgives?
It may be said that justice is surely more than restored by the

[31] The two arms or hands of God: St Albert, 'Serm. in Dom. XII post
Trin.' St Thomas, 'In Rom., c. 4, lect. 1. Sermon in Lent (ed. Vives, vol.
29, p. 226). St Francis de Sales, 'Sermon for the feast of St Thomas', 21
April 1622 (*Oeuvres*. ed. Annecy. vol. 10, p. 409)—Two daughters of
God: J. Rivière, 'Le conflit des *filles de Dieu*, dans la théologie médiévale',
in *Rev. S. R.*, 13 (1935), p. 59. J. Leclercq, 'Nouveau témoin du *Conflit
des filles de Dieu*, in *Rev. Bénéd*, 58 (1948), pp. 110–24. The list could be
lengthened, for example Nicolas of Cusa (R. Haubst, *Die Christologie des
Nikolaus von Kues*, Freiburg, 1956, pp. 76–9).
[32] St Thomas, *In III Sent*., d. 1, qu. 1, art. 2, ad 4. 'Quamvis Deus sit
summa misericors, sua tamen misericordia nullo modo justitiae suae
obviat. Misericordia enim quae justitiam tollit magis stultitia quam virtus
dici debet; et ita Deum non decet'; Ia, qu. 21, art. 4; IIa IIae, qu. 21,
art. 2; *In Rom*., c. 15, lect. 1; *In Hebr*., c. 2, lect. 4. Earlier, Peter Lombard,
IV Sent. d. 46, c. 5 (ed. Quaracchi, 1916, No. 421, p. 1017); Robert Pulleyn,
Sent., lib. 1, c. 13 (*PL* 186, 701).
[33] IIa IIae, qu. 21, art. 2; qu. 163, art. 4, ad 3; *In Rom*., c. 2, lect. I fin.

sacrifice offered by Jesus Christ. But the fact that this sacrifice was offered by the man Jesus Christ, and that it was thus, through our Head, the sacrifice of mankind, does not mean that God was not involved in it or that he was not at work in Jesus.[34] God pays the cost of his justice, and *his payment is mercy*. But the renunciation implied by the complete forgiveness of mercy in no way diminishes God's reign. On the contrary, it displays its supremacy with greater splendour, because forgiveness is a more regal attribute than justice.

May not the hymn of God's elect, the hymn they sing when they come out of Egypt and cross the Red Sea (Rv 15:3) be described as essentially a hymn to mercy?

---

[34] Cf. 2 Co 5:18–19; Jn 3:16; 1 Jn 4:10, and my *Lay People in the Church* (London and Westminster, Md., 1957), pp. 148, 149. Ambrose accepted the notion of a sacrifice made *by God* cf. J. Rivière (who was personally unfavourable to such an idea), 'Le sacrifice du Père dans la Rédemption d'après St Ambroise' in *Rev. S. R.*, 1939, pp. 1–23.

CHAPTER SIX

Christmas is, first of all, Jesus Christ[1]

WE ARE WITNESSING A KIND OF SECULARISA-tion of Christmas. Christmas, it is said, is the children's feast, the feast of family intimacy. Who, on that day, fails to feel kindness stirring in his heart, the wish to be good, to bring comfort to the ailing or to those in trouble, to make some gesture of peace and friendship? Even in war a kind of truce is arranged on that day; it would be shameful to kill and natural to offer the enemy a drink.

There is the Christmas tree, and lights, and presents. And yet, in those illuminated cities, Christmas is tending to become the conclusion and pretext for a huge commercial season that begins in the early days of December. Advent is becoming a season of commercial advertising. Recently in a roomfull of soldiers, one of them, a Mohammedan, was celebrating Moulond, that is the Birth of the Prophet. A conscript seminarian took the opportunity of saying, 'We too celebrate the birth of our God as saviour of mankind.' He was startled to realise that many of his comrades simply did not know that Christmas was just that.

Goodness itself has its dangers. For instance, it is becoming increasingly common for Christian families, on that day, to welcome to their table those who have no home of their own. They call to mind that once there was a mother and her young husband, the birth of whose child was at hand; they were told that there was no lodging available for them, so, friendless, the only welcome awaiting them was among the animals in a cave used as a stable.

[1] First published in *La Croix*, 21 December 1960.

We have heard this theme developed in sermons to the effect that for the proper observance of Christmas we should invite a refugee, a coloured student, a poor man, to spend it with us. Of course there is truth in this and yet Christmas is first of all Jesus Christ. A friendly gesture of this kind only becomes truly Christian when faith's teaching about this day has been accepted as true. Once that has been done light and warmth can radiate unchecked.

Confronted by these dangers and in view of the secularisation in progress Christians have been neither inert nor passive. The title of this article was itself taken from a poster, pasted on the walls, or displayed in shop windows, in Strasbourg, as a result of a Catholic and Protestant initiative approved by the authorities of each. This fact suggests one of the main reasons for our joy as Christians: Christmas is an ecumenical feast. For us Christians, who are at present divided, Christmas is something common to us all, not only as regards the calendar or the social customs connected with it but because we agree on the essential meaning of the festival: Christmas is Jesus Christ, first of all: Jesus Christ who 'is always the same yesterday, today and for ever' (Heb 13:8).

We are now beginning the year 1961. It will be, in a very special way, a year of ecumenical grace. In the Catholic Church the work of preparation for the Council will continue, and although in itself the Council is concerned with the internal affairs of the Church its ultimate aim is of importance for the ecumenist in the wide sense, that is, for that effort which the Holy Spirit has aroused in all Christians to make in order that they may rediscover themselves within the unity of the visible Church of Christ and the apostles. Now the ecumenical movement, in that form of its development which is taking place within the framework of the World Council of Churches with its central organs at Geneva, is to hold its third World Assembly in November–December 1961 at New Delhi, India.

Its theme will be: *Jesus Christ, light of the world.* The theme of its first World Conference (Amsterdam, 1948) was: 'The disorder of man and the purpose of God'; that of its second Conference was: 'Jesus Christ, the hope of the world'. Thus, in different forms, the question is always about the same thing, or rather, about the same two things, each involving the same relationship. On the one side there is the world; that world is a world of disorder, without hope, existing in darkness, and in great need of light. On the other is Jesus Christ who is the expression of God's saving purpose, and hope and light for the world: Jesus Christ himself and not any form of humanitarian message whatever. If Protestantism had at one time lulled itself with that dubious melody, it has now to a great extent returned to a position that accepts not only the apostolic testimony but also the dogmas of the great councils of the fifth century. In his recent Christmas message, with the New Delhi Conference particularly in view, M. Visser t'Hooft, the Secretary-General of the World Council of Churches, wrote:

> St John speaks of the *true* light that lightens every man. Christmas has nothing to say about light in general, about the unbroken alternation of day and night, winter and summer. It is concerned with the true, the authentic light which God sends, and this light is Jesus Christ, God who came to take flesh among us. If we keep Christmas on December 25th, the reason is that in the ancient world this was the day of the *Sol invictus*, the Unconquerable Sun. Christians therefore fixed their feast in opposition to this feast of the natural order.
>
> Christmas is the universal feast. But it can only retain its universality on condition that its joy springs from a realisation that God has intervened in history in a unique way. Its real universality depends upon its roots being planted in God's great work in Jesus Christ.

The victorious sun which rises today and sheds its light upon this Christmas of 1960 is that which Isaiah, the prophet of Advent, had foretold: 'I have appointed thee to be the alliance with my people, and the light of the nations' (Is 42:6).

How great our need that he should come! He came once in the humility of the flesh: he will come back one day in the power of his glory. He comes each day, spiritually, through the ministry of the Church, through the priests and the laity who are his witnesses. For us Frenchmen, our fair France has at this time become France in distress, a France at war in Algeria, and therefore in mourning. The whole world is a world in distress, for it, too, is everywhere at war whether the war be hot or cold. Such are the conditions in which this year we must say, and say courageously, with the energy and the accent of truth: Glory be to God on high, and on earth peace to men of good will (Lk 2:14).

What does that mean for us?

It means something which at first sight seems too sublime, too spiritual to be applicable to our human situation, and yet which is the absolute and decisive truth about that condition. This is the truth which the Church offers in the gospel of a votive Mass which I, personally, have often celebrated, the votive Mass for peace. This gospel is taken from St John (20:19–23). Again it is not peace in general, the peace which men arrange and violate; it is the peace of Jesus Christ. It is inseparable from that forgiveness of sins of which the astounding ministry was entrusted to the apostles. In short, its profound source is the radiation of God's love upon us, within us and through us upon other men, just as the profound source of war is sin. It is often said that if there was a good God there would be no war. But would it not be truer to say that if we obeyed God, if we put the gospel into practice, there would be no war? Christmas can, once again, become the origin of that peace which we desire, or rather, which mankind *absolutely needs*.

On one condition: that it is authentic, not a mere word, not a ceremony, not folklore. In short, on condition that it is Jesus Christ coming in his real personality into our hearts as into a living crib. And this time may he be listened to and obeyed with absolute sincerity.

CHAPTER SEVEN

Dum Visibiliter Deum Cognoscimus: A Theological Meditation[1]

CHRIST THE REVEALER OF GOD

The preface of the Mass for Christmas, which may have been composed by St Gregory,[2] gives thanks to God in these words: 'Through the mystery of the Word incarnate a new light from your brightness has shone into our hearts, so that now that we know God visibly we may be caught up through this into the invisible realities.' We may disregard the fact that St Gregory himself seems to seek in his view of the incarnate Word chiefly a moral exemplar, an invitation to us to contemplate heavenly things. Here I prefer to concentrate on the function of the incarnate Word as the revealer of God or, more exactly, on the significance of the actual *fact* of the incarnation with regard to this revelation.

It is essentially a biblical idea. St Paul who had not known Christ according to the flesh considered him rather as the *content* of that revelation of which he, Paul, had been granted the understanding. And yet he deliberately applies to Christ the biblical themes of Wisdom: Christ is the image of the visible God, the flawless expression of his nature.[3] An early hymn, quoted in the

---

[1] First published in *La Maison-Dieu* 59 (3rd quarter, 1959), pp. 132–61.
[2] B. Capelle, 'La Préface de Noël' in *QLP*, December 1933, pp. 273–83; 'La main de S. Grégoire dans le Sacramentaire grégorien' in *Rev. Bénéd.*, 1937, pp. 13–28.
[3] Cf. Col 1:15; Heb 1:3; 2 Co 4:4 and 6; 3:18; Rm 8:29 and the parallels Ws 7:25–6; Si 24:3.

first epistle to Timothy, reads: 'Great indeed, we confess, is the mystery of our religion' (3:16). The synoptic gospels describe Jesus as the master. The justice he teaches is different from that of the Pharisees and even from that of the Law. At the transfiguration Jesus was accompanied by Moses and Elijah, the Law and the Prophets, but when the apostles ventured to look up again after their awed prostration they could see only Jesus and they heard a voice from heaven saying, 'This is my Son, my Chosen; listen to him' (Lk 9:35).

This is one of the main ideas in St John's gospel. The first three gospels record the spread of the word after its beginning with the preaching of John the Baptist—'The beginning of the gospel of Jesus Christ . . . John the baptiser appeared in the wilderness' (Mk 1:14). The fourth gospel, on the other hand, shows that this beginning did not occur only in history and in this world. The word that resounded in Palestine nineteen hundred years ago had its its real beginning in the eternal Word: 'In the beginning was the Word, and the Word was with God, and the Word was God.' It is *this* eternal and divine Word that took flesh and dwelt among us. As a result the teaching we receive from him is the teaching we receive from God. 'No one has ever seen God; the only Son, who is in the bosom of the Father, he made him known' (1:18; cf. 6:46). When the Jews asked how a man who had done no (rabbinic) study could know all these things, Jesus answered: 'My teaching is not mine, but his who sent me' (7:15–16). And he claimed to know and to be able to make known the one who sent him.[4] For long past God had been speaking, that is, manifesting himself. But he made himself known through the events of sacred history and through the prophets as from afar off; he manifested himself through his deeds alone. Was he never to be heard, was he never to be *seen*? For sight and not hearing only, had been the desire of Moses before it was the desire of the Greek soul (Ex 33:11). And every religious soul yearns to pass from the shadows to the reality, from obedience to presence.[5]

God's purpose consisted wholly in this movement towards this

---

[4] Cf. Jn 7:29; 12:49–50; 14:1–9.
[5] St Bernard describes the righteous of the Old Testament as anxious to hear not the prophets but God himself: *In Cant. serm.* 7, 1–12 (*PL* 183, 789–90).

perfect reality of his self-communication. The real nature of the new and eternal alliance is to be found in the transition from those things which are simply gifts from God to God's own gift of himself, 'from the God who speaks to the God made man'.[6] St Epiphanius attributes the following *agraphon* to Christ: 'The person who spoke in the prophets is myself, here am I'.[7] The liturgy adapts a phrase from Isaiah (52:6) in the same: *Ego qui loquebar, ecce adsum.* And the same idea fills the solemn prologue of the epistle to the Hebrews to which we shall return: 'In many and various ways God spoke of old to our fathers by the prophets; but in these last days he has spoken to us by a Son' (1:1-2).

When God no longer confined himself to speaking through men but made himself the human utterance of revelation, he obviously introduced the final revelation. The prophets had spoken about another Person than themselves; in Jesus Christ, *God himself* speaks about himself. The early Christians and the Fathers had a vivid and joyful sense of this great new reality: Jesus Christ has enabled us to know God. Today we are scarcely conscious of the value of this knowledge as such. For us religion seems rather to be a matter of intention and sincerity of heart or of good works. Salvation without any knowledge of God would suit us just as well. The early Christians were living in a pagan society that had no knowledge of God, no wish for it and no idea that such knowledge was possible.[8] They experienced the joy and confidence of having passed from ignorance to the knowledge of God through the work of Jesus Christ: it was one of the constant themes of their thanksgiving. Christ, the Word made man, was, for them, the revealer of God, that is of the Father who dwells in unapproach-

[6] This is the sub-title of L. Bouyer's *La Bible et L'Evangile* (*Lectio divina*[8]), Paris, 1951 (English transl., *The Meaning of Sacred Scripture*, London, 1960.) This difference between the two dispensations is brought out in Appendix 3 of my *Mystère du Temple*, Paris, 1958 (English transl., *Mystery of the Temple*, London and Westminster, Md, 1962); see also J. de Baciocchi, 'Présence eucharistique et transsubstantiation' in *Irénikon* 32 (1959), pp. 139-60.

[7] A. Resch, *Agrapha* (*Texte u. Unterschg· XXX*, 3/4), Leipzig, 1906, p. 207.

[8] Witness the indignation of Celsus at the claims of the Christians. Cf. M. Harl, *Origène et la fonction révélatrice du Verbe incarné* (Patristica Sorbonensia, 2), Paris, 1958, p. 76.

able light (1 Tm 6:16; cf. 1:7).[9] God, who is by nature invisible, said St Leo, has in our nature become visible.[10] Christ is the supreme revealer and what he revealed contains no shadow of error; he disclosed, at least *ex parte*, the fundamental elements in the mystery of God and the Primal Truth.

But he did more than reveal God, he also revealed the meaning of communion with him and the way to such communion. Ignatius of Antioch, writing to the Ephesians in 116–17, remarks: 'Ignorance was dispelled, its former kingdom destroyed, when God appeared in human form in order to manifest eternal life in a new way'. These three things are complementary: the revealer, the revealed truth, that is, the nature of the life or salvation involved, the means or the way of access to that life. Jesus who revealed the Father also reveals the means by which the Father may be reached. Jesus who is the truth of God revealed is also the means of access: 'Philip, he that has seen me has seen the Father.' 'I am the Way' (Jn 14:9 and 6). Jesus reveals the world *of heaven*, a world that is really the world above, and at the same time he reveals the ways in which we may acquire a life of communion with God, a mode of existence that is different from ours on earth, a life according to the Spirit and the ways of Christian life.

This revelation is not contained in his teaching alone; it is also, and perhaps we ought to say mainly, in what he *did*. If we restricted ourselves to his teaching we might easily conclude that his manhood was merely a mouthpiece of the Word, and the Word alone would be the revealing instrument of God. There is some element of this in Origen, who, despite an attempt to correct it, never quite eliminated Alexandrine Platonism from his system. That

[9] This theme of early Christology, often neglected of late years, has received attention in some recent works, especially that of M. Harl, *op. cit.*, p. 78, n. 27, and the bibliography therein. Cf. the passages quoted at the end of this article.

[10] *Sermo* 23, 2; *Epist.* 28 to Flavian, n. 4 (Denze. 144).

[11] Ep 19:3. St Cyril of Alexandria from the same point of view emphasises the sanctification of Christ's *body*; for God's indwelling in that body is quite different from a mere metaphysical relationship; its purpose is directed to the creation of a 'new man', a renewal of human nature in the Spirit. Cf. his Commentary on St John and the *Sixth Dialogue on the Trinity* (*PG* 75, 1017): P. Galtier, 'Le Saint-Esprit dans l'Incarnation du Verbe d'après S. Cyrille d'Alex.', in *Problemi scelti di Teologia contemporànea*, Rome, 1954, pp. 383–92.

philosophy was interested solely in that aspect of reality which is translucent to the mind, and, in Origen's view, the coming of the Word *in the flesh* had no higher significance than the other comings of the Logos that were entirely spiritual. The flesh conceals more than it reveals.[12] In fact, however, the coming down of the Word into our flesh, God's acceptance of the status of a servant, the washing of the disciples' feet, the obedient love that led to the death of the Cross—all this has the force of a revelation and of a revelation *of God*: 'Philip, he that has seen me has seen the Father'.

In the New Testament and more explicitly in the Fathers and the early liturgies the knowledge of God which Christ brought is not mere knowledge. It is simultaneously instruction and holiness. It is not just information as a preliminary to salvation; it is salvation already in action. St Paul connects the idea of being saved with that of coming to the knowledge of the truth (1 Tm 2:4). It is not by chance that baptism is so often called 'illumination' or 'faith' (Tertullian), but it is also as often called 'initiation'. This is due to the fact that on the one hand this saving knowledge is not only of aesthetic significance: it is the beginning and therefore the reality of the communication of his life and glory which he intends for us. On the other hand the coming down of God to us is inseparable from our ascent to him. Christ reveals the Father to us but only that he may draw us to the Father. The Word is not without its fruit (cf. Is 55:10–11). In the New Testament descent (*katabasis*) implies ascent (*anabasis, analepsis*): more accurately the coming down of God to us sets in motion our return to him.[13] The Fathers had a profound realisation of this fact and it is one of the reasons why the redemption seemed to them to have been accomplished at the moment of the incarnation: what is called the 'physical theory' of the redemption is fundamentally the expression, and a most authentic and profound expression, of this aspect of the mystery.

[12] Cf. M. Harl, *op. cit.*, pp. 185, 201f, 205–18, 336–8
[13] See among other texts: Jn 1:51; 3:13; 6:51 and 52. Ph 2:7–11; Rm 1:17. It is a truth remarkably expressed by St Fulgentius, *Sermo in Festo Stephani* (PL 65, 729–30); the effect of Christ's descent = the ascent of the Saints, celebrated on the day after Christmas in the person of the first martyr.

THE INCARNATION CANNOT BE SEPARATED
FROM THE WHOLE WORK OF REDEMPTION

The Council of Chalcedon (451) sealed the faith of the Church on the subject of the incarnation: 'true God and true man, consubstantial with the Father in his godhead consubstantial with us in his manhood . . .'.[14] To see in this definition merely the formulation of a physical or rather a metaphysical fact would be to fall short of the faith of the Church and unduly restrict the thought of the Fathers and the New Testament. That there are two natures united in the being of a single person is, of course, true but that does not exhaust the mystery. Even if we regard this metaphysical fact of the incarnation as the necessary condition for a real redemption, making possible an act of infinite amendment to God and of infinite worship, it would still be only a part of the truth. It would be a fuller and less inadequate account of the mystery but still somewhat narrow. It would be an advance on the previous theory in as much as it brings the metaphysical fact of the incarnation into relationship with God's purpose of redemption, and yet its idea of that purpose remains arid, unilinear and almost impoverished.

The incarnation is essentially a fact, the most decisive fact in the history of salvation. That history includes ontological problems but it cannot be reduced to them. Its mysteries can only be understood in relation to a purpose or a plan; we have to make the effort to grasp them as moments in the development of an economy. From a theological point of view the most interesting aspect, in my opinion, of the project for a kerygmatic theology drawn up between 1936 and 1938 by Fr J. A. Jungmann and Fr H. Rahner, is their attempt to revise '*theo*-logy' in the light of the 'economy' of salvation.

For God does not reveal himself for his own sake, he revealed himself to men and in the way in which he desired to be for *them*. Similarly in the teaching of the Fathers and of the New Testament epistles the incarnation does not exist on its own apart from what it is meant to be *for us*: 'propter nos et propter nostram salutem', as the Council of Chalcedon, repeating the Nicene creed, affirms.

[14] Denz. 148.

Ignatius of Antioch envisaged the whole divine economy or plan as moving towards 'the new man, Jesus Christ'.[15] The purpose of the incarnation is the formation of a new man which we too have to become through our incorporation in Christ.[16] It is a common-place that the Fathers are never tired of repeating: 'The Son of God became man in order that men might become God'.[17] This means that we miss the meaning of God's intention in the incarnation if we fail to realise the connection which he wished to establish with creation as a whole and with man, as its synthesis and summit, in particular.

On the one hand, the incarnation is intimately related to the world, it sets it on its right course again—despite its importance I do not intend to dwell on this aspect. On the other hand it is also intimately related to Christ's redeeming work in its entirety. St Thomas Aquinas understood this with remarkable thoroughness. He introduces the third part of his Summa with the words: 'Our saviour and Lord Jesus Christ, by delivering his people from

[15] Ephes. 20:1; and cf. *supra* fn. 11.

[16] Cf. St Hippolytus. Antichr., 3 (ed. Achelis, G.C.S., p. 6, l. 17–19): 'The Only-begotten is the Child of God, it is through him that we too have received the new birth of the Holy Spirit: so that what we hope for most in this world, we who are many, is to be joined together with this unique heavenly being'. From this thoroughly biblical point of view the two phrases in Jn 1:13 'nati sunt' and 'natus est' can be seen in their full implications.

[17] Some examples: St Irenaeus, A.H. 3, 10, 2 (*PG* 7, 874); 3, 19, 1 (*PG* 7, 939); 4, 44, 2 (*PG* 7, 1062A); 5, preface (*PG* 7, 1120B); St Athanasius, *Orat I contra Arianos*, 39; 2, 70; 3, 34 (*PG* 26, 92, 296, 397); *De Incarn. Verbi* 54 (*PG* 25, 192B); Amphilochius of Iconium, *Oratio in Christi Natalem*, 4 (*PG* 39, 41A); St Gregory Nazianzen, *Orat.* 2, 22; 40, 45 (*PG* 35, 432 and 36, 424); St Gregory of Nyassa, *Orat. catechetica magna* 27 (*PG* 45, 69); St John Chrysostom, *In Joan.* 1, 14 (*PG* 59, 79); St Ambrose, *In Luc.* Bk. 5, n. 46 (*PL* 15, 1648); St Augustine, *Serm.* 125, 5; 127, 6, 9; 166, 4; 184, c. 3; 186, 2; 192, 1; 194, 3 (*PL* 38, 680, 710, 909, 997, 999, 1012, 1016); *Epist.* 140, 4, 10 (*PL* 32, 541f); 187, 20 (*PL* 33, 839–40); *Enarr. in Psalm*, 34, 21 (*PL* 36, 507); *De Civ. Dei* 9, 15, 2; 21, 15 (*PL* 41, 269, 279); St Augustine, *Serm.* 128, 1 (*PL* 39, 1997, quoted by St Thomas, IIIa, qu. 1, art. 2); St Fulgentius, *De Incarn.* (*Maxima Bibliotheca Patrum* 9, 310); St Leo, *Serm.* 23, 4; 25, 2; Theophylact, *Enarr. in Ev. Joan.* C. 1 (*PG* 123, 1156). And see the studies by J. Gross, M. Lot-Borodine, on deification in the Greek Fathers; A. Spindeler, *Cur Verbum caro factum? Das Motiv der Menschwerdung und das Verhältnis der Erlösung zur Menschwerdung Gottes in den christologischen Glaubenskämpfen des 4 u. 5 Jahr*, Paderborn, 1938; J. Loosen, *Logos und Pneuma im begnadeten Menschen nach Maximus Confessor*, Münster, 1941; K. Bornhaüser, *Die Vergottungslehre des Athanasius u. Joh. Damascenus, 1903*.

their sins, as the angel foretold, has disclosed himself to us as the way of truth through which it has now become possible to arrive at the resurrection and the beatitude of immortal life.' Within the confines of a single treatise he includes first the mystery of the incarnation in itself, 'which is the mystery of a God made man for our salvation', then the *acta* and *passa* of the incarnate God, that is, the whole of Christ's redeeming work, accomplished in the saviour's life and 'Passover'. If the mystery of the incarnation is that of 'a God made man for our salvation' then it is impossible to keep it apart from everything which its redemptive purpose achieved. The *acta et passa Christi in carne* are included in this mystery. I believe that the Fathers would have welcomed Péguy's phrase (in the first *Clio*): 'The agony, the death of Jesus, his cry, "Eli, Eli . . ." all this is the completion of the incarnation, because in all this God was becoming "truly man".' It may even be said in addition that since the incarnate word is the revealer of God, his *acta* and *passa* are also an authentic revelation of God.

In the perspective of Scripture, the liturgy and the Fathers, the nativity in itself implies the series of the mysteries of salvation that lead up to their consummation in the passion and resurrection.

St Paul sees the Lord's coming in the flesh solely in the light of his passion and resurrection: sacrifice (Ph 7:11; Heb 10:5–17); resurrection (Rm 1:34) and glory (Ph 2:7–11); redemption (Ga 2:4–5). And even, since Christ's existence in the flesh had no interest for him, the apostle considered the Lord's divine sonship to have been first manifested in his resurrection and then by his sitting at the right hand of the Father.[18]

J. Pinsk pointed out, some years ago,[19] that the Roman liturgy for Christmas does not separate the historical fact or the memory of that fact, which is such a distinctive feature of this feast, from the whole mystery of redemption, the whole plan of redemption, envisaging man's deification and ultimately the mystery of God himself. In the three Masses for Christmas Day, St Thomas' suggestion[20] that each of them applies to one of the three births—

[18] Cf. Ac 13:32–3; Rm 1:4; cf. 8:11; Heb 1:5; 5:5.
[19] 'La venue de Seigneur dans la liturgie de Noël', *QLP*, December 1933, pp. 259–72.
[20] IIIa, qu. 88, art. 2, ad 2.

eternal, historical and spiritual—seems somewhat artificial and,
as the context shows, he himself was not deceived by it. For the
fact is that the liturgy unites in one act of remembrance the
transcendent originating principle, its historical sacrament and its
final result; in short, the threefold and interconnected reality of
our adoption through grace, Christ's birth in time and his eternal
generation.[21] Christmas envisages our deification and therefore
our redemption through the Lord's Passover, and these can become a reality because he who was born, died and rose again was
no other than the Son of God. All this constitutes one single
mystery of alliance; and indeed the *admirable commercium* of
the incarnation is related in its entirety to that of the ascension
and Pentecost, the final stages of a Passover, that is, a passing over, of which the cross is the beginning.[22] The liturgy of
Christmas speaks again and again of the redemption as a present
reality.[23]

The eastern liturgy interprets the mystery in the same way.

[21] Cf. E. Flicoteaux, 'Le mystère de Noël', in *Vie Sp.* 7 (December
1922), pp. 282–304. The liturgy celebrates only those births that originate
in the eternal world and only the earthly births which are in immediate
relationship with the incarnation—those of St John the Baptist and of the
Mother of God.

[22] Cf. P. Miquel 'Le mystère de l'Ascension' in *QLP*, June 1951, pp.
105–26, esp. pp. 122f. The author who quotes the prayers for the feast
of the Ascension (Leonine) might have connected them with the prayer
super oblata in the midnight Mass: 'ut tua gratia largiente, per haec
sacrosancta commercia, in illius inveniamur forma, in quo tecum est
nostra substantia' (Feltoe, p. 161; Mohlberg, no. 1249).

[23] E. Flicoteaux, *op. cit.* quotes the relevant passages. One of the most
striking is the *De Profundis* for Vespers. St Leo calls Christmas 'salutis
nostrae sacramentum' (Serm. 22, 1), 'sacramentum humanae restitutionis'
(25, 1). The liturgy in the West, as thoroughly as that of the East, is
penetrated by the idea that the incarnation (Christmas) is the beginning
of the redemptive restoration of all things: cf. G. B. Ladner, *The Idea of
Reform, its impact on Christian Thought and Action in the Age of the
Fathers*, Cambridge, Mass. 1959, p. 2845; E. Weigl, 'Die Oration
"Gratiam tuam, quaesumus, Domine", zur Geschichte des 25 März in
der Liturgie' in *Passauer Studien*, 1953, pp. 57–73 (the prayer we use for
the Angelus). The comparison between the crib and an altar is common
in the Greek Fathers (St John Chrysostom, Theodotus of Ancyra, etc.).
It was often reproduced pictorially in western medieval iconography:
E. Mâle, *L'art religieux du XIIe siècle en France*, ch. 3; 'L'art religieux du
XIIIe siècle en France', 7th ed. 1931, pp. 185f. In her fine poem 'L'attente
de Jésus' Marie Noël has shown the cross as in some sense overshadowing,
point by point, the preparations which Mary made for her infant's needs.

The liturgical calendars announce Christmas with the phrase: 'The Passover, a feast to be observed for three days'.[24] The triodons and canons of the days before the feast may have been composed by Simeon Metaphrastes (eleventh century); they interpret the feast in a way that is fully supported by early patristic and liturgical evidence and the interpretation is very profound. Christmas—and that means the incarnation—is the beginning of the *kenosis* or God's self-abasement to the condition of a servant. This is wholly in line with St Paul's hymn in his epistle to the Philippians (2:7–11). Here are some examples:

The Word of God, incorporeal, immortal and containing infinite reality with no extraneous admixture, has come into our world; not that he was far from it beforehand—for he was absent from no part of creation; coexisting with his Father he penetrated all things (cf. Ep 1:23; Col 3:11)—and yet he has come, he has come down from love of us, that we might behold him unveiled.[25]

Our Lord Jesus Christ, his only Son . . . who in these last days, for our salvation, took the form of a slave and was made man, became involved in human nature, was crucified and rose again the third day.[26]

He whose equality with God was not an usurpation shows himself to all men in the form of a servant.[27]

The unaltered image of the eternal Father takes the form of a servant.[28]

The anaphora of the Liturgy of St Basil contains a similar reference to Ph 2:65 preceding Rm 5:12, and we find the same thing in the Liturgy of St Gregory Nazianzen, in the catechistic

[24] Cf. Th. Spasskij, 'La Pâque de Noël', in *Irénikon*, 30 (1957), pp. 289–306. I have only indirect knowledge of *Das Weihnachtsfest im Orthodoxen Kirchenjahr. Liturgie u. Ikonographie*, by K. Onasch, Berlin, 1958.

[25] St Athanasius, quoted by Suicer *Thesaurus ecclesiasticus*, s.v. συγκαταβασις

[26] St John Chrysostom, 'Eight Baptismal Catecheses'. Cat. 1, 21.

[27] Introduction of the 1st Troparion inserted in the canon of 20 Dec., the preliminary feast to Christmas.

[28] Sticheron for the vespers of Christmas: 8th c. (quoted by Th. Spasskij, *art. cit*).

homilies and the anaphora of Theodore of Mopsuestia, etc.[29] This relation of the incarnation to the plan of salvation, the destiny of death of the first Adam, through recapitulation in Christ, the second Adam, is a fundamental theme in the liturgical and dogmatic tradition of the Church. In the Fathers this inclusion of a reference to the Lord's passion and resurrection already in the mystery of Christmas is expressed in different ways. It appears first of all in the soteriological argument so frequently used in the trinitarian and Christological disputes of the fourth and fifth centuries, but previously explicit in St Irenaeus and germinally in St Ignatius of Antioch.[30] The Alexandrine Fathers, Athanasius and Cyril, the Cappadocians, and Tertullian, Ambrose and Augustine also, repeatedly use the following argument: No man is saved who has not been incorporated by the Son of God into his incarnation; our resurrection, the supreme article of Christian faith and hope, is guaranteed only if Christ's resurrection is true, that is, if God *really* became man.

The idea of connecting our birth through grace with Christ's birth in the flesh was particularly cherished by St Leo and also by St Maximus, or whoever it was whose works are attributed to him.[31] A mind formed on the teaching of St Paul might, at first sight, be surprised at finding our *heavenly* birth, *according to the Spirit*, connected with Christ's nativity *according to the flesh*. For the person who quickens us is not Christ in his conformity with the first Adam, 'born of a woman, born under the Law' (Ga 4:4; the only occasion when St Paul mentions the Virgin Mary); it was precisely under this aspect that *he died*, and he only became a 'quickening spirit', the origin of the new, heavenly life through his resurrection according to the Spirit.[32] This is a point of New

---

[29] Cf. the passages quoted by L. Ligier, *Autour du sacrifice eucharistique. Anaphores orientales et Anamnèse juive de Kippur* in *NRT* 82 (1960), pp. 40–5 (pp. 49–50).

[30] Ignatius, Smyrna, 4, 2; Irenaeus, A.H. 5, 1, 1–3 (*PG* 7; 1121f); Epidexis 39 (Patr. Or. 12, 775). Cf. E. Mersch, *Le Corps mystique du Christ. Études de théol. histor.*, 2 vols. 3rd ed. 1951. Index, s.v. *Argument sotériologique*.

[31] St Leo *Sermo* 26, 2; 29, 3; St Maximus, *Hom.* 15 (*PL* 57, 254); Pseudo-Maximus, *Hom.* 9 (*PL* 57, 245).

[32] The epistle to the Galatians as a whole. Rm 1:3–4 (with St Augustine's commentary: *Ep. ad Rom. inchoata expose.* (*PL* 35, 2091); 4, 25; 6,1–11; 8, 1–13; 1 Co 15:20–3, 45–50; 2 Co 5:16–21; 13:4; 1 Tm 3:16; 2 Tm 2:8; cf. 1 P 3:18.

Testament doctrine that demands more attention from those who would base Mary's spiritual motherhood of the Mystical Body directly upon her quality as Mother of God according to the flesh. St Leo does not draw this conclusion, and his reasoning was exact. He connects the spiritual (and ultimately heavenly) birth of Christians, that is, the integral creation of the new man, with the birth of the word in time and also with his eternal birth as the only Son. But this Christian birth comes about through Christ's passion and resurrection and through baptism which incorporates Christians into that passion and resurrection and not specifically into the mystery of Christmas.[33] It is by including within its scope the whole redemptive course of Christ's abasement leading to his death and beyond death to his exaltation in heaven—his Passover in its entirety—the triumphant conclusion of his life as a servant, that Christmas really becomes the mystery of 'a God made man for our salvation' (St Thomas, IIIa, prol.).

This work of redemption is permeated by gracious self-giving (*sugkatabasis*), filial obedience and loving service. It is the 're-capitulation', in St Irenaeus' sense of this word, of the fall, that is, the integration, but in the opposite direction, of all those elements in history through which man had become a lost being and was continually adding his own consent to being lost. Self-exaltation had caused his degradation and loss. He is enabled to rise up and, in Christ, regain his path to glory, when he shows himself willing to come down.

Before proceeding further there must be mentioned two important consequences or applications of this New Testament and

---

[33] Cf. Serm. 26, 2 (*PL* 54, 213): '. . . today's feast renews for us the sacred advent of Jesus, born of the Virgin Mary, and we find that when we revere our saviour's birth, we are also celebrating our own origins; for the birth of Christ is the beginning of the Christian people and the anniversary of the head is also that of the body. It is true that each individual is individually called, and the children of the Church have come into her during the various periods of time, and yet all believers who have emerged from the baptismal fonts and are crucified with Christ in his passion, risen with him in his resurrection, at his side in his ascension to the right hand of the Father, are on this day brought to birth with him . . .' Cf. *Serm.* 21, 3; 25, 5; *Epist.* 16, *ad epsic. Sicilliae*, 'nisi proprie voluisset intelligi regenerationis gratiam ex sua resurrectione coepisse' (*PL* 54, 699). On this relationship between the incarnation and redemption according to St Leo, cf. the Appendix 1 in *Le mystère liturgique d'après S. Leon*, by M. B. de Soos, Munster, 1958.

traditional way o regarding the incarnation as inseparable from the work of redemption as a whole, and from the object to which it is directed—man's salvation or deification.

1. In the theology *De Ecclesia* first of all. It is a commonplace that the mystery of the Church follows a course parallel to that of the incarnate word and should reach a similar equilibrium in a kind of Chalcedonian dogma devoted to the Church. The Christological idea developed above may suggest a further parallel the full significance of which will be realised by those who follow the thought of the ecumenical movement. In the mystery of Christ we may not separate his being from his mission, or, if the expressions are permissible, his morphology from his physiology, and even from his external activity. Similarly, in the Church such a separation is impossible. The mystery of the incarnation is not a mere metaphysical fact and cannot be reduced to its ontological formula. So, too, the mystery of the Church, and even its unity, cannot be conceived as something static, a mere organisation or institution existing in the world. The mystery of the Church envisages and includes a missionary work of salvation to be communicated. When we speak of the Church, or simply of its unity, we should never forget that she was not brought into being for her own sake, but for an apostolic service to the world.

2. In the theology of created or earthly reality. This theology also, closely related as it is with that of the incarnate word, cannot be separated from God's purpose which is Christological and redemptive.[34] It must also be affirmed that we should be careful not to confine ourselves to the plane of abstract and formal analysis; this is a legitimate and even necessary stage in the process of reflection, but if we are bent on describing things as they really *are*, then we must envisage them in the way they concretely exist. With this in mind we find ourselves confronted by a world foreseen from its origin, sinful and redeemed *in Christo* and *ad Christum*.[35] In God's eternal purpose the word is conceived as *Incarnandus*. . . . From my own personal experience, I know that for one formed in the school of St Thomas it requires an effort to accept these truths

[34] W. Kunneth, *Theologie der Auferstehung*, 4th ed., Munich, 1951, and the criticism of the views of Canon G. Thils by D. V. Warnach in *Theologische Revue*, 1952, col. 172.

[35] Cf. Ep 1:4; Col 1:16–17; Heb 1:3; 1 Co 8:6. Cf. 2 K 7; Ps 89; Is 9:6; Dn 7:14; Lk 1:32.

fully. But it is no more possible to stop at a purely formal onto-logical consideration of things than it is to remain satisfied with a metaphysical account of the hypostatic union. A complete theo-logy of the realities of this world cannot simply be a theology of incarnation: it must ultimately become Christological, redemp-tive, eschatological.

GOD REVEALED IN HIS 'MANHOOD'

'In many and various ways God spoke of old to our fathers by the prophets; but in these last days he has spoken to us by the Son, whom he appointed to be the heir of all things, through whom also he created the world' (Heb 1:1-2). This passage is read as the epistle for the third Mass on Christmas Day. Between the two stages of God's manifestation which it distinguishes there is both continuity and opposition. We may profitably support our medi-tation by as solid and concrete description as possible of the con-text of these manifestations and of the content of these two stages: the prophets and the Son.

The prophets form a long procession from Moses to John the Baptist; thirteen or fifteen centuries during which these men drew near to God. Consider Moses, the Moses of Michelangelo, or of the Chartreuse of Champmol now in the art gallery at Dijon, or better, the Moses of the Bible. He is the man who confronted Pharaoh; the man who, relying in faith on God's promise, was the solitary leader of an obstinate and carnal people throughout the forty years in the desert. He was the man of Sinai who encountered God and spoke to him as it were face to face in a locality which even today looks convulsed, volcanic and lonely. Or consider Isaiah—also depicted in the gallery at Dijon or among the sculp-tures of Chartres—a seer who saw Yahweh Sabaoth in his regal majesty within the sacred precincts of the Temple (cf. 6:1-4, quoted below). These prophets are figures of impressive grandeur, giants among men. Strength, intransigence, reckless courage and austerity—these are the characteristics that mark them through and through.

When we turn from their personalities and the context of their visions and consider their message, we find it dominated by the proclamation of the reign of God in an absolutely exclusive sense:

Yahweh is King; he alone is Lord. This is a reality with formidable demands and consequences. And yet it is remarkable that the imperative and sometimes even frightening features of this reign are, as it were, tempered, or rather, completed by a declaration of tenderness, intimacy and mercy. We are told that the Messiah will rule over the nations with a rod of iron like a military conqueror,[36] but also that he will be 'the good shepherd', tending his flock with care even at the cost of difficulties which he will not evade (Ezk 34; Jr 23:1–8). The Messiah is described as a new David, with a mission to reign,[37] but also as a meek and suffering servant taking upon himself and bearing the iniquities of us all in order that all might be reconciled.[38] 'The Lord your God is a devouring fire, a jealous God' (Dt 4:24), and yet he has a love for his people that nothing can extinguish, nothing can turn aside. Its tenderness and unbounded willingness to forgive are illustrated in the astounding account of Hosea and his 'wife of harlotry'— surely one of the supreme moments of God's self-revelation in the Old Testament.

'A prophet is a man who brings justice down upon this earth,' said Léon Bloy. The justice and the fire of heaven! But now something entirely new emerges. God himself speaks in his own person, makes himself personally manifest. He no longer speaks from afar through the mouths of other men controlled by the might of his power. He himself speaks, in person: *Ego qui loquebar, ecce adsum.* We are all attention, wondering what we shall hear. We draw near, wondering what we shall see. We discover that when God himself becomes the speaker, when he shows himself in person, when he discloses the hidden depths of his being, when the invisible makes himself visible, what appears is 'his goodness and loving kindness': *Apparuit benignitas et humanitas salvatoris nostri Dei.*[39] What appears when God himself in person is a man,

---

[36] Ps 2:9. Cf. Dt 28:4–8; Jr 28:13–14; and also Rv 2:27; 12:5;14:15.
[37] Is 42:1–3; 50: 4–9; 52:13–53j 12.
[38] Tt 3:4: the epistle for the Mass at Dawn on Christmas Day.
[39] St Athanasius, *De Incarn. Verbi*, 16 (*PG* 25, 124D–125A), St John Chrysostom, 'Eight unpublished baptismal Catecheses', ed. A. Wenger (*Sources chrét. 50, Paris, 1954*), Cat. 1,3 (p. 110); 1, 8 (p. 112); 2, 1 (p. 134). Fr Wenger also quotes from an unpublished homily of Severian of Gabala for Maundy Thursday: 'God's mercy and lovingkindness (*philant.*) is manifest throughout creation, but especially in the mystery of the economy . . .'. See J. Lécuyer, *Théologie de l'initiation chrétienne d'après*

and, first of all, a child.

The word *Philanthrôpia* used by St Paul was of pagan origin, and it does not occur elsewhere in the New Testament. But in that incorporation of Hellenistic culture into Christianity which it was the mission and the grace of the Fathers to effect, this expression which signified the gracious kindliness, or the generosity tinged with mercy and benign good will of a sovereign, God's gentle 'Philanthropy' became a key word at the head of all catechetical instruction. The Fathers liked to begin with an account of God's good deeds to men and his love for them, as shown in the creation, and then in his treatment of men, not leaving them to be lost but coming down to help and save them.[40] The eastern anaphoras, that of St Serapion for example, were fond of invoking God with the fine title, 'Friend of Man'.

Of course, if he was to manifest himself to created beings bound up in the life of the body and in historical time, God was obliged to take some other form than his *forma Dei*. He could unveil himself only by assuming another veil, reveal himself only through a kind of disguise. Only veiled can he become unveiled to earthly eyes. This is a dialectic which alone makes revelation possible. But its paradoxical nature should not be allowed to conceal the fact that the reality and positive value of revelation are bound up with the form it borrows, with the veil under which that revelation is made.

Now, the nearer God's Wisdom draws to man, the more human

---

les Pères, MD, no. 58, 1959, pp. 5–6. For the first four centuries, cf. H. Petre, *Caritas. Étude sur le vocabulaire latin de la charité chrétienne*, Louvain 1948, pp. 200–21. G. Downey, '*Philanthrôpia* in Religion and Statecraft in the IVth century after Christ', in *Historia*, 4 (1955), pp. 198–208 (numerous refs. to the Greek Fathers, pp. 204f; to the eastern liturgies, pp. 205–7). For the later development in the East, cf. J. Schweigl, Der Kult des *Philanthropus Soter*, vom 1–15. Jahrh.' in *Gregorianum 22* (1941), pp. 491–502. It was with this title that the feast of the Sacred Heart was introduced into the Roman edition (1942) of the 'Liturgicon'. Cf. J. Schweigl, 'De cultu liturgico "Dulcissimi Domini et Dei et Salvatoris nostri Jesu Christi, Amatoris hominum" in ritu byzantino' in *Gregorianum*, 23 (1942), pp. 255–65.

[40] Cf. Ba 3:38: '. . . he committed it to Jacob his servant, to Israel his beloved; thus it appeared on earth and conversed with men' (a passage quoted by St John Chrysostom in order to show that God's human coming had been foretold): Quod Christus sit Deus, n. 2; *PG* 48, 8:15; cf. Si 24:8f; Pr 8:31; Ws 9:1of, then finally, Jn 1:14.

it becomes.[41] Not only does God speak a human language—he
could not otherwise be understood by men—he also shows himself as human. We are not merely referring to those cases when the
Lord appeared in human form to the great heroes of the faith,
under the old dispensation; to Abraham under the oak of Mambre
(Gn 17) to Joshua (Jos 8:13–15), to Daniel (7).[42] We take the same
view of the inner meaning, noted by many exegetes, of the per-
sistent anthropomorphisms in the Bible.[43] God is constantly
represented as endowed with sense faculties, performing physical
actions, experiencing emotions similar to the senses, actions and
emotions of men. These metaphors were of service in directing
men's minds away from an image of a God involved in nature
worship, but they had a positive aim and content: they are bound
up with the revelation of God as a *moral* God. Their employment
was fundamentally justified by the fact that God had made man
in his own image and likeness (Gn 1:26). This fact, with its far-
reaching consequences, provides the basis for any possibility of a
relationship between the living God and man: if he speaks to us,
if he communicates his Spirit to us, this is because between him
and ourselves there exists a radical resemblance. 'We also are his

[41] This fact was noted by Eusebius (H.E. 1, 2, 7; 11–12; 24–25) and, as
regards Abraham, by almost all the Fathers (for the Ante-Nicene Fathers,
cf. refs. in Bardy's edition of Eusebius, *Sources chrétiennes*, 31, 1952, p. 7.
[42] Cf. among others, J. Bonsirven, *Le Judaisme palestinien au temps de
Jésus-Christ*, Paris, 1935, vol. 1, pp. 145f; 221; J. Pedersen, *Israel: Its
Life and Culture*, London, 1940, vols. 3–4, pp. 647f; N. Michaeli, *Dieu à
l'image de l'homme*, Neuchâtel–Paris, 1950. T. Boman '*Das hebraische
Denken im Vergleich mit dem Griechischen*, 2nd edition, Göttingen, 1954,
pp. 84f, 91; L. Bouyer: *La Bible et l'Évangile*, Paris, 1942, p. 143 (English
transl. *The Meaning of Sacred Scripture*, London, 1960). M. T. L. Penido,
on the other hand, in *Le rôle de l'Analogie en Théologie dogmatique* (*Bibl.
Thomiste, 13*), Paris, 1931. pp. 81, 100, takes a purely Greek and metaphysical view of this question.
[43] Cf. this fine passage of Karl Barth who, having so powerfully cham-
pioned God's transcendence, discovers his 'manhood'. 'How is it possible
to *eliminate* the manood of God, when we have just observed that his
divinity means precisely his freedom to love, and consequently his power
of being not only in the heights but also in the depths, of being great and
at the same time little, self-contained and yet in fellowship with others
and for their sake, so that he may give himself to them?' K. Barth,
L'humanité de Dieu (*Cahiers du Renouveau, 14*), Geneva, 1956, p. 27. St
Bonaventure remarks profoundly: 'Hoc est maximum miraculum, ut
quod Deus sit homo, primus sit novissimus'. (*In Hexaemeron* Coll. 3, 13:
Opera, ed. Quaracchi, vol. 5, p. 345b.

offspring', says St Paul, quoting Aratus (Ac 17:28). And, there-fore, in God there exists, in a state of divine perfection, what may be called an exalted form of manhood.

And yet the moment we have said this, we have to contradict it. For 'an exalted form of manhood' suggests the idea of one and the same nature with the same qualities merely transposed to a supremely high level, but 'state of divine perfection' signifies a positively infinite distance, a radical and unalterable disparity. God is God; between him and us no common reality exists, noth-ing vast enough to embrace both terms. 'My thoughts are not your thoughts, neither are your ways my ways. For as the heavens are higher than the earth, so are my ways higher than your ways and my thoughts than your thoughts' (Is 55:8-9). The difference is, in fact, far greater even than this. For, after all, there is a yard-stick shared by both the heavens and the earth; we can measure the distance between the stars and calculate the sun's temperature, but between God and us no such yardstick is available. God is God.

And yet the expressions we use about him, based on what he has previously communicated to us, correspond to a reality. Note the phrase: based on what he has previously communicated to us. For without his revealing word, we should never have presumed to say, for example, that begetting and birth, fatherhood and son-ship are realities existing in him. These are characteristics that belong to man. The Church, nevertheless, has sought to under-stand the affirmations of the New Testament in such a way that their full significance is retained, by always keeping in mind the transcendence and the mystery of the super-eminent manner in which they are verified in God. It is under the aegis of this kind of dialectical knowledge, discussed in philosophy or theology in the treatise on analogy, that what follows will proceed. We shall try to grasp the element of *theo*-logy, that is, of revelation of *God*, contained in the event of Christmas which is pre-eminently a feast of the redemptive 'economy'.

This *theo*-logy is expressed in the well-known phrase: what is most remarkable is not that Jesus Christ is God, but that *God IS Jesus Christ*. There must therefore be something in God which enabled him to become that man; and this is not simply his omni-potence which, in itself, is only infinite possibility; nor is it only

the freedom of his grace which allows him to come down from his
great height to our own lowliness.[44] No, it is something positive
which impels him to this gracious deed and to become man.

Throughout the Bible God shows himself as being both transcendent and self-giving, utterly exalted and intimately near. He
exists in absolute perfection in his own realm of holiness, and yet
he is wholly concerned with us, wholly engaged in self-communication. It is indeed most remarkable that, in the biblical revelation,
these two apparently contradictory aspects not only co-exist but
are affirmed together in the same texts or the same episodes which
ultimately acquire their total truth in Jesus Christ. It follows that
transcendence, if it is the transcendence of the God of faith, cannot exist without also implying God's gracious condescension and
familiarity and vice versa. I shall discuss only three passages
taken from the Old Testament.

Jacob left Beersheba, and went toward Haran. And he
came to a certain place, and stayed there that night, because the
sun had set. Taking one of the stones of the place, he put it
under his head and lay down in that place to sleep. And he
dreamed that there was a ladder set up on the earth, and the top
of it reached to heaven; and behold, the angels of God were
ascending and descending on it! And behold, the Lord stood
above it and said, 'I am the Lord, the God of Abraham your
father . . .'. Then Jacob awoke from his sleep and said, 'Surely
the Lord is in this place; and I did not know it.' And he was
afraid and said, 'How awesome is this place! This is none other
than the house of God, and this is the gate of heaven'. (Gn 28:
10–13, 16–17)

Terribilis est locus iste! The liturgy repeats this exclamation in
the Introit for the dedication of a church. God's presence produces
that religious fear which springs from the sense of his absolute
holiness. Those who have had such close experience of it feel it to

[44] It is unnecessary to have recourse here to the analysis made by R.
Otto and historians of religion, of the conjunction, in the experience of
the 'holy' of the elements of the *tremendum* and the *fascinosum*. The experience of the saints is sufficient. At the Last Supper St John rested on
Jesus' breast, but when the Lord appeared to him in the Apocalypse, he
fell prostrate to the ground like one dead (Rv 1:17). St Francis of Assisi,
who made the first crib at Greccio, on Mount Alverna could only say,
'Who are you, Lord, and who am I?'

be immense and infinitely above them.[45] Jacob experienced dread; the place at which God came into contact with the earth is a place to be dreaded. But it *was* the point of divine contact, where communication and therefore proximity had been established, where a constant coming and going, from above to below and from below to above, is in operation. This verse was quoted by Jesus as applying to himself (Jn 1:51), to his own body as the place at which God really touched the earth, the unique situation wherein the two-way process of grace and thanksgiving, of prayer offered and the gift received, was in active motion.

> In the year that King Uzziah died I saw the Lord sitting upon a throne, high and lifted up; and his train filled the temple. Above him stood the seraphim; each had six wings: with two he covered his face and with two he covered his feet, and with two he flew. And one called to another and said, 'Holy, holy, holy is the Lord of hosts; the whole earth is full of his glory.' And the foundations of the threshold shook at the voice of him who called, and the house was filled with smoke. And I said, 'Woe to me! For I am lost; for I am a man of unclean lips, and I dwell in the midst of a people of unclean lips; for my eyes have seen the King, the Lord of hosts!' (Is 6:1–5)

Isaiah had seen God's majesty and he, too, became afraid. How could he face the presence of the thrice-holy God and yet not die? The narrative goes on to give the answer: 'Then flew one of the seraphim to me, having in his hand a burning coal he had taken with tongs from the altar. And he touched my mouth and said, "Behold this has touched your lips, your guilt is taken away, and your sin forgiven".' (Is 6:6). God's holiness and purity that establish him apart and at a vast distance from man, have now been communicated to the prophet, and later they will be communicated to the people to whom he is sent, to whom he will go in the obedience of faith. The result is, that in Isaiah, the title 'the Holy One' acquires a special meaning as 'the Holy One of *Israel*.' Immanence and communication are associated with transcendence and are inseparable from it.

The liturgy has made the hymn of the angels in Isaiah its own,

[45] Cf. E. Petersen, *Le Livre des Anges* (French transl. Cl. Champollion, Paris, 1954, pp. 45–54).

and with its instinct for the fulfilment of prophecy, it has added
the words: 'Blessed is he who is coming in the name of the Lord.'
It realises that the Most High has come and will come again. It
also realises that when Isaiah saw Yahweh in the temple, he had a
vision of Christ in glory (Jn 12:41). For since the incarnation, since
Calvary and the resurrection, God's glory dwells in Christ's now
glorious body, and Christians participate in it when the Eucharist
is celebrated and received.[46]

Now we go back five centuries. Moses had come to Sinai for the
first time. He sought refuge there. It was in the midst of a desert,
completely empty. Suddenly he saw a bush on fire and the bush
went on burning but was not consumed. He drew near.

> When the Lord saw that he turned aside to see, God called to
> him out of the bush, 'Moses, Moses!' And he said, 'Here am I.'
> Then he said, 'Do not come near; put off your shoes from your
> feet, for the place on which you are standing is holy ground.'
> And he said, 'I am the God of your Father, the God of Abraham,
> the God of Isaac, and the God of Jacob.' And Moses hid his
> face, for he was afraid to look at God. (Ex 3:4–6)

Thus Moses, also, was afraid. Once again the place of God's
self-manifestation was a place of dread, unapproachable. Nevertheless God *did* manifest himself there, and he not only manifested himself, he called. At that moment Moses received his calling
and his mission, and also at that moment God revealed his name:

> Moses said to God, 'Who am I that I should go to Pharaoh
> and bring forth the sons of Israel out of Egypt?' He said, 'But
> I will be with you . . .'. Then Moses said to God, 'If I come to
> the people of Israel and say to them, "The God of your fathers
> has sent me to you", and they ask me, "What is his name?"
> What shall I say to them?' God said to Moses, 'I AM WHO I AM'.
> (Ex 3:12–13)

[46] Cf. St Augustine, *Enar. in Ps. 101, serm.* 2, 10 (*PL* 37, 1311): 'Vade,
inquit, et dic filius Israel: "Qui est" misit me ad vos . . . "Ego sum",
inquit, "Deus Abraham, et Deus Isaac, et Deus Jacob" ' (Ex 3:13–15).
'Audisti quid sim apud me, audi et quid sim propter te . . .' *In Ps 134*, 6
(*PL* 37, 1742–3): 'Quod enim "ego sum qui sum", ad me pertinet, quod
autem "Deus Abraham, Deus Isaac et Deus Jacob", ad te pertinet. Et si
deficis in eo quod mihi sum, cape quod tibi sum.' But God is already, in
what he is in himself and for himself, what he desires to be for us.

This sublime passage which includes God's answer, may, it is agreed, be translated in three or even four different ways. It may be translated, with the Septuagint, the *Bible de Jérusalem* and most other Bibles: 'I am who am'. God replies to Moses who has asked him to declare his name, in a way that is indeed mysterious but is also positive. Etienne Gilson calls the metaphysics of Exodus that of 'Aseity'. It may also be translated: 'I am what I am', 'I am who I am'. In this case God would be refusing to reply, refusing to give his name and withholding his mystery. Finally, it may be translated: 'I will be who (or what) I will be', for the verb used in v. 14 is the same as that in v. 12 which all the Bibles agree to be translated: 'I will be with thee'. In this case, God is not considered in his being but in his activity; activity in relation to us and for our sake, always imminent, always prevenient. Whom am I? My deeds will show you. I shall be what you shall see when I deliver you from Egypt, feed you in the desert, guide you to Sinai to receive my Law, there to enter into a covenant with me and thus become my people; when I lead you to the Promised Land and bring you into it. I shall be the one who will punish you for your sins, bring you to nought through defeat and exile, but also the one who will deliver and re-establish you and bestow indestructible life upon you.

On this latter view the Living God, the God of Faith, is identical with the Being who, in the final Book of Revelation, again describes himself as 'Who is, who was, who is to come' (Rv 1:4, 8; 11:17; 16:5). He not only *is*—Aseity; he not only *was*—Eternity; *he comes*! He does not exist simply in himself and for his own sake in his transcendent perfection; he exists for us also, he is with us, opening out for us the way of life and accompanying us along it as the giver of being and life.[47] 'I shall be who I shall be'; this you will see from my deeds. In the end, in the fullness of time, when all those incomplete and transient comings are over, I shall be the

[47] A German mother told me (in Stuttgart, 1958) of the following question asked by her small son; it raises a theological point of importance and, incidentally, demolishes Marcion's whole system: 'Ist der *grosse* Gott auch der liebe Gott?' Cf. St Irenaeus: 'They (the Gnostics) believe that they have discovered a "great God" whom no one can know, who has no communication with men, who does not administer the affairs of this world. In reality, this is the God of Epicurus whom they have found, a God without a function, either for himself or others—a God without a Providence' (*A.H.* 3, 24, 2).

one who will come to you in person, who will dwell bodily in your midst and remain with you for ever. I, personally, will be your Passover, I myself will be the pathway through the Red Sea; I shall be the true Manna, the true Bread of Life, the true Serpent raised up in the desert, the true deliverer and the ransom for your sins. I myself will be the covenant of my people. I SHALL BE JESUS CHRIST. For when God is not only 'He is, he was', but also, as his mystery reaches its completion, 'He comes', he is called Jesus Christ. And he says to us, 'You will die in your sins unless you believe that I am he' (Jn 8:24).

The perfect reality of the Living God, of the God of Abraham, Isaac and Jacob, of the God of Moses, of the God 'who is, who was and who comes', in short, of the God 'for our sakes', is Jesus Christ, 'For in him, the whole fullness of the deity dwells bodily' (Col. 2:9). On Mount Sinai, in the apse of the little church erected on the top of Djebel Musa where Moses encountered God and received the Law, there is depicted, between Moses and Elijah, the burning bush in the form of a circle emitting flames surrounded and interspersed with green foliage. Within the flaming circle we see the Virgin and her Child upon her breast. This is the way that He-who-is appeared, in the place, at the moment when 'visibiliter Deum cognoscimus'.

It is clear that the God-for-our-sakes is the God of the 'economy' of redemption and everything done in that economy is done freely and gratuitously. As such they do not belong to the necessary mystery of God's nature. Nevertheless they imply and reveal something of his nature. They are theophanic. Christmas, which already implies the whole redemptive mystery from the agony to Pentecost and even to our final glorification, and which is the culmination of those communications that are scattered throughout the course of sacred history, is a revelation of the fact that the Absolute does not exist only in and for itself but that it is self-giving Love, that is, *Agapè*. 'God is Love' (Jn 4:8 and 16). 'In this the love of God was made manifest (*ephanerôthè*) among us, that God sent his only Son into the world, so that we might live through him' (1 Jn 4:9). No Absolute exists which is not also Love, no mighty God who is not the loving God, God turned towards us, God for us. There is no 'I am', no *Ens a se*, no Aseity, that does not contain within itself, not only the possibility, but

D

also the positive desire to be 'I will be (for your sake, moving towards you, acting with you)'. There is no 'He is, he was' that is not simultaneously 'he comes'. Eternally, 'He is, he was' and this is the reality that he became when he came to us, and that is the reason why 'and this is eternal life, that they know thee the only true God, and Jesus Christ whom thou hast sent' (Jn 17:3).

As I have already remarked the economy of redemption inevitably raises ontological problems, problems of divine ontology—the words sound presumptuous and I venture to use them only because the word of God exists, and with its assistance we may try at least to stammer—and problems of general ontology also. For if the Being *a se* is *Caritas*, this must have repercussions in the ontology of his whole creation and expecially in that of those created beings whom he made in his own image. In the revelation of the supreme Being something is also revealed about the real nature of all being. All study, all appreciation of what can be called the Christian or Judaeo-Christian specific characteristics raises the question of the Christian or Judaeo-Christian meaning of ontology. It is a problem of overriding importance. It was discussed by Fr L. Laberthonnière, though unfortunately he came to it with a misunderstanding of and a morbid prejudice against scholasticism. He asserted that a Christian ontology can only be an ontology of charity. I am sure that this is true, but the separate stages in an approach to such an ontology must not be telescoped. It is true that only in charity does nature itself, through grace, find its salvation, that is its meaning and integral completion. But before reaching this point it would be opportune to have recourse to the Augustinian analysis of *esse vere esse* rediscovered or reproduced by M. Blondel in terms of the degrees of being.[48] We may distinguish 'being' as implying mere existence, and 'being' with its full content and 'consolidated', having attained its right relationship with the Supreme Being. The finality of any created being, its reference to a norm, its destiny, belong to its integral, ontological constitution. It is possible *to be* and still be lacking in the *truth* of one's being; and it is possible to attain that truth.[49]

[48] *L'Être et les êtres*, Paris, 1936.
[49] That this is in fact the ontology of the Bible, and that it is in agreement with some aspects of Platonism (one of the reasons for the Platonism of the Fathers) is clearly shown by T. Bowman, *op. cit.*

Heaven, that is salvation, is when the relationship between the beings that form the entire universe with the Supreme Being, have become perfect. St Paul refers to this consummation in the words, 'when . . . God may be everything to everyone' (1 Co 15:28). And since in Judaeo-Christianity it is the end that sheds light on the beginning, just as, biblically speaking, the truth of things is eschatological, it is this that points the way to the truth of all the ontological situations that exist on a level lower than that of the ultimate ontological reality.

One of the metaphysical problems confronting the mind is that of knowing how there can be beings who exist apart from Being itself? This is one of E. Du Bois-Reymond's 'enigmas', and Lachelier also asked himself the question. It is clear that Being can only refer and reduce to itself everything that comes into existence —we will not say, apart from itself or outside itself but distinct from itself. The *fiat* 'Let the world be', at the beginning includes in its imperative the 'God who is all in all' at the end. But the very act by which the Absolute relates all things to itself is that by which it communicates being, life and happiness. Between this self-reference and the bestowal of happiness there is no contradiction, but identity—a truth expressed in the profound remark of St Irenaeus: *Gloria Dei, vivens homo. Vita autem hominis, visio Dei.*[50] The Absolute *is* Love, and Love is self-giving, self-communication.[51] The Absolute is Generosity.

It is in Jesus Christ, in God's coming in our flesh, that we are made to realise both the extent and the manner in which the Absolute is Love and Generosity. Not only and not straightway as glory and victory, but first as humility and self-abasement. We have seen that Christmas is the beginning of that movement, through which the Son of God, 'the splendour of God's glory, the

---

[50] *A.H.* 4, 20, 7 (*PG* 7, 1037). Biblically speaking the glory of God consists in communicating glory: Is 55:5; 62:7; Ba 4:37–5:1; Rm 9:22–3; Ep 1:18; 3:16; Col 1:27. On the problem arising from an apparent opposition between the glory of *God* and *my* happiness cf. de Lubac, 'Le motif de la création dans "L'Être et les êtres" ' in *NRT* 65 (1938), pp. 220–5; H. Boüessé, 'Théologie et Doxologie' in *L'Année théolog.* 11 (1950), pp. 193–212, 269–303; J. Huby, 'Salut personnel et Gloire de Dieu' in *Études* 204 (5th Sept. 1930), pp. 513–28.

[51] St Thomas in his theology of the motive of the incarnation uses the principle he found expressed in Pseudo-Dionysius: 'Bonum est diffusivum sui' (IIIa, qu. 1, art. 1). See C. V. Héris, *Le Mystère de Dieu*, Paris, 1946.

flawless expression of his nature', reduced himself to the condition of a servant. The Absolute being absolute necessarily relates all things to itself, but it does this with an unimaginable graciousness set in motion by love. The relative would not be reintegrated in the Absolute nor time be consummated in eternity, nor created beings find their Creator, nor all beings become unified in Being itself, if the Absolute had not come down into the relative, Eternity into time, the Creator into created being, Being itself into the world of beings, the Holy into the world of sin. The Absolute is love that reaches as far as this; the *Ens a se* is *Caritas* of this dimension. God's graciousness, as shown in the whole series of his comings and supremely in the *kenosis* of Jesus Christ, has also its *theological* truth: in God, in the being of God as made known to us in the economy of salvation.

Mankind's entire history has gone astray and been shattered because Adam formed a false idea of God. He wanted to become like God. I hope that you have never made Adam's sin consist in that. For what other ambition could he have had? And was it not this to which God had precisely called him? No, Adam had simply mistaken his model. He has thought that God is an independent, autonomous, self-sufficient being and in order to become like him he rebelled and disobeyed.

But when God revealed himself, when he wished to show what he really is, he revealed himself as love, tenderness, self-sharing, infinite delight in another, attachment, dependent, obedient, obedient unto death.

By believing that he could become God he was in fact becoming totally different from him. He fell back into his solitude, whereas the reality of God is communion.[52]

What remains to be said? Only a conclusion whose theological and pastoral significance is, I believe, extremely important.

The modern world, considered as beginning with the Renaissance—its new anthropology has been analysed by Dilthey and Cassirer[53]—is like a man who is working intensely and even

[52] L. Evely, *Notre Père. Aux sources de notre fraternité*, Paris, 1956, p. 43.

[53] W. Dilthey, *Weltanschauung und Analyse des Menschen seit Renaissance und Reformation* (Ges. Schriften, 2), Leipzig, 1914, 3rd edition, 1929; E. Cassirer, *Individuum und Kosmos in der Philosophie der Renaissance Studien Bibl. Warburg*), Leipzig, 1927.

successfully, and yet suffering unawares from a cancer, undetected even by those responsible for his health. The world is nursing a tragic equivocation of which few of the Christian laity or priests —the salt of the earth!—seem to be aware. This consists of a separation between the Absolute and Love. Love has become humanised, secularised, reduced to a naturalistic level. I shall not say, deploring it, that *agapè-caritas* has become *humanitas*;[54] there was no need for it to become that; it was so already. What is needed, rather, is that it should so remain. Christmas is for ever the day 'when the goodness and loving kindness of God our saviour appeared' (Tt 3:4). The truth is, however, as Maritain explained in *Humanisme intégral*, that modern humanism is not constituted by the discovery of human values after a long period during which man had been misappreciated, but by a humanism without God, and the incarnation, a non-theocentric humanism.

It may be said that the modern world, wholly focused on man, has developed a *humanitas*, a 'philanthropy' that is merely human and terrestrial, not theocentric. On the other hand Christians have to some extent lost the sense of the inclusion of God's *humanitas* or 'philanthropy' within theology. As a consequence the dialectic of theology ceased to be the perfect expression of that Absolute who is Love. It tended to become theology as a cultus— a cultus, a duty performed for an Absolute considered as enthroned in the remote heavens, in a kind of heavenly Versailles. This development is perceptible in the religion of the French classical period, as it evolved—while still retaining plenty of grandeur and vitality—after about 1660, then in an even more moralistic and human form which found expression in the eighteenth century, and finally in the less mystical religious or apostolically committed sections of the middle class in the nineteenth century. To demonstrate this with the necessary documentation would be too lengthy a procedure.

This putting asunder of what God has joined together has had serious consequences. When we examine the ambiguities, the objections which for many of our contemporaries form the stumbling block on the road to faith, we always arrive, by different routes, at the same difficulty: 'God? But what for? I prefer

[54] This is one of the themes of M. Fuerth, *Caritas und Humanitas. Zur Form und Wandlung des christlichen Liebesgedankens*, Stuttgart, 1933.

ordinary men to religious people. Religion is simply a higher and subtler egoism. What has religion to do with work, with the realities of marriage, with the problems, great or small, of real life?'

Men desire a humanity without God because—as Yahweh explained to Samuel: 'They have not rejected you but they have rejected me from being king over them' (1 Sam 8:7). To some extent also because we have too often presented them with a God without 'philanthropy', a theology that did not call for an anthropology or its immediate concomitant, a first commandment that could be observed with the second.

The solution, inasmuch as it depends on us, is not to pay an exaggerated attention to mankind and to the world, but to return to the integral truth about the Living God, the God of the Bible and of Faith and of the History of Salvation. There is nothing more urgent than to strive to know and make known the *true* God, the God whose last word is Jesus Christ.

APPENDIX

An anthology of patristic texts on Christ, the Revealer of God

Clement of Rome (Co 36:2): 'Through him (Christ) we know as in a mirror the unblemished and sublime countenance (of the Father)'; 59:2: 'Through Christ, God calls us to pass from darkness to light, from ignorance to knowledge of the glory of his name.'

Ignatius of Antioch (Ep 19:3): 'Ignorance was scattered, its former kingdom overthrown, when God appeared in human form to bestow the new reality of eternal life'.

Polycarp, tied to the stake for his burning (Martyrium Polycarpi, 14): 'Lord, God Almighty, Father of Jesus Christ, thy well beloved and hallowed Son, who has taught us to know thee . . .'.

Irenaeus, A. H., 3.62 (*PG*, 7, 861): 'Thus through *the Son* who is *in the Father* (Jn 14:10–11), the Father became manifest *bearing testimony to the Son*, and the Son declaring the Father. As Isaiah also expresses it: "And I, saith the Lord God, am the witness, together with my Child whom I have chosen, so that you may recognise and believe and understand that it is I".' A.H., 3, 11, 5 (*PG*, 7, 883): 'The God *who made the earth* and commanded it *to bear fruit*, and who *created the waters and made the springs to well up*, this same God in these last days has given the human race the blessing of food and the grace of drink, through his Son—God "incomprehensible", through him who is "comprehensible", God "invisible" through him who made himself "visible".' A.H., 4,6, 5–7 (*PG*, 7, 989–90). 'Et ad hoc Filium relavit Pater ut per eum omnibus manifestetur, ut eos quidem qui credunt ei justi, et incorruptelam, et in aeternum refrigerium recipiat (credere autem ei est facere eius voluntatem) . . . Omnibus igitur revelavit se Pater, omnibus verbum suum visibile faciens.' N.7: 'Et sine illo (Filio) nemo potest cognoscere Deum. Agnitio enim Patris, Filius, agnitio autem Filii in Patre, et per Filium revelata, et propter hoc Dominus dicebat: Nemo cognoscit' (Mt 11:27). A. H., 5, 1 (*PG*, 7, 1120–1): 'We should have no other way of coming to know the things of God if our Master, who is God's Word, had not become man. No one else, save his own Word, can tell us about the Father. "For who has ever known the mind of the Lord, or who has been his counsellor?" ' (Rm 11:34; Is 40:13). In the *Presentation of the Apostolic Preaching* (*Epideixis*) 92 (*PO*, 12, 796), Irenaeus applies to the incarnation the verse of Isaiah (65:1): 'I have shown myself to those who did not ask for me' (cf. Rm 10:20).

Clement of Alexandria: 'Christ is the face (*prosôpon*) of God' (Paed., 1,7,51).

Origen, *In Joan.*, 6, 32 (*PG*, 14, 821–2): 'the Son glorifies the Father by making him known'. *De Principiis*, 1, 2, 8 (*PG*, 11, 136): 'Verbum quoniam non solum splendor gloriae esse dicitur ab Apostolo, sed et figura expressa substantiae vel subsistentiae ejus . . .'. Why is Christ called this? Because he reveals the Father and also because of the equality between the eternal Word and the Father. Also *Contra Celsum*, 1, 97 (*PG*, 11, 1445).

Anaphora of Serapion, 1, 3: 'We praise thee who art known through the only Son, through him revealed, explained and made known to the created world . . .'.

Athanasius, *De Incarnatione Verbi*, chapters 14, 16, 45, 46 (*PG*, 25, 120–1, 124–5, 176–7, 177–80).

Hilary, *De Trinitate*, Bk 5, n. 20 (*PL*, 10, 142 and 143): 'God manifests himself, God speaks of the God whom he has seen. Only by God can God be understood.'

John Chrysostom, *In Joannem*, Lom. 12 (*PG*, 59, 81–4); Hom.

15 (*PG*, 59, 97–102): Christ the image of the invisible God (Col 1:15); God, invisible even to spiritual creatures, has been manifested in the flesh (1 Tm 3:16).

Cyril of Alexandria, *In Joannem*, Bk 1, chapter 10 (*PG*, 73, 177); Bk 11, chapter 1 (*PG*, 74, 461); chapter 3 (*PG*, 74, 493–6); chapter 7 (*PG*, 74, 500): Jesus has made God known *as Father*.

Leo the Great, Sermo 26, 2 (*PL*, 54, 213).

Finally, reference may be made to the following studies: F. Amiot, 'Deum nemo vidit unquam' in *Mélanges bibliques A. Robert*, Paris, 1957, pp. 470–7; J. Alfaro, 'Cristo Glorioso, Revelador del Padre' in *Christus Victor mortis* (*Gregorianum, vol. 39*) Rome, 1958, pp. 222–70; R. D. Luckhart, 'Matthew 11:27 in the *Contra Haereses* of St Irenaeus' in *Rev. de l'Univ. d'Ottawa*, 23 (1953), pp. 65–79; R. Latourette, 'L'idée de révélation chez les Pères de l'Église' in *Sciences ecclésiast.*, 11 (1959), pp. 297–344 (from St Ignatius the Martyr to St Augustine inclusively); A. Van der Bosch, 'Le mystère de l'Incarnation chez S. Bernard' in *Citeaux*, 10 (1959), pp. 83–92; 165–77; 245–67 (Majesty and condescension); *idem*, 'Dieu devenu connaissable dans le Christ d'après S. Bernard', in *Collectanea Ord. Cisterc. Ref.*, 22 (1960), pp. 11–20; 'Le Christ, Dieu devenu imitable d'après S. Bernard', *ibid.*, pp. 341–55.

CHAPTER EIGHT

Jesus Christ, Lamb of God[1]

I. THE TEACHING OF THE BIBLE

The Lamb of the Passover. 'Let this month be for you the beginning; it shall be for you the first month of the year. Speak to the full assembly of Israel and say: On the tenth day of this month let every man take a lamb, one lamb for every family, for every house. . . . A lamb without a blemish, a male of the first year, you shall take it from the sheep or the goats. You shall keep it until the fourteenth day of this month, and the whole assembly of Israel shall kill it in the evening. And the blood shall be taken and sprinkled on the two side posts and the lintel of the doors of the houses in which it will be eaten. The flesh shall be eaten on that night, roasted by fire, with unleavened bread and bitter herbs. . . . This is the way you shall eat: your loins girt, sandals on your feet, your staff in you hand, and you shall eat in haste. This is the Passover of Yahweh.

'For on that night I shall pass through Egypt, and I shall strike all the first born of the land of Egypt, both man and beast, and I will bring judgement upon all the gods of Egypt. I am Yahweh. The blood shall be a sign for you in your houses; I shall see the blood and I shall pass over you, and the plague shall not fall on you to destroy you. When I strike the land of Egypt, you shall keep the memory of this day, and celebrate it by a feast in honour of Yahweh; you shall celebrate it from generation to generation

---

[1] Conference given to the ecumenical Study Congress of Protestant Youth, Versailles, 4 Sept. 1946. Text published in *Cahiers bibliques de Foi et Vie.* Jan.–Feb. 1947, pp. 46–7.

as an institution for ever.' (Ex 12:2, 3, 5–8, 11–14). This is one of those narratives in which the difference between a Judaic interpretation of the Old Testament and a Christian interpretation amounts to a Christological interpretation, an interpretation in the spirit of Christ and pointing to him. I had occasion to verify this personally when, as a prisoner of war, on the approach of the Jewish Passover, we asked one of our Jewish fellow prisoners who was acting as rabbi to explain the meaning of the ceremony then being prepared, I realised that this Passover which for us implies so great a mystery was for them merely an anniversary, at most something like the relief of Orléans or the armistice of November, an anniversary of national liberation. For us, on the other hand, the lamb of the Exodus is lit up with all the later light shining on it from the mystery of the Lamb of God, as it was disclosed in the Servant of Yahweh, the person and above all the death of Jesus Christ, the visions of the Apocalypse.

In the Bible, as in the general activity of God, everything is first presented in images that foreshadow the reality, as a seed that will develop into a full grown organism. The Bible as a whole grows from a seed to its full unfolding, from a genesis to an apocalypse, and it is the final reality that shows the meaning of the initial revelation. At the time of the Exodus when Israel's constitution was first truly established the whole process began with the lamb that was sacrificed; it ended with the lamb that was victorious, with that marriage of the lamb, participation in which enables us to see God (Rv 21:23). Its sacrifice marked the beginning of the year, but it is far more than a chronological beginning, it is the true origin of the whole development of the people of God. That movement consists of men who are constantly leaving Egypt, crossing the Red Sea, entering the Promised Land. The Church is the constant succession of this people of God who give up the world's allurement and live in the desert from the bread that is given daily and who take possession of the promised inheritance. But at both the beginning and the end of this pilgrimage, there stands the Lamb. It is through the power of the blood of the Lamb that the people of God has been delivered from slavery; it is through the power of this blood that the people receive their inheritance and, in the mystical marriage, become one Body with the Lamb. As a result, in Christ, the world's heir, there will be

Christ alone, only the total Christ, and love will be love within that body.[2]

This story records one of God's judgements on the world, 'on the gods of Egypt'. And yet one race escaped that judgement, the people whom God had chosen to be his own. It was the blood of the lamb that marked them out as God's people in the midst of Egypt. The Bible contains other instances of signs bestowed as a mark of grace or protection; Cain and his descendants bore a mark of grace even in their punishment (Gn 4:15). When Jerusalem was to be punished, those who had been faithful were marked with a 'tau' (a letter in the form of a cross) on their foreheads, and the Apocalypse mentions several times a sign by which the servants of the Beast are distinguished (13:16; 14:9; 16:2; 19:20; 20:4), whereas God's servants are marked with a seal—the prefigurement of the mysterious sacramental 'character'—on their foreheads.

The deliverance and salvation given to Israel were entirely the result of God's grace; Israel was literally *spared* and *saved*; it did not spare itself. But although the blood of the lamb was the source of salvation, it had to be applied. 'And the blood shall be taken and sprinkled on the two side posts and on the lintels of the doors . . .' (v. 7). There was something *to be done*: the blood had to be taken and one had to show oneself to God, as it were imbued or marked with it. This is a feature that frequently recurs in the life of the people of God; the land of Canaan, for example, was *given* as an inheritance, given by grace, and yet it had to be conquered. God's gift is bestowed on us in such a way it behoves us to do something if we are to profit by it. This is the economy, prefigured in the lamb of the Passover, of the Christian sacraments; these are indeed gifts of grace, but gifts that through personal effort we have to make our own.

The servant of Yahweh (Is 52: espec. v. 7; cf. Ac 8:32; Jr 11:19). The Christian intepretation of the Old Testament is again, in this instance, singularly helped by the reality of the gospel. We know the meaning of the servant of Yahweh because we knew who that servant was; this was the content of the deacon Philip's explanation to the eunuch of Queen Candace, who did not understand

[2] 'Erit unus Christus, amans seipsum', St Augustine (*In Ep. Joan,* 10, 3).

what he was reading because he did not know the person whom it was about. The servant of Yahweh is compared to a lamb in the sense that, being sacrificed for us, he submitted without complaint.[3] Christian religious feeling has been drawn to the contemplation of the Man of Sorrows bearing the iniquity of us all, and in his passion maintaining a silence and a gentle tenderness that confounds our pride. One intense aspect of medieval devotion can be wholly explained by its contemplation of Christ as the suffering servant. An entire aspect of its theology, i.e. its Anselmian development of the theology of the redemption, originates from the same source, for if the redeeming sacrifice came to be considered as a 'vicarious substitution', this was due to the prophecy of the servant Yahweh. But on this point I prefer the testimony of a Protestant exegete whom I shall again quote later on.

Oscar Cullmann has observed[4] that God's plan, centred as it is on the unique fact of Jesus Christ, entails for the time before Christ that leads up to him a kind of progressive concentration upon him, and for the time after him a progressive expansion originating in him. Not mankind but one particular race is chosen and out of this race a remnant is set apart to carry out God's purpose, and finally the choice is narrowed to one man, one individual: the servant of Yahweh in Isaiah, the Son of Man in Daniel (7). The process is one of substituting an increasingly particularised reality, that finally arrives at Jesus, who in his death bears the full weight of man's salvation alone. Old Testament prophecy thus opens up wide avenues of insight into the reality of the gospel.

Jn 1:29 and 36. At the transitional point of prophecy and fulfilment we encounter a man who is indubitably a prophet, and who is yet surpassed by the least in the Kingdom—John the Baptist, the Forerunner. 'The Law and the Prophets were enough till John

---

[3] In Aramaic, the word *lamb* may also mean *servant*: cf. C. F. Burney, 'The Aramaic Origin of the Fourth Gospel'. Oxford, 1922, pp. 107f. J. Jeremias in *Zeitsch, f.Ntl.Wiss.* 1935, p. 115 and art. 'amnos' in Kittels Wörterbuch; Oscar Cullmann, *Christologie du N.T.'.* Neuchâtel–Paris, 1958, pp. 64f.

[4] Oscar Cullmann, 'La royauté du Christ et l'Eglise dans le N.T.' (*Cahiers bibliques de Foi et Vie*, Christmas, 1941), pp. 35f. *Christus und die Zeit*, Zurich, 1946, pp. 99–103.

appeared. But ever since, the kingdom of God has been proclaimed and everyone is storming his way into it' (Lk 16:16). John stands at the threshold of the gospel as one who personally bears witness to that which the Law and the Prophets in their entirety indicate as to what Christ should be, and at the same time points out *who* he is.

Mathias Grünewald's picture of the Baptist is well known: it is grimly realistic and hence likely to be considered historical, with profound overtones of doctrine and mystery. He is erect, cloaked in a large red mantle, and pointing with a huge forefinger, that is in marked contrast with sombre background of the picture, to Christ on the cross: Behold the Lamb of God!

In the beginning of the gospel as recorded by John who was then one of the Baptist's disciples but who thenceforward was to 'follow the Lamb wherever he went', Jesus is described as the Lamb of God. This title was probably meant to refer to the lamb-like characteristics which Isaiah attributed to the servant. Sometimes, the name lamb, ascribed to Jesus, is considered to be a testimony to his innocence, and in fact in the Bible the idea of innocence and that of a lamb are interconnected.[5] But apart from the probable reference to Isaiah there are two reasons that impel us to emphasise the idea of victim. First, the words themselves describe the Lamb as bearing the sins of the world and taking them away. Secondly, this is the aspect which is given special prominence in St John's gospel. There is the well-known problem of the chronology of this gospel with regard to the Last Supper and the crucifixion in comparison with that given by the Synoptic Gospels. St John's chronology, of course, is meant to bring out the fact that Jesus died at the hour when the Passover Lamb was eaten, and that he is the true Passover Lamb, just as he is the true life and light and the bread of heaven, etc. This is why St John records and stresses the fact, which the Passover Lamb prophetically foretold, that the soldiers pierced the side of Jesus but did not break his bones (Jn 19:36; cf. Ex 12:46; Nb 9:12). But together with blood, water flowed from Jesus' side; and the Fathers and the theologians agree in regarding this as a symbol of the sacraments that constitute the Church. These sacraments, they

[5] Cf. e.g. Ex 12:5; Lk 10:3, and especially P 1:19, which actually links together the two ideas of innocence and sacrifice.

say, issued from the side of the saviour sleeping in death, just as
Eve was drawn from Adam's side. So we also, the new Israel, the
true and ultimate people of God, receive existence from this Lamb.

The Apocalypse. In the Apocalypse Christ is described as a lamb
with the utmost emphasis, as a lamb, as *the* Lamb. The word used
is not the same as that which the Baptist used in order to denote
Jesus (ἀμνός), but ἀρνίον, which perhaps stresses the precise
idea of a lamb as distinct from sheep in general. A lamb is young
and weak—the idea has innumerable applications. And yet this
lamb is the centre of worship in heaven.

It is the lamb who has been sacrificed. 'Then, standing in the
very centre of the Throne and of the Four Living Creatures and
of the Elders, I saw a Lamb that seemed to have been slaughtered.
He had seven horns and seven eyes, which are the seven Spirits of
God, and are sent out into every corner of the earth. Then he
came and took the book from the right hand of him who was
seated upon the Throne' (5:7). 'There were myriads and myriads
and thousands of thousands, crying in a great voice, "Worthy is
the Lamb who was slain, to receive power and riches and wisdom,
and strength and honour and glory and blessing" ' (5:12, cf. 9).
Cf. also 13:8. The blood of this sacrificed lamb exerts power over
its followers. These owe their redemption to the lamb (v. 9); to
the lamb they owe the fact that the Accuser has been overcome.[6]
Through the lamb their garments have been whitened, and access
to the worship and the cool joys of heaven has been granted to
them (7:14).

The sacrificed lamb is also the conquering lamb. The Apocalypse was written when the persecution of Diocletian was at its
height, and its aim was to instil courage into believers undergoing
the 'Great Opression', (7:4). To them and to us it says: the Lamb
who was sacrificed reigns from henceforth. Soon, sacrificed and
conquering he will return and enable us to reign with him and
quench our thirst at the source of life. 'They will all go to war
against the Lamb, but the Lamb, with his called, chosen and
faithful followers, will conquer them. For he is Lord of lords and
King of kings'. (17:14).

---

[6] The Holy Spirit, on the other hand, is the intercessor and the
advocate.

This is why, although the Lamb appears to have been sacrificed, he is erect (5:6; 14:1); he stands 'before the throne of God', but he shared in the worship given to the Being upon the throne (5:13; 7:9, 10; 14:4) and he was himself enthroned. Thus the worship of believers, the adoration of those who have not succumbed to the beast is also a worship and adoration of the Lamb. This became a dominant theme in Christian art from the time of the ninth-century gospel illuminations to that of the famous reredos of Van Eyck.

The Lamb is not only a conqueror, he rules and is enthroned, he receives the adoration of believers and yet he is in a relationship of the closest intimacy with them. His transcendance is shown by his position as conqueror and King, but this transcendence is also shown as including communion in his life. Under a different metaphor the Lamb of the Apocalypse is thus seen to be identical with that person who is the Vine, we being the branches, whose body is the Church or the Bride, we being the members. The aspect of immanence is added to that of transcendence. In communication and life in common, God's self-revelation and his purpose for creation are consummated.

That purpose has unity as its goal. From the start it aimed at forming mankind into a people that would be *his* people. That people was Israel, and in the end the new and true Israel, the Church. That is why, in the Apocalypse, the Church is described as a people composed of every tribe and nation and tongue (7; cf. 14:1–5), as a city, the new, the final Jerusalem, in opposition to 'Babylon the great' upheld by the beast with the seven heads. Jerusalem is even personified, and the unity of all mankind within her is conceived as the unity of a single person.

But this purposeful unity goes further than unity among men; it entails communion between mankind and God, a communication and a sharing of life. The life given to the people of God issues from the throne of the Lamb, (7:17; 22:1). Ezekiel had seen the waters flowing from the new temple (Ezk 47). And Jesus explained that the true temple was the temple of his body (Jn 2:19, 21); he also said that the time was coming, in fact had come, when God was to be worshipped not in Jerusalem or in any confined place whatever, but in the Spirit and in truth (Jn 4:23–4). That time has in fact come in the Church, the body of Christ, the spiritual temple, in the Church wherein every soul, as a member of Christ, receiving life from his Spirit, becomes Jerusalem and God's temple. But this 'time' will only be fully realised in heaven, where John 'could see no temple in the City, for the Lord, the Almighty God and the Lamb are themselves its temple' (21:22).

'I saw the Holy City, the New Jerusalem, descending from God out of heaven, prepared as a Bride dressed in beauty for her husband. Then I heard a great voice from the throne crying, "See! The Home of God is with men, and he will live among them. They shall be his people, and God himself shall be with them and will wipe away every tear from their eyes . . ." ' (21:2-4). The new and final temple, wherein the worship of the new and eternal alliance occurs, is simultaneously God himself and the new Jerusalem, adorned for the marriage of the Lamb. 'For the wedding day of the Lamb has come, and his Bride has made herself ready. She may be seen dressed in linen, gleaming and spotless—for such linen is the righteous living of the Saints. . . . Happy are those who are invited to the wedding feast of the Lamb!' (19:7-9). The Bride of the Lamb is the Church, the final, the true Jerusalem with its twelve gates on which are inscribed the names of the twelve tribes of Israel and twelve foundation stones bearing twelve names, the names of the apostles of the Lamb (21:9-14).

Thus God's purpose reaches its completion and consummation in the final chapters of the final book; its seeds had been chosen in the first chapters of the first book. It is a single great movement from Genesis to the Apocalypse and its meaning, its entire meaning, is the formation of a people of God, a people united with God in the reality of a common life. It was *for this* and *in view of this* that 'in the beginning' man was made in the image of God, and made as man and woman (Gn 1:27). These great realities—being in the image of God, being a son of God—and the nuptials with God—[7]are all attempts to express the idea of a life in common, of a single life communicated to many and led by many. This is the mystery of the Mystical Body which, in the New Testament, is disclosed in various forms of expression about God's indwelling

---

[7] The intimate relationship between *'being a son'* and *'being in the image of'* is evident from St Paul's remarks on the Son as the image of the Father (2 Co 4:4; Col 1:15, etc.), and from the connection, which I think should be made, between Lk 3:38 and Gn 1:27 and v. 3.

and his life with his people, in that wedding which unites him with them, and is consummated in the marriage of the Lamb wherewith revelation terminates.[8] Christ and redeemed mankind will be two people in one flesh: the body of Christ, which is also the true and final temple of God.

The two aspects, brought out in the Apocalypse, of the Lamb as both sacrificed and conqueror, are intimately connected, and this connection needs clarifying.

The victory of the Lamb springs from its sacrifice. This is proclaimed in the canticles of both the elders and the angels: 'Worthy are thou to take the book and break its seals, for thou hast been slain and by thy blood has purchased for God men from every tribe and tongue, and people and nation'. 'Worthy is the Lamb who was slain, to receive power and riches and wisdom, and strength and honour and glory and blessing'. (5:9, 12).

The Apocalypse in this instance expresses the unanimous theology of the books of the New Testament which unite Christ's triumph and glory with his humiliation and Passion. The Son of man had to be lifted up as the serpent was lifted up in the desert in order that whoever believes in him may have eternal life (Jn 3:14–15). 'He humbled himself by living a life of utter obedience, even to the extent of dying, and the death he died was the death of a common criminal. That is why God has now lifted him so high and has given him the name beyond all names . . .' (Ph 2: 8–9). But no words more aptly express the connection between the cross and glory than those in the story of the disciples of Emmaus on the evening of Easter Day: 'Was it not fated that the Christ should suffer thus, and then should come into his glory?' (Lk 24:26; cf. Jn 7:39; Ac 8:32–5; 1 P 1:11).

The factor that is common to these passages is the affirmation of a conjunction between the cross and the self-sacrifice on the one hand, and the power of communicating life on the other, i.e. between Good Friday and Easter Day, on the other. Thus in our 'new creation', the cross—Christ, the second Adam being its originating power—becomes the true and new tree of life. Adolphe Diessmann, with this in mind, ends his study of the theme of the cross in St Paul with a reminder of Christ as the living vine, and of

---

[8] All these elements obviously need to be developed and expounded independently.

the cross as the tree of life.[9] This again is illustrated in Christian iconography; it frequently depicts the cross as the tree of life. Personally I think that this is one of the earliest and most comprehensive themes, and that the cross in full foliage which is distributed in the four sections of some of the ceilings of the catacombs, should be considered as an artistic expression of this interpretation of Christianity.

This connection between sacrifice and victory, death and life, seems to me to express a kind of inner law that is natural to life 'in Christ'. I have been amazed at the constant recurrence of life springing from death,[10] at the fact that the cross, and the cross alone, destroys the pride of life in us and releases the energies of that life which is hidden with Christ in God. Trial is the condition of renewal and progress. 'For thy sake we are killed all the day long; we were accounted as sheep for the slaughter. But in all these things we win an overwhelming victory through him who has proved his love for us' (Rm 8:36–37; cf. 2 Co 12:9–10).

II. CHRISTIANS CONFRONTED BY THE LAMB OF GOD

This doctrine, or rather this reality, of Christ the Lamb of God is for all Christians the centre of their faith and life. In fact it is this that makes us 'Christians'. As in the time of Moses, in Egypt, a people of God has been marked off from the world by the blood of

[9] Cf. his *Paulus*, 2nd ed. Tübingen, 1925, pp. 157–8, and 250–1. Out of a number of possible references I shall select only; Fr de Lubac 'L'arbre cosmique' in *Mélanges E. Podechard*, Lyons, 1945, pp. 191–8.

[10] In the discussion after my conference at Versailles this formula was criticised. On the one hand my suggestion that it was a law, almost a natural law, was disputed. On the other hand, it was said that life is *not the product of death*; it is God who brings life from death and Rm 6:23 was quoted: 'Sin *pays* its servants: the wage is death. But God *gives* to those who serve him: his free gift is eternal life through Jesus Christ our Lord'.

If I regard and continue to regard this connection between life and death in terms of a general law, and particularly as a law of the spiritual life it is because this is in agreement with both St Paul and personal and pastoral experience (cf. 2 Co 4:10–12, 16; Ph 3:11). Death, the process of dying, is constantly at work in us, promoting life, committing us to life, so much so that it tends to appear as originating life. But life obviously does not spring *from* death; it originates, by way of death, death to the obstructing elements, and beyond death, from the Living Being who died and rose again.

the Lamb. Since the gospel, membership of this people has been acquired not through carnal, racial relationship with Abraham's descendants but through a personal act of belief in the proclamation of salvation in Jesus Christ, which it is the duty of the Christian apostolate to transmit to the whole world. The specific point of the apostolic message and of the Christian faith is the forgiveness and newness of life that come from the sacrificed and conquering Lamb; that Lamb is 'our Lord Jesus Christ, who was delivered to death for our sins and raised again to secure our justification' (Rm 4:25). The essence of Christianity consists in participation in this forgiveness and newness of life, in making the work done for us ($\acute{v}\pi\grave{\epsilon}\rho\,\acute{\eta}\mu\hat{\omega}\nu$—for our benefit) by the Lamb of God a practical reality within us.

This is our common need, and from it we live. And since it is the great unifying factor that exists even among Christians who are otherwise separated, it may be useful to note the way in which each of the great Christian communities proclaims this essential truth and derives its life from it.

(a) *The Catholic Church.* The ministry of the Church is wholly concerned with communicating to mankind the mystery of the Lamb and its achievement. This she does by means of two great activities: the preaching of the word to which our faith corresponds, and the celebration of the sacraments of faith which are wholly and exclusively an application through time and space of the unique work of our salvation accomplished by the sacrificed and risen Lamb. The function of the sacraments, their only function, is to re-present and to apply to Christians who celebrate them and approach them in faith, the work of salvation accomplished on the cross. Far from claiming to add some new and independent human efficacy to Christ's work on the cross they are simply the application, under symbolical signs to which God has attached a promise, of the fruits of the saviour's unique mediation. The Church in her entirety is the actualisation and the sacrament of Christ's unique mediation; she may be called—using the phrase with its utmost literal force—the great sacrament and sign of the cross. She presents the reality of the cross and applies it to mankind.

It is erroneous to interpret the function of the Church, the sacraments, the Virgin Mary and the saints as obscuring Christ's unique mediation, in the sense of adding something of their own to what they had been entrusted to do through Jesus Christ sacrificed for our sins and risen for our justification. These 'mediations' are subordinate; they only exist, only work in the shadow of the work and mediation of Christ. The sacramental action of the Church is the representative sign, the means of application, and, if we may so express it, the realisation in this world of that work and mediation. In this sense R. Will is right when he says, 'It is the "spiritual" Christ himself who is the object of worship and the active character in the Mystery. . . . His redeeming work is constantly in action in the Church. The Church is not a secondary mediator; she is the Lord made visible'.[11]

Our Protestant friends, as we shall have occasion to repeat, are always afraid that this 'visibility' of the Lord in the Church, may become for Catholics purely and simply the visibility of *the Church* herself and that thus restricted, will cloud the sovereignty of our Lord.

This is why our Protestant friends appreciate all those elements in the life and ideas of the Catholic Church which explicitly direct souls to Christ. I remember the frankly sympathetic reception given to a number of papal pronouncements, the Jubilee of the Redemption, for example, in 1933, and the encyclical *Summi Pontificatus* of Pius XII. From this point of view, there can be no doubt that modern Catholic devotion is deeply and broadly Christological. Dom Marmion's excellent books have sustained the spiritual life of countless men and women. It is not simply the result of the present liturgical movement whose Christological orientation has not escaped the notice of 'Foi et Vie';[12] it is also the result of the catechesis and preaching which for the last thirty years have magnificently regained their centre in Christ. And now a biblical movement is emerging which will itself be profoundly Christocentric.

'How closely Christians are drawing together!' wrote R. Chapal reviewing the work of the liturgical pastoral movement now in full swing.

[11] R. Will, *Le Culte*, vol. 2, Paris, 1929, p. 194.
[12] Cf. R. Chapal, in *Foi et Vie*, March–April, 1946, p. 341.

(b) *Anglicanism*. It is common knowledge that Anglican theology and devotion are both Christological and sacramental. Here I shall mention only one Anglican publication—because it seems to me representative of one of those middle positions, critical and at the same time 'catholic', historical but also theological, biblical and yet respectful of tradition, which are characteristically Anglican, and also because it takes us to the heart of our subject. I intend to discuss *The Gospel and the Catholic Church* by M. Ramsey (Longmans, London, 1936).[13] I must confess that to me this book seems too consciously systematic. Scholasticism is not confined to the Middle Ages; the modern age and the historical sciences sometimes exhibit it in a form of their own. But although Ramsey's book has an element of the *a priori* and occasionally comes close to being arbitrary, it has the merit of making as its centre and the criterion of its form two ideas which are at the heart of the gospel and of Christianity: Christ dying for our sins and rising again for our justification; and the unity of his Body. It is in the light of these two ideas that Ramsey examines and justifies all the essential elements of the Church: the ecclesiastical administration, including the episcopate, the Church's worship, ecclesiastical unity, the Reformation, Christian reunion.

This book, therefore, provides us with a completely Christian and ecumenical theology, worked out in the light of the mystery of Christ who died and rose again, that is, ultimately, in the light of the mystery of the Lamb.

(c) *The Orthodox Church*. Need I recall that the great treatise on Christology (recently translated into French) by Fr Bulgakov, is entitled 'The Lamb of God',[14] and that its sections on ecclesiology and eschatology (published in Russian after its author's death) is entitled 'The Bride of the Lamb'?

(d) *Protestant theology and devotion*. It is wholly and fervently centred on salvation in Jesus Christ alone. 'Where it is a question of our justification, we must discard all notions of the Law and of

---

[13] In 1961 its author became Archbishop of Canterbury.
[14] The French translation, which omits the first 120 pages, is entitled *Du Verbe incarné* (*Agnus Dei*), Paris, Aubier, 1943.

our own activity, and turn to God's mercy alone, withdrawing from the contemplation of ourselves and becoming converted to Jesus Christ alone'.[15] But need we give quotations? They are superabundant, and on this question I have nothing to teach my readers; they know more than I do about it.

This soteriological and Christological point of view has been further developed and emphasised in the most recent trends of Protestant thought. We may consider, for instance, the dogmatic development which has issued from the work of Karl Barth—I am thinking of a book like *Le grand oeuvre de Dieu* by Pastor Maury, or the biblical studies written with the spiritual life and preaching in mind, e.g. the brochure 'Que veut dire la Bible?' by R. de Pury, and the admirable commentary on the Scriptures, still unfortunately not completed, by M. W. Vischer, *Das Christuszeugnis des Alten Testament*.[16]

When I read these robust works I receive an impression of one-sidedness. It would be the height of discourtesy for me to return the hospitality offered to me with such friendly kindness, first by the Congress of Ecumenical Studies and then by the 'Cahiers biliques de Foi et Vie', by engaging in controversy. On the contrary, I believe that I am sharing in the spirit of that hospitality by initiating a dialogue which is the very reverse of controversy, and, as its name indicates, is an aspect of dialectic and therefore of an opposite point of view. This is why I allow myself to express what I have so strongly felt. It is a one-sidedness that emphasies:

1. The theme of sin-forgiveness, condemnation to death and grace, at the expense of that new life which has an equal primacy in Scripture. It is a great merit of R. de Pury's little book that it shows how the whole Bible is in movement towards Good Friday and Easter Day, and therefore to the mystery of the Lamb. Throughout the period of the Law, Israel was a people endlessly condemned to death on account of its faithlessness, and endlessly brought back to life by the grace of God. The Church, similarly the true and final Israel, is the people whose men and women have been condemned to death for their sins and restored to grace through Jesus Christ risen from the dead. I agree wholeheartedly

[15] Calvin *Inst. c. 14*, ed. Budé, 4, 130.
[16] Evangelischer Verlag, at Zollikon-Zürich; 2 vols., so far published.

that this affirmation, the subject of the apostolic witness, is indeed central, and de Pury has helped me to realise this. At the same time, we should not forget that Easter cannot be separated from Pentecost—only fifty days after Easter. The work of grace extends to our re-creation as children of God (cf. 1 Jn 3:2, 9), our resurrection from condemnation to death involves a new life breathed by God into believers. There is not only the baptism of repentance, the baptism of John, but also the baptism of the Holy Spirit, the baptism of water and fire. When de Pury writes, in his characteristic poetical style: 'We are still travelling through the night, but we know that death is dead and that the morning is at hand',[17] he seems to me to be making too decisive a separation between Easter and Pentecost, to leave Christians in the condition of John the Baptist, and fails to mark how truly we have passed from death to life and from darkness to light (cf. 1 Jn 3:14; Ep 5:8; Col 1:12–13, etc.).

2. A similar one-sidedness, and connected with the previous one, seems to me to be the constant and exclusive emphasis, with respect to the biblical revelation, on God's transcendence, and what may be called his externality, and the neglect of that aspect which is his self-giving. Its intention is to make quite definite the inalienable sovereignty of God and Christ, but it runs the risk of missing the fact that all Scripture bears witness to God's desire to communicate himself to mankind, to establish a fellowship with them, a fellowship in *his* life. This desire is achieved 'in Christ', through our existence in Christ, and his existence in us, that mystical Body and marriage of the Lamb discussed above. In 'Que veut dire la Bible' we are clearly made to realise the Bible's entire progress towards Christ, towards his death and resurrection; it is less clear that its progress is also, and as completely, towards *the Church*, to that result of Good Friday and Easter, which is the work of Pentecost, a work which, when completed, will mean that God will be 'all in all' and in the marriage of the Lamb, and that this begins in the 'first fruits of the Spirit' from which the Church now lives and that makes her the Body of Christ and even now his Bride.

Even W. Vischer's very fine and very profound commentary

[17] 'Je suis le Seigneur ton Dieu' *Catéchisme réformé de seconde année*, 8, 21, p. 26 (Dec. 1937).

shows traces here and there of a position based too exclusively on the aspect of transcendence and externality, to the detriment of the aspect of self-giving and intimacy. I have in mind, for example, his way of explaining Gn 1:27: 'God made man in his own image'. Instead of seeing in this—as, in my comment above I have explained why I think we should—the basis and the germinal origin of all that great movement of God's self-communication to us, Vischer only emphasises the aspect of separation and transcendence: not the fact of man's being *in the image of God*, but that of his *being created*; and he goes on to develop the Barthian dialectic.[18] Or, to take another example: the commentary on ch. 13 and 15 of Genesis in which together with the promise or alliance between God and Abraham, we are given a description of the actual formation of the people of God, and therefore the whole process of his self-communication to his people whose development penetrates Israel's life in its entirety and leads up to its complete fulfilment in Jesus Christ and the Holy Spirit. Vischer, however, concentrates exclusively on a theme of transcendence and sovereignty; what is impossible to man is possible to God: Abraham believed in the promise even though all human probability was against it: Isaac's birth was due to God alone, etc. In short, the whole set up of Barthian paradox, which is undoubtedly most real and true. But he nowhere discusses the aspect of God's self-giving and communication, and the promise of giving himself to us, hailed by Mary and Zechariah as fulfilled in Jesus Christ.

Other examples of such one-sidedness would not be difficult to discover. In my view, these could be found for example in M. J. Ellul's contribution to the collective work 'Protestantisme français' (*Paris, Plon*). And my reason for mentioning this article is that its depth and attractiveness are likely to make it widely influential. But I am more concerned to welcome other tendencies and manifestations in which I perceive a balance and totality of great ecumenical value. I am thinking, for example, of that liturgical, sacramental and ecclesiastical renewal which in contemporary Protestantism is emerging against a background of explicit fidelity to the Reformation. I also have in mind, in the sphere of biblical and theological research, the very notable

[18] *Op. cit.*, vol. 1, pp. 60–61.

studies of O. Cullman.[19] Through his criticism of pure or 'consequent' eschatology, Cullmann seems to me to have restored reality to the 'time' of the Church, to the period of her duration, and thus to the Church herself. Between Good Friday and the *Parousia* there extends the 'time' of the Church—which is also that of Pentecost, its foundation is Jesus Christ, not now merely expected and hoped for but already come, already given. In him there is a divine fullness and totality; and thanks to that, what Christians do and the way they now live in the Church has a positive meaning with reference to the consummation of all things at the end of time.

Although I consider that the criticisms of the Catholic Church, pp. 108, 129, 148–9, are invalid, I am in profound agreement with his positive assessment of things, and I am glad to find, even in the actual modes of expression, ideas which, to my mind, are central to the whole doctrine of the Church. Thus, in the light of Scripture (a profound bond, an inestimable piece of common ground), we may travel a long way together. I am convinced that historical and biblical studies—conducted not only in a spirit of objectivity, but of complete integrity and universalism, avoiding the one-sidedness, that we may inherit, even unconsciously, from our own particular background—may prove of great significance in the cause of Christian unity. Books such as Cullmann's or Hebert's 'Throne of David', seem to me to be preparing the ground for an encounter in the light of truth.

I am not unconscious of the fact that although some Protestant studies leave an impression of one-sidedness, Catholic theology and devotion, in their turn, create apprehension to our Protestant brethren, an apprehension which is almost a scandal, a stumbling-block to their deepest Christian loyalty. It seems to them that in what we affirm about the image of God, with all that it entails in man with regard to his capacity for God, natural theology and 'analogy', incurs the risk of ending up as an affirmation of continuity between man and God, and a forgetting of the deadly nature of the wound caused by sin. Pastor P. Maury, who had ex-

---

[19] 'La royanté du Christ et l'Église dans le Nouveau Testament' (*Cahiers bibliques de Foi et Vie*, Christmas 1941) *Christus und die Zeit*, Zollikon-Zürich, Evangelischer Verlag, 1946. Cullmann quotes among other works of similar inspiration, those of L. Stähline, de Kummel, etc.

pressed this fear to me in the course of a dialogue in 1937,[20] repeats it in the dialogue with Fr Daniélou with which 'Protestantisme français' concludes. Our Protestant brethren feel that, with us, the aspect of death and condemnation to death is smothered and obscured by the aspect of the communication of life, and that we construct a 'theology of glory' without warrant. It also seems to them that with us the unique mediation of Christ is denied and made pointless by secondary mediations, that of the Virgin Mary in particular.

I consider that the two tendencies I have just defined and which, if I am not mistaken, represent what we consider to be a dangerous trend in Protestantism, and what Protestants consider to be a dangerous trend in Catholicism, may become the two poles of the ecumenical dialogue and of that mutual tension through which Christendom is striving to attain complete loyalty to the complete truth. In the early days of Barthian theology there was considerable discussion of the 'question' which the Churches had to put to each other. In Germany before and during the war, especially from the Catholic side, much was heard about the 'Gesprach' to be held between the different denominations. Today the more favoured words are 'dialectic' and development. I consider that beneath these various labels a most authentic reality is present. Whether it be questions which each asks the other or of engagement in a dialectic, I pray that the dialogue between us may not stop, and that it shall not merely be the more or less acrobatic showmanship of a few specialists but also involve the activity and receive the attention of the mass of believers in the Church herself. Its atmosphere should be one of that prudence which any responsible task demands, and of loyalty and obedience with respect to the Church, apart from which ecumenical activity can easily be the superficial activity of dilettantes.

At the conclusion of this study, I should like to stress once again the urgency of the ecumenical movement, in the spirit of which I have written it. We have observed that already we are all united, profoundly united, in our belief in Christ, in the faith in him. But we have also seen that the mystery of the Bride is united to that of the Lamb: do not the two expressions together form that

[20] Two brief notes published in English in *The Student World*, 1937 No. 2, and in French in *RSPT*, July 1937.

single mystery which St Paul calls 'great' (Ep 5:32)? The bibilical revelation, as a whole, leads up to both of them. If the ecumenical movement has a meaning, that meaning is the promotion and the sealing of our unity in Christ, a unity that is already in existence, but hidden, a unity destined to be made visible in the Church, the people of God who are called to sing with one voice the canticle of the Lamb.

CHAPTER NINE

'The Cross of Jesus' by
Fr Louis de Chardon, OP[1]

IN THE BEGINNING OF THE EIGHTH VOLUME OF
his *Histoire littéraire,* Henri Bremond records the neglect into
which Chardon's masterpiece had fallen, even in his own religious
order. In fact it needed *La Métaphysique des Saints* before
Chardon regained the company of those who have something to
say to our time. A re-publication of the original text became imperative. Fr Florand, with the threefold competence of a theologian, an historian and an artist, has devoted several years to producing it. The new edition whose format and typography—perfect of their kind—accurately reflect the original, and provide us
not only with an accurate text, faithfully restored, with references
and a table of contents, but also with an Introduction of more than
160 pages.[2]

In this Introduction Fr Florand has assembled all the available
information about Chardon's life and about the environment in
which his work was produced. Little about his life but more about
the environment, that of a religious 'congregation' in process of
reform in a period of transition. All this is of importance for the
explanation of Chardon's book. That 'masterpiece' is studied

---

[1] Article published in *Vie Sp.*, Suppl. vol. 51 (April 1937), pp. 42–
57.
[2] *La Croix de Jésus* . . . by Fr Louis de Chardon, of the Order of Friars
Preachers. New edition with an Introduction, by Fr Florand, of the
same Order, *Paris, Ed. Cerf.* 1937, 17x22; CLXII—590 pp. (Fr Florand
was recalled to God in the night of 28 Feb. 1961.)

critically with respect to some of its main themes. It is a strictly doctrinal study, continuing and deepening Bremond's analysis, and generously providing what, in the absence of any monograph or even reference to Chardon, had been completely lacking.[3] The difficult question of sources is considered with precision and competence, and adds in conclusion, a paragraph on Chardon the writer, which adds little to Bremond's remark, but again does justice to the many pages of such attractive harmony in which a sensitivity for words perfectly reflects that of the soul.

We can only refer the reader to the text itself, and to the comments on it which historians will not fail to make.[4] Our purpose here is simply to make a twofold comment on Chardon's work, first, on its doctrine, and then on its general characteristics, on what may be called its theological quality.

The doctrine of the 'Cross of Jesus' is entirely homogeneous. (I shall not here consider its applications and extensions, especially those tragic and debatable chapters on the theology of Mary which which take up the whole of the first section.) The general thesis is that the Christian life involves the cross both as a life of faith, hope and charity, and simply as Christian life. It is a unified outlook made explicit and based upon two considerations; that of Christian life as such, with its grace derived from Christ and its logical consequences, and the fact that Christ's grace naturally tends towards the cross (this is the subject of the first section); and that of the life of faith, hope and charity in itself, by virtue of the purifying and crucifying necessities that result from the 'divine missions' (this is the subject of the third section, the second develops the

---

[3] Nothing in Hurter, *Nomenclator Litt*; nothing in the great *Année Dominicaine*; nothing in Touron; nothing in Michaud, *Biogr. Univ.*; nothing in *DTC*; a mere mention in Pourrat, *La spiritualité chrét*, 4, 2, p. 261, n. 2, 1928, and a short notice, due however to Bremond's work, in the *Lexikon für Theol. U. Kirche*, 2, 1930.

[4] There is one already in the *Bull. thomiste*, 1936, pp. 869–75, in a most interesting review by Fr Féret, of that part of the Introduction which appeared in the form of articles in *Vie Sp*. Keeping strictly to the point of view of the history of Thomism, Fr Féret brings out, by quoting characteristic passages, the contrast between two opposing tendencies, genuinely represented by Chardon and Massoulié; that which develops in 'affective' or 'mystical' theology for its own sake, in which St Thomas is used together with other sources but is not followed exclusively; and that in which no other spiritual master is sought than St Thomas studied literally.

theme of love, the principle of separation). My own remarks will be confined to the first section.

'The grace of Jesus constitutes the subsistence of his mystical Body and thus creates a quasi-personal unity between Christ and Christians which explains *the crosses* which they endure' (Intr., p. 75). This statement, which summarises the first section, incorporates two affirmations: that of our quasi-personal union with Christ, that of the natural movement of Christ's grace towards the cross.

The first, considered generally, is a part of the common Christian inheritance, but Chardon expresses it in a way that is both attractive and somewhat startling: by virtue of our communication of Christ in grace, we are, he says, 'one and the same substance with him . . . so that he with us together forms a single Jesus Christ' (pp. 26–7). Christ is the real constitutive principle, the real subject of attribution of all that we become through grace: 'Since grace, which is the intrinsic principle of our adoption, is the same grace that, in its abounding infinity, is subsistent in Jesus Christ in the Person of the Word, it is clear that it is through grace that Jesus is the subsistence of his mystical body, and that, through the relationships produced by this grace, which flows from him as Head, we are united, as dependent members, to the principal member so as to form one mystical person in him, and, with Jesus form a single Jesus, mystically' (p. 30).

Are not such phrases exaggerated? Does not Chardon's teaching contain a false and unacceptable notion of the mystical body, imagining that it is the actual grace of Christ, numerically the same reality, in its fullness as it exists in his soul and as it is communicated to us? Whereas, in fact, between Christ's grace and ours there is a specific unity only, that of a spiritual reality, produced (incidentally, in varying degrees) in subjects who retain an independent substantial existence. And if it cannot be literally maintained that we form in Christ and with Christ a single person, a single substance, what is left of these fine pages?

I agree, however, with Fr Florand, that the doctrine of 'mystical subsistence' is basically sound, and, even, that it is supported by the best Thomist theologians. For what is Chardon *really* saying?

What reality has he in mind when he speaks of the 'same substance' and of 'mystical subsistence'?[5]

This, first of all: that our grace is specifically Christian, 'Christic', we should say. It is a grace of which the connatural and homogeneous subject is not mankind as such but the saviour's manhood hypostatically united with God. It is to him and to him alone that this grace belongs, as a 'property' belongs to a nature. Now, although this grace remains in Christ and it would be foolish to picture it as flowing from him into us as from an overfilled vessel, it is nevertheless in the likeness and through its creative power, personal to the incarnate, saving Word, that we are re-created in grace. It is as though a genius like St Thomas has the power of creating in a worn-out mind an intellectual activity like his own and deriving from it.

There is this also, which on reflection seems to be one of the chief elements in the mystery and one of the foundations of Chardon's thought: by virtue of the infinity of Christ's grace, itself grounded in the twofold necessity of his divine personality and his function as universal saviour, the whole content of Christianity is already in Christ. Christ with Christians added to him do not, in a sense, amount to more than Christ himself alone. For Christians, who are the members, the body and the *pleroma* of Christ, only make explicit, in numerous ways of life and activities, that which exists in undivided perfection in Christ. There is a slight resemblance between this and the way in which the world makes explicit, in multitudinous and varied forms, that which in God exists in undivided perfection.[6]

[5] The actual word is not used by St Thomas. Fr Florand quotes as an ideological literary source Nacliantus and Nazarius. For the idea itself he refers to Cajetan. But Cajetan also uses the very word: 'Christus est velut hypostas issui corporis mystici, quod est Ecclesia' (Comm. on 1 Co 12:12), and not only in this passage which, being written towards the end of his life, might be thought to be due to the impact of the problems raised by Luther, but also as early as November 1512: 'Christus non solum caput mysticum eius sed mysticum suppositum ipsius est' (*Apologia de comparata auct. papae et conc.,*, c. 6, ed. 1514, Fol. 23vb; ed. Pollet, 1936, p. 223).

[6] As regards the world and God, cf. e.g. De malo, 5. 1. ad 4; and Metaph, 12. lect. 12. 'Totus enim ordo universi est propter primum moventem ut scilicet explicetur in universo ordinato id quod est in intellectu et voluntate primi moventis' (ed. Cathala, no. 2631). As regards Christians and Christ: 'In Christo autem spiritualis non est particulatum, sed est totaliter et integrum; unde ipse est totum Ecclesiae

The action of Christ and that of the natural order, of the first and second Adam, are wholly different. When the first human being communicated life in the natural act of begetting he did not do so through any power peculiar to himself, but by virtue of a principle of life which is that of the species. In himself this life of the species was only imperfectly and fragmentarily present; the species was a more ample reality. Through his action it was continued and propagated in other individuals, who themselves only partially represented it. Thus the first human being did not produce another being identical with himself and living from his own life, but a being resembling him in specific likeness and living from the life of the species.

Christ, on the other hand, intrinsically possessed the full perfection of grace, the total reality of the species *grace*. When he communicates the life of grace to others, what he communicates is truly his own, he introduces us into communion with his own life, not with the life of any species. Neither the act of begetting nor the society resulting from this communication of life are entirely similar to the parallel phenomena in the natural order. If the Christian life has come into existence in us, that does not mean that we have had to be begotten through division of substance apart from Christ in order to continue and make perfect a life which is already perfect in him, not that we must make a common effort to achieve, a mode of existence which is already fully achieved in him. The begetting of a Christian is assimilation to Christ and Christian communal life is essentially participation in the life of a single being. Considered in isolation it is that of a member sharing in a single life and the social phenomena are necessary only for that communal-incorporation while it is in process of development.

And, of course, the life of Christ achieves its ultimate reality in a multitude of different beings, each having its own substantial

---

bonum, nec est aliquod majus ipse et alii quam ipse solus' (*4 Sent.* d. 49, q. 4, a 3, ad 4); 'et quia Christus in omnes creaturas rationales quodammodo effectus gratiarum influit, inde est quod ipse est principium quodammodo omnis gratiae secundum humanitatem, sicut Deus est principium omnis esse; unde sicut in Deo omnis essendi perfectio adunatur, ita in Christo omnis gratiae plenitudo et virtutis invenitur . . .' (*De Verit.*, qu. 29, art. 5).

existence and personality, but nevertheless it retains its unity. Even on the natural level human life, lived by individuals who are so many independent substances, has a real unity, but since no individual accomplishes that life in its fullness, its unity remains anonymous; it is the life of *mankind*. But this is sufficient to enable St Thomas to describe it as a kind of personal unity, and, before Pascal, to compare it to 'a single man';[7] it is sufficient that even a single sin that infects the species can be communicated to other individuals. But what we are now considering is something in addition to this. For this new specific unity, in which a number of different individuals are to participate, has an existence apart from those individuals, whereas the natural life of the species has no such separate existence. This new life is the life of a person; it has its homogeneous existence in the Lord's most holy soul. It is no longer an anonymous life; it is the life *of Christ*.

All this, however, remains entirely mysterious. How is it possible, on such a view, for us to retain our personality not only as corporeal beings but as Christians? What exactly is this unity comparable indeed to a substantial unity, but not to any kind of substantial unity known to us, comparable to a personal unity, but not to any kind of personal unity known to us? It is impossible to answer this question, because our only terms of reference are natural realities whereas this is a unique and absolutely original reality without parallel in our world. We may, with due caution, discover analogies with it—as did St Paul. But these analogies are most imperfect, and when we look to them for an explanation of the *how* of this reality, they steal away; they are bound to steal away.[8]

On this point, we may perhaps attribute a certain weakness to Chardon; more concerned with practical spirituality than critical accuracy, he has perhaps expressed with excessive clarity things which cannot be clearly expressed. Perhaps he did not sufficiently

[7] *Sum. Theol.* I[a]–II[ae], 81. 1, with precise reference to original sin.
[8] If this criticism is to be expressed in a more technical manner, it might be said that Chardon seems to have misunderstood the significance of the 'improper' and metaphorical analogy of proportionality involved in St Paul's image of the mystical body: an analogy of proportionality does not relate forms or essences but only modes of action. Cf.. M. T.–L. Penido, 'Le rôle de l'analogie en théologie dogmatique' (*Bibl. Thomiste*, 15), pp. 42f.

E

keep in mind the fact that in this sphere of reality the purpose of utterance is not so much to say something as to avoid saying nothing.[9] He has driven a defective vocabulary to a point where it becomes too lucid—or not lucid enough. And, while accepting his teaching as fundamentally sound, we have to admit that he gives a meaning to the word 'subsistence' which is considerably in excess of its strict definition.

'Mystical subsistence' provides the explanation of the crosses that Christians endure; for Christ's grace, communicated to us, has an intrinsic tendency to the cross, since it is a saviour's grace: 'because this grace was given to him for that purpose which was the reason for his coming down into this world, and because the function he had to fulfil concerned the "Satisfaction" he had to make as Head for the sinful members (of his Body), we must conclude that the plenteousness of grace gave to his soul a disposition and an inclination to obey the decree issued in the counsels of the most glorious Trinity, and which include the cross . . .' (p. 46). From ch. 5 to ch. 15, Chardon examines in detail the subtle ways in which Jesus' whole life is marked by this inclination to the cross, not only to the point of death but beyond death, since he now lives in us who are his members.

Chapters 16 and 17 mark the transition from Christ to Christians, from the cross of the one to the crosses of the other: 'Jesus, for ever in heaven, and on earth until the end of the world, makes it plain that his inclination to the cross has not passed away'. (I. ch. 16, p. 121). The inclination towards the cross inherent in the soul of Jesus finds its activity in the holy souls of those who form his mystical body. (I. ch. 17, p. 126). We have now reached the very centre of the book, because its aim throughout is to explain and glorify the suffering of those who lead the spiritual life by relating it to the very nature of Christian grace. Chardon summarises his doctrine as follows:

> We have set forth the doctrine of the mystical body of Jesus and of its mystical subsistence, we have noted the directives of his grace and the harsh obligations of his ministry, we have seen with awe the insatiable and violent yearning of his spirit for the

[9] Cf. St Augustine with reference to the use of the word *persona* in the theology of the Trinity: 'Dictum est Tres personae, non ut illud diceretur, sed ne tacentur' (*De Trinitate*, Bk. 5, c. 9, n. 10; *PL* 42, 918).

cross. We now have plenty of time to consider the way in which he arranges its distribution among the souls that belong to him, through the bonds of grace, as mystical parts and members. We shall also see how it is that the more closely these souls are raised to his spirit, the more they are obliged to suffer . . .(p. 126).

Here again the modern editor asks whether Chardon is not exaggerating and whether he can claim the authority of St Thomas. The editor concludes, in our view correctly, that although Chardon may have over-emphasised the inner sadness of Christ's soul, his fundamental teaching on the intrinsic tendency of Christian grace towards the cross belongs to authentic theology.

On this point Fr Florand most opportunely refers to a series of very precise passages in which St Thomas delineates, between the redeemer and ourselves and ourselves and him, what may be called a circuit of exemplarity. The point at issue is to discover how far the efficacy of our baptism effects renewal and transfiguration, and, more generally, why, now that we have been redeemed, we are still subject to trials, to suffering and to death. Among the reasons he adduces St Thomas gives the primacy to the following: because Christ came to save sinners he entered into the logic of sin with its results, temptation, suffering and death. Now, however, all things have been restored; we have been grafted into him by baptism and our final glorification has been acquired *de jure*, for we have fellowship in his crucifixion and death. In this life, however, we must tread the path Christ trod for us, fashion ourselves in likeness to our Head, make 'satisfaction', suffer and finally die, as he made 'satisfaction', suffered and finally gave his life.

If we reflect on the realism implicit in these statements of St Thomas, on their existential nature, on what such purposive activities mean to him, I think we must admit that the idea that movement towards the cross is imprinted in the very tissue of the Redeemer's grace, conforms to the essential principles of his thought.

St Thomas also provides a serious basis for the idea that 'the movement towards the cross in the soul of Jesus dimmed the reality of his glory' (title of ch. 6, p. 52). It is common knowledge that for St Thomas everything relating to Christ, his prerogatives, his weakness is to be gauged by his function as redeemer.[10] In the Summa, in particular, the whole treatise on Christ is illuminated by one of the early articles on the motive of the incarnation, (1 3). It is because he came as mankind's saviour, and its saviour through the cross, that, in Christ, the glorious prerogatives which naturally belonged to his manhood on account of his hypostatic union, were as though restrained, and, so to say, put into parenthesis, in order that the limitations and weaknesses which are normal for his condition as saviour through the cross might be seen to be authentic.[11]

All this has important consequences not only for Christology but also for the theology of the Church. We hope to return to them on some future occasion. And it certainly provides the basis for Chardon's better insights. But if some may be described as 'better', the obvious implication is that others are less good. When he speaks of 'the dimming of the reality of glory through the movement towards the cross' (ch. 6), or when he says 'that the concrete knowledge of the circumstances of his death which Jesus had throughout his life guided him to the cross', the remarks are excellent. But when he says that 'the movement towards the cross, produced by grace in the soul of Jesus, means that his awareness of the splendour of the cross impelled him to martyrdom' (ch. 8, p. 56), or that 'this inner drive towards the cross is the reason why Jesus preferred the thought of death to the thought of his being the Son of God' (ch. 8, p. 66); or, lastly, that 'charity, going contrary to its nature, instead of being the cause of joy in the soul of Jesus, was the source of sadness' (ch. 11, p. 85), we may consider these sentiments less excellent. Indeed one may ask whether the demon of art for art's sake did not have a hand in some of these passages of fine writing, just as he seems to have had much to do with those fine prayers with their elaborate and rhythmic cadences so plentiful in the religious heritage of the seventeenth century. More definitely we may ask whether Chardon did not

[10] 'Oportuit animam Christi perfectum esse quantum ad habitus scientiarum et virtutum, ut habeat facultatem satisfaciendi; et quoad corpus ejus subjectum esse infirmitatibus ut ei satisfactionis materia non deesse'. (*Sum. Theol. III*ᵃ, *14, 1 ad 1*); cf. art. 4, and *46, 4. ad 2*. Questions 7 or 9–15 of the 3rd Part are entirely governed by this principle.

[11] Cf. IIIᵃ. 14, 1, ad 2; 15, 5, ad 3; cf. Ch. V. Héris, *Le mystère du Christ*, ed. Rev. des Jeunes, *passim*.

yield to the temptation to give a 'psychological' account of Christ, that is, to try to form an idea of what his feelings, his inner life— as the French School would call it—must have been. In reality, however, although the 'psychology' of Jesus Christ is truly human, it is also theandric, and the least of his actions, his least movement, is a mystery. The gospels are more sober. They tell us what Jesus did; they make hardly any attempt to express what he felt. And what can we know of the trials, the suffering and the joy of a soul bathed in the perfection of light and love, when we do not even know what these are like in those nearest to us and cannot isolate their elements from the incomprehensible complexity in which they exist in ourselves.

This leads us naturally to a few comments on Chardon's attitude as a theologian, with which we shall conclude.

There can be no doubt that he intended to be a theologian,[12] and beyond question he was a good theologian. But it is also obvious that he had his own way of being a theologian, and it is that that we shall try to appreciate.

Before we reach the actual text of the book, which is sufficiently explicit, nothing is more instructive on this matter than the authorisations printed at its head; the authorisation from the Masters in Theology (De Launoy and Loisel): 'Its author has successfully conjoined the theology of the Scholastics and the Fathers with that of the Spirit and the heart . . .'—the authorisation from the Dominican Order (Fr Philip Bordereau): '(it displays) great ability in successfully conjoining mystical with scholastic theology, "affective" theology with speculative, establishing the maxims of the former upon conclusions of the latter.'

Thus his contemporaries, referring to theological distinctions whose exact meaning and origin it would be interesting to investigate, characterise his work as an alliance between two 'theologies', that which is an intellectual pursuit and that which is concerned with prayer, that of the theological Schools and that of spiritual direction. It is a distinction which would have been understood then (and also widely accepted now) as indicating the position of

---

[12] 'I am speaking as a theologian on this matter . . .' (Avert., p. 7). Note, however, that he is here claiming to be a theologian, because he does not want to be a philosopher, that is to employ the processes of reason alone.

St Thomas on the one hand, and that of Tauler or even St Catherine of Siena on the other. But Chardon claimed that his achievement was no hybrid mixture. His critics said that he, and those who followed him, had added to St Thomas and to unalloyed theological intellectuality, an element that belongs to the sphere of 'affectivity' which is that of 'mysticism' and the mystics, and not to theology as normally understood or to St Thomas himself.[13] Chardon defends himself in his Foreword, in a very personal and moving way, with regard to the theological work which he claims to have produced:

> I know only one theology; the circumstance of making it 'effective' does not destroy its nature; it perfects it. Knowledge of God without charity is lifeless; love is its centre. Without love it is out of orbit. By what I have done, I am not separating scholastic theology from mysticism; they will become the two men of the emblem (p. 9).

But a page earlier, in this same Foreword, he defines the purpose and status of this single theology in the following way.

> In these discussions I am enquiring about the knowledge of God and of the things of God. My object is to love them and through loving them to try to unite myself to them and to transform myself into them. The arguments I use, the problems which I discuss, the difficulties on which I shed light, the truths I establish, the authorities that guarantee their infallibility, all have as their single purpose the arousing of desire, the perfecting of prayer, the kindling of the heart, the mortification of the senses and the mind, and the inducement to the sacred practices of the acts of religion and of all the virtues (p. 8).

Thus Chardon is not simply aiming at knowledge. His aim is to know God and the things of God in order to love them and to make them loved. And, of course, every theologian in some sense hold this position; he works in order to love God better, and he is convinced that his theology will assist him in this purpose. But Chardon seems to go further. In his case, the purpose of love and of union is not simply a stimulant to the theologian's activity: it appears to determine the nature of his work, not a mere factor

[13] Cf. the Introd. by Fr Florand, p. LXXIV, and Féret, *loc. cit.*

adding to his momentum, a circumstance affecting what he is doing, but an element that specifies his activity, modifying it and inwardly qualifying it. He was not concerned simply to analyse and as far as possible explain the mystery of Christ, of the mystical body, of grace, of the divine 'missions'. He was concerned with awakening souls, with giving them light that they might learn to love, and with strenghtening them through enabling them to understand themselves in Christ.

Moreover the use of the special principles of theology are here kept subordinate. Neither the theological sources as such nor even the mysteries as such control the development of the teaching without more ado; they are at the service of a form of contemplation whose true and primary principle is an inner state, an experience, a most vivid awareness of the mystery of Christian life on the cross. Under the aegis of such an inner state, a theologian with Chardon's great qualifications, seeks a theological explanation taken from the nature of things; he contemplates the mysteries, reads the theological sources, has recourse to St Thomas, in order to clarify, provide a reasoned basis for the experience lived by souls and to justify it.[14] In this sense the subject matter of the 'mystical theology' he develops is 'regulated by the maxims of scholastic theology' (third section, ch. 21, p. 495), but the regulation is in a sense that which 'mystical theology' bestows on itself, for it has made its own selection of the sources, of the maxims and of the order in which they are utilised. The theological principles he adopts are not considered strictly according to the order, content and balance which intrinsically belong to them, but only from that angle and with those contents which affect the spiritual life. The result is undoubtedly of theological significance but the point of view is not that of a professional theologian. It is that of a shepherd of souls, putting at their disposal and at the disposal of his own pastoral work, the resources, in his case, the magnificent resources, of authentic theology.

Fr Florand's Introduction once again illustrates the text. He gives us an account of the conditions under which Chardon worked

[14] Fr Florand observes correctly: 'Abbé Henri Bremond clearly realised the psychological origin of this work and very rightly assigned it to a desire to explain the sufferings of "holy souls", that is, souls on the way to holiness' (p. LXV).

the setting of a novitiate house in the fervour of the reform initiated by Fr Michaëlis. He had been a novice in it, then acting novice master and later returning to it to carry out, without apparently any official function, the work of director of souls. This indicates one of the 'theological sources, *loci*' that determined the nature of his work: 'fervour' and 'spiritual direction'.[15] So it is not excessively surprising to find that the spiritual theme organises the most ample theological material it assimilates, and that Chardon finally describes his work as 'a short Summa of mystical theology' (p. LXV).

Does this diminish the worth of a book which its editor rightly calls a 'masterpiece?' In no way; it gives it precision and defines it. The only error would be precisely this: to consider it absolutely as a 'Summa of mystical theology', i.e. a synthesis in which *all* spiritual truths are incorporated and given the order intrinsically due to them. The truth is that only many of them are, and these not on account of their particular value but with reference to a central theme, that of the drive towards the cross which is inherent in the Christian and divine substance of grace. It is desirable that the Church should have many theologians and works of this kind. In order, however, that they should be really sound and perfectly balanced, one condition is essential. A theology that is nothing but theology must exist; a *study* of God and of the things of God, conducted for its own sake, along the lines, the specific direction and content of these subjects as they intrinsically exist. For experience constantly verifies the saying of one of my former masters (Fr Ambrose Gardeil): 'Among us, the intellectual is the ptorector of the spiritual'.

[15] Fr Florand mentions several times (pp. LXVI, c) the connection, which seems historically certain, between the growth of spiritual direction and the theme of 'dark nights' and 'crosses', at least as regards their literary description (and therefore one that we can grasp). This connection, which has struck me also, deserves an historical and theological study.

CHAPTER TEN

Are we still waiting
for Jesus Christ?[1]

WE HAVE NO DOUBT ALREADY WONDERED WHY
the liturgy selects as the gosepl for the first Sunday of Advent the
passage which describes the end of the world and the return of the
Lord in glory: 'There will be portents in sun and moon and stars.
. . . Then they shall see the Son of Man coming in a cloud with
power and great glory . . .' (Lk 21).

Advent is indeed the preparation for Christmas, a kind of symbolical reproduction of the long waiting for the Messiah by the
people of God throughout the Old Testament: Christmas is the
memorial, almost the anniversary, of the birth of Jesus. The
expectation of the coming of Jesus Christ was a characteristic of
the Jewish race, it was shared by Mary. I cannot help calling to
mind in this regard the delightful and sensitively religious poem
by Marie Noël, 'Waiting for Jesus':

> 'I must hurry and get ready
> For Advent is at hand
> I must hurry and get ready
> The clothes to greet my child . . .'

The Church, in fact, asks us, during Advent, to enter into the
feelings of the Jewish people awaiting the good news of their salvation. That being so, why does she choose for the gospel the passage
that foretells the end of the world and Christ's return as judge
and ruler of the world?

[1] Conference given on *Radio-Luxembourg*, 7 Dec. 1947; published
in *Vie Sp.*, Dec. 1949, pp. 451–5.

The intention behind this is to remind us that waiting for Jesus is not over, because his coming is not only a thing of the past. The Lord will come again; he comes every day. The Christian life establishes us precisely in the condition of waiting for him; it is itself a kind of Advent that will only end when there is nothing more to be expected, i.e. when Jesus has fully come, or, in St Paul's words, when God will be all in all.

Jesus Christ came in the flesh; he was born in Bethlehem, when Quirinus was the governor of Syria, Herod the king of Judea, and Augustus ruler of the Roman world. This is the coming which we commemorate, and so to say, keep the anniversary at Christmas, even though we do not know the exact date of that birth, 25 December being simply a conventional date.

But Jesus Christ, who has already come in the flesh, will return in glory to judge both the living and the dead, and he spiritually returns every day in our souls. Similarly his resurrection is an historical fact, occurring when Caiaphas was high priestd an Pontius Pilate governor of Judaea in the service of Tiberias, and we commemorate this fact and, so to say, keep its anniversary on Easter Day. But at the end of time there will be the glorious resurrection of our bodies, and between Christ's resurrection and that of our bodies every day bears witness to the spiritual resurrection of a great number of souls.

It follows that Christianity, in its entirety, is the celebration of the past events of redemption, of the expectation of the fulfilment of all things in that eternal life, invoked at the end of the Creed, and the present reality of a spiritual life in Christ and in God, with Christ and with God, and through the grace of both.

I have just quoted the Creed. Is it not remarkable that beginning with the words 'I believe', it ends with 'Expecto', I look for. Christian life comprises inseperably both faith in the present reality of Christ's presence and an expectation of the reality to come. It is both faith in Jesus Christ and waiting for Jesus Christ.

It awaits him, we have said, coming gloriously at the end of time to reward each man accordingly to his works and to establish a new order of absolute justice. As Christians, is our belief in this sufficiently strong? Or, although we accept it in principle, do we realise that in doing so we are affirming a matter of importance? In our time, history is much in men's minds. Many of our contemporaries are genuinely moved by the hope of a goal, remote perhaps, but towards which they want to direct the historical process. We also have our hope, but we know to what conclusion the world is moving. Its whole process is tending towards Christ's final victory over death. A new order of things, that began with his resurrection on Easter Day, moves to its consummation in the resurrection of all men and in the establishment of a total and undisputed reign of God. Whether this is far off or near, no one knows, and those who imagine they can work out how long it will be delayed or when it will happen—facts known to God alone—are only fooling themselves. But sooner or later it will come about. Jesus Christ will return in order to incorporate us with himself in his kingdom. In the evening of our lives he will come for each of us, as a thief in the night—this comparison is from the gospel. He will, however, pre-eminently return at the end of the world, not then as a thief but in power and glory. Do we really believe this? Are our hopes really turned towards that moment when, as the Apocalypse affirms, he will wipe away all tears from our eyes? When it is a question of some national victory or temporal deliverance we realise soon enough what constitutes desire and hope. If it is a question of the coming of some human friend we know very well what it is to wait for him and want him. Religious feelings are naturally more reserved and tranquil. But they should be equally real, and of practical account in our lives. Let us live in the expectation and desire of the Lord's return, of his justice and his reign.

He will come as a conqueror and judge at the end of the world; he comes as a thief at the end of our lives, but he also comes every day, most intimately and gently, as a friend, in our souls. This is a fact of our experience. Who has not had illuminating and generous moments in his life sometimes corresponding to a period of suffering and struggle? Who has not experienced, after prayer, a heartfelt prayer, in Church or at home, that kind of certainty, of quiet exaltation, of profound peace—even in the midst of suffering—which results from God's visitations? Who has not heard within himself that voice which is God's as well as that of conscience, and that, with astonishing precision, calls for some sacrifice from us, an act of generosity or forgiveness, and then, if we have obeyed its inspiration, gives us beyond any human certitude the witness of its uplifting and consoling power. No; it is a fact that we are not alone. We are constantly being visited by Jesus.

But there is more to it than this. Do you know this verse in the Apocalypse, manifestly written by the disciple whom Jesus loved —a voice once heard, never forgotten? It is the Lord speaking to his disciple and through him to his Church: 'See, I stand knocking at the door. If anyone listens to my voice and opens the door, I will go into his house and dine with him, and he with me' (Rv 3:20). The gentleness of these words! Jesus stands outside our door and he knocks. Sometimes his knock is quite faint but loud enough for the sensitive to recognise it and to open their door. If, however, one turns a deaf ear, he may go away, having knocked in vain, and that is surely sad. But it also happens that if he is determined to come into our house and for us to dine with him, he knocks more forcibly, with his powerful hand, e.g. in grief or in the unleashing of fearful events. Disease, mourning, the great tribulations of existence, have thus a warning function in God's purpose; they open the way to the comings of the Lord. Happy the man who can discern their meaning! He will open the door, welcome his visitor, and they will dine together on the provisions the guest supplies, those provisions which sustain a life of friendship with God.

In conclusion, I should like to underline that this twofold expectation or awaiting—the Lord's glorious return and his hidden visits to the souls of men—fulfils the expectation of the Jewish people and of Mary. For it was salvation that the Jewish people looked for from its Messiah, and it is the ultimate reality of this same salvation that we look for in the resurrection of our bodies, the joy and glory of the kingdom of God. With regard to Mary, we know from the gospel that her happiness came from the spiritual presence of God and of his word within her. Her expectation of Jesus, her joy in bearing him, receive their consummation in our waiting for his visitation, our joy in his presence, just as Israel's expectation is consummated in our hope for the Lord's triumphant and final return.

And thus our initial question—why does the Advent liturgy begin with the gospel of the end of the world and Christ's return in glory?—receives this answer.

Are we still expecting Jesus Christ?

CHAPTER ELEVEN

David and Solomon; the Foreshadowing of Christ's Two Comings[1]

WHEN WE READ IN SEQUENCE I K 16–3 K 11, which record the history of David and Solomon, it is impossible to avoid a twofold impression of unity and contrast. On the one hand, the two kings seem inseparable; David needs his immediate fulfilment in Solomon; Solomon presupposes David, so united to him as to be included in the light of the same divine regard and blessing.[2] On the other hand, it is difficult to imagine persons more unlike than David and Solomon or two more different political systems than those represented by their reigns.

Both monarchs prefigure Christ. Not indeed, as St Irenaeus noted,[3] in all their actions, but in the gifts they received from God and in the great deeds they performed. David's significance as a prefiguration of the Messiah is one of the great abiding themes of Scripture, from the prophecy of Nathan (2 K 7) to the gospels which explicitly declare that the 'type' of the messianic king was

---

[1] An article published in *Vie Sp.*, 91 (Nov. 1954), pp. 323–40.

[2] Solomon is a continuation of David to such an extent that it was his work to fulfil the promises made to David and to avenge his wrongs: 3 Kings 2:1–12; similarly in 5:17, it is in a sense David who, victorious in the end, found his fulfilment in Solomon's building of the temple, which his constant wars had long prevented him from undertaking. Cf. also 11:12 and 34; the affliction he deserved did not affect Solomon personally and directly, because of his identity with David, the faithful and hallowed King.

[3] *Adv. Haer.* 4. 27. 1 (*PG* 7, 1056 SV).

fulfilled in Jesus.[4] Scriptural tradition made Solomon the 'type'
of the sage and attributed the composition of several wisdom
books to him.[5] The queen of Sheba and other monarchs came to
listen to him (cf. 3 K 10; 2 Ch 9, 23), and the Fathers saw in this
episode a prefigurement of the adoration of Jesus by the Magi.
Solomon's reign was spectacular, and it is through an insistence on
the special features of this reign that several psalms proclaim the
future messianic reign—especially Psalms 2, 45 and 72 (Hebrew).[6]
But Solomon is pre-eminently the builder of the first temple, itself
a prefigurement of the true and nobler temple, the Body of Christ
(Jn 2:19f). Yet when Jesus surveyed all this past history he remarked, 'Something greater than Solomon is here' (Mt 12:42 and
parallels). He himself is Wisdom personified,[7] the centre of reference of everyman seeking for salvation, the true temple not made
with human hands.

After these explanatory remarks I shall try to show that David
and Solomon foreshadow Christ in his two comings or, what
amounts to the same thing, in the two phases of his existence, as

[4] Cf. in particular Am 9:11; Ho 3:5; Mi 5:1–5 (the Messiah related to
Bethlehem); Is 9:5–6; 11:1–5. On the eve of the destruction of Jerusalem,
Jr 23:5–6; 30:9; 33:15–17. During the exile, Ezk 34:23–4; 37:21–5.
After the exile, Zc 12:8; the Psalms—89, 132, etc. In the New Testa-
ment: Mt 1:1; 9:27; 15:22; 22:42; Lk 1:69; 2:4; Rm 1:3; 2 Tm 2:8;
Rv 5: 5; 22: 16.

[5] E.g. Proverbs, The Song of Songs, and Ecclesiastes. Cf. also 3 Kings
5:12. On the messianic significance of Solomon, cf. H. M. Féret, L'éco-
nomie providentielle . . .' in *Forma Gregis*, March 1951, pp. 57–70.

[6] On Solomon considered by the Fathers as a 'type' of Christ, cf. e.g.
Origen 'Com. in Cant. Cant., Prol.' (*G.C.S. Orig.* 7, p. 84). So Augustine
Civ. Dei Bk. 17, c. 8. n. 2 (*PL* 41, 541; commentary on Ps. 72).

[7] On the gable of the main door of Strasbourg Cathedral, Solomon is
presented enthroned and above him the child Jesus on Mary's knees.
P. Perdrizet, *Negotium perambulans in tenebris*, Strasbourg, 1922, p. 34,
quotes on this subject an Ethiopian work, *Kebra Nagast*, which calls
Christ Solomon. He also refers to the *Speculum humanae salvationis*, c. 9,
which says: 'Thronus vero Salomonis est beatissima Virgo Maria. In qua
residebat Jesus Christus, vera Sophia', (ed. of the *Speculum* by Perdrizet,
pp. 53–4). The theme of Solomon, the 'type' of Christ as Wisdom, would
appear to have been particularly attractive to religious minds in Alsace.
It is repeated on the south door of Strasbourg Cathedral. The 'Hortus
deliciarum' by Herrade of Landsberg (end of the 12th c.), represents
Christ—Solomon on his state bed and the banquet of Christ—Solomon
(miniature 35 *a* and *b* in the edition of *Canon Walter*, 1952). Solomon is
also depicted in a window of the Church of the Dominicans (now above
the main door) at Colmar.

ruler of the world; his first coming in humility, and his final coming at the end of history, at his *parousia*, when he will come in power.

I have shown elsewhere,[8] how Christ's regal power was universal and absolute from the first instant of his life, when his work was to be a saviour and a conqueror through the cross rather than the victorious man of glory. The moment when the word of God took flesh in Mary's womb in order to be the saviour of the world he possessed in his manhood the fullness and the practical power of those energies with which God intends to restore all things and to bring them into sacred fellowship with him. The completed reality of this fellowship and restoration, the natural consequence of Christ's regal and priestly power, is that kingdom which he will establish and then offer in homage to the Father (1 Co 15:24–8). It is the kingdom, the consummation of the messianic activity foretold by the prophets and which formed the subject of the hope and expectation of the Jews, including the apostles before Pentecost. The prophets foretold and the Jews hoped for a restoration in which Israel was to be the principal beneficiary and which would extend from the inner realm of men's hearts to the outward order of things. Very characteristic in this respect is an anecdote recorded by K. Stern: a rabbi was told that the Messiah had come. The rabbi went to the window and looked out, then, coming back, shook his head in negation. 'No,' he said, 'I see nothing changed.'

When John the Baptist, when Jesus himself began their ministry they proclaimed that the kingdom of God was at hand, had come. In a sense, what the prophets had foretold did come into existence with Jesus Christ: the messianic signs became manifest, the blind received their sight, the lame walked and a time of renewal was proclaimed for all (cf. Lk 4:18f; Mt 11:2f; Lk 7:18f). And yet we also might go to the window, look down into the street and observe that nothing has been changed: men suffer and make war just as though the kingdom of God had not come down upon earth. Each year when the feast of Christmas returns and it is my duty as a priest to proclaim to men that on that day their saviour was born, I am troubled by a problem of truth: have I the right to say this when apparently nothing is changed in the world?

[8] *Jalons pour une théologie du laïcat*, Paris, 1953, pp. 101f (Engl. trans. *Lay People in the Church*, London, 1957).

The answer to this question is to be found in a consideration of God's will and of his plan of salvation as these are made known to us through revelation. For the gospel and the apostolic writings show us that God's plan has two stages. Its purpose was first to give us that which causes salvation and the restoration of all things, but to reserve the full unfolding of its power and the totality of its effects for a final period still to come, which is called the *parousia* (Christ's return) or the eschatological era (the time and order of the end). Jesus Christ has indeed come and with him the activating principle of a total renewal, but he is to return again and, as St Peter said on the day after Pentecost, 'until the whole world is re-created, he has to remain in heaven. The holy prophets under God's inspiration have pronounced about this event since the beginning of the world '(Ac 3:21). Like the Jews we too should like to see a new order of things: it was, however, a person who came. This is the reason why at Christmas we celebrate our saviour in the form of a little child, something weak but also some-thing germinal and promissory.[9] We wanted the establishment of the kingdom, whereas, if the expression is permissible, we only receive the King! He is, of course, powerful, and henceforth we praise him as bearing imperial authority upon his shoulders (Is 9:5; the Introit for Christmas), but he did not unfold his full power to begin with, for he had to be our saviour through the cross and he had no wish to coerce our freedom by a display of his irresistible authority which we should have had to accept. Christ-mas is the inauguration of his coming in gentleness; he has yet to come in power and majesty.

Now the first thing that strikes one from a perusal of the stories of David and Solomon is that with the former we have to do with a man, with the latter we are confronted by a social order. The first incident in David's career is significant; he faces Goliath alone, his strength being his courage. David's whole reign is summarised in the person of the king; Solomon's is expressed in the organisa-tion of society and the grandeur of a kingdom. This is partly due to David's vivid, attractive, compelling personality that reaches us through the details of many an incident without parallel in Solomon's Story. But, as the sequel will show, there is more to it

---

[9] Cf. 'Encore une fois, Noël', in *Ecclesia*, Dec. 1951, pp. 3–6.

than that. David in fact symbolises Christ's regality in that stage
in which Jesus reigns personally in human souls: Solomon symbolises that regality in its triumphant conclusion when he will set
up his rule supremely and create a new order in the external world.

David's reign was a period of struggle and humiliation; that of
Solomon was a time of peace and glory. David was always at war,
always fighting; the capture of Jerusalem, war against the Philistines, Moabites, Ammonites, Edomites, frequent internal dis-
turbances and revolts. David had the historical mission to crush
Israel's enemies, to ensure that the people should be free to serve
Yahweh faithfully in a land previously occupied by other races
that were culturally and militarily more powerful, but idolators.
In like manner Christ was to overcome Satan, casting down the
prince of this world and delivering us from slavery. It is said of
David that he was unable to build the temple on account of his
wars, until Yahweh had put all his enemies under his feet (3 K
5:3). In this way David symbolises the present reign of Christ that
will endure until God has put all *his* enemies under his feet, as St
Paul says (1 Co 15:25f), referring to Psalm 100 (*Dixit Dominus*),
a psalm of the king's enthronement whose messianic implications
were emphasised by the apostles.

Of Solomon, on the other hand (whose very name means
Peaceful) it is written: 'He reigned over all kingdoms from the
Euphrates to the land of the Philistines and he had peace on all
sides round about him. Judah and Israel dwelt safely, every man
under his vine and under his fig tree, from Dan to Beersheba, all
the days of Solomon.'[10] Solomon himself, when he declared his
intention to begin building the temple, remarked, 'Now the Lord
my God hath given me rest on every side; I have no adversary or
opposition of any kind' (3 K 5:4). There was no longer a *Satan*, a
contradictor or opponent. This foreshadows the eschatological
era when the evil one, the contradictor, the opponent of the reign
of God will not simply be overcome—*that* he has been since the
cross—but also effectively silenced and made impotent.

[10] 3 K 4, 21, 25. Cf. Qo 47:13, and 1 Ch 22:9, adapted to show the
continuity between Solomon's and David's work: 'A Son shall be born to
thee who shall be a man of rest, and I will give him rest from all his
enemies, for his name shall be Solomon, and I will give peace and quiet-
ness in Israel during his life'.

Kingship in Israel was only granted by God on the request of the people who wished to have a king *like other nations*. At first God looked with disfavour on this wish of his people to be like others; then he allowed the monarchy to be established, but made it clear that he did not intend kingship in Israel to be identical with that of the gentiles: it could only be the kingship of *his* people if its existence was according to *his* will, communicated or interpreted in *his* word by *his* prophets. David was a king wholly according to God's heart because he was obedient to the directives of the prophets. His great religious sensitivity was inseparable from his function as king: he maintained an attitude of constant dependence upon God, wanting, like John the Baptist later when with Jesus (Jn 3:27), only what was given him from heaven. Thus, by his character, David fulfilled the type of king God wanted and that the prophets had tried to fashion, the kingly type that Jesus was to bring to perfection and most explicitly reveal in his person: a king, meek and humble of heart, sensitive to God's desires and to the service of mankind (cf. Mt 20:25f; Mk 10:42f; Lk 22:25f; Jn 13:12f).

Most striking, however, is David's extraordinary prefigurement of the humiliations of Jesus Christ. When one re-reads the account of Absalom's revolt, with the help of the geographical or topographical details given in 2 K 15f it is impressive to realise the extent to which the long episode of David's sufferings has a prophetic and messianic significance, prefiguring the beginning of the passion down to its details; Achitophel's betrayal so closely resembles that of Judas that Jesus explicitly referred to it when he spoke of Judas.[11] Like Jesus, David left the city, crossed the brook Cedron, climbed and went beyond the Mount of Olives. Like Jesus also, he was insulted and mocked by those to whom he had been especially kind. Lastly, like David who regained his kingdom —this time more thoroughly than before—after passing through these humiliations, Jesus began his reign through the agony in the garden and the cross. 'It was right and proper that in bringing many sons to glory, God (from whom and by whom everything

[11] Jn 13:18 quotes Ps 41:10 which definitely refers to the time when David was in flight from Absalom (J. Calès, *Le livre des Psaumes*, vol. 1, Paris, 1936, p. 445). Jn 15:25f refers to Ps 35:25 (on David in flight from Saul) and to Ps 69:5 (on David, reprinted later: Calès, pp. 667–8).

exists) should make the Leader of their salvation, a perfect Leader through the fact that he suffered'.[12]

Characteristics of this kind are totally absent from the reign of Solomon. Solomon was never a type of a humiliated and suffering king; on the contrary, he was the type of a monarch enjoying the fullness of his power in peace and glory. From the day of his coronation, effected by the combined authority of priest (Sadoc) and prophet (Nathan) (cf. 3 K 1:32f). Solomon is a perfect symbol of plenitude. His reign is one of glory and total triumph: its structure is characterised by his complete enjoyment of power and wisdom and by the perfect union between these two. Later legend inflated his personality and attributed to him, especially in the sphere of magic, knowledge which simply as knowledge was potent, and was combined with uncontested dominion.[13] These are typical features of an eschatological situation. Here on earth, power and knowledge are not necessarily combined, although their tendency is to become so. It is the same with power and holiness. Often indeed there exists a wounding conflict between them. Often the holier man or the more learned is oppressed by the more powerful. The 're-establishment of all things' will also entail the re-establishment of order and justice in this respect. The Son of man, eschatologically, will not be betrayed; he will judge. Solomon is more typical of this aspect than David, the betrayed and suffering king, weak in face of the wicked who persecute him.

Nothing is more striking than the way in which David exercised mercy. On occasion, of course, after a complete victory, he would practise repression with a brutality that reflects the customs of his age and which alas! has very far from disappeared from our own (cf. 2 K 8, 12, 31). And yet if we compare his conduct with Solomon's, it is evident that David's is mainly marked by mercy and Solomon's by sheer and rigid justice. Is this a consequence of

[12] Heb 2:10. The verses that follow apply to Christ one of David's sayings in a psalm composed precisely during his flight from Absalom (Ps 22:23; cf. Calès, *op. cit.*, p. 275). Calès considers the Davidic origin of the psalm doubtful, but B. F. Westcott, *The Epistle to the Hebrews*, p. 51, accepts its Davidic origin.
[13] In legend Solomon is presented as a kind of magician, and a Seal of Solomon (*Sphragis Salomônos*) was supposed to put evil spirits to flight; Solomon was regarded as being victorious over such spirits. Cf. P. Perdrizet, *Negotium . . .*, pp. 7, 34; H. Leclercq in *DACL*, vol. 15, 589f.

their character? No doubt it is, but it is also a sign of their difference as 'types'.

With scrupulous conscientiousness, David twice spared Saul's life when he had him at his mercy (1 K 24 and 26). In the king's person, even though unworthy and fallen, he respected Yahweh's anointed, and also he committed the enforcement of justice to God,[14] with that care, characteristic of his religious soul, to make sure that the entire initiative should be God's alone. No doubt, when he ascended the throne, his outlook, politically, was as cunning as that of Henry IV of France. But on the typological plane his accession prefigures Christ's coming in his ministry of reconciliation and pardon. David's captains imagined they were fulfilling his wishes when they murdered his opponents, somewhat as James and John imagined they were fulfilling Jesus' wishes when they called down fire from heaven against *his* opponents (Lk 9:54). But Jesus said to them, 'you do not know to what spirit you belong, The Son of man did not come to destroy men's lives, but to save them'. And when Jesus was rejected in one place, he went to another; he did not resist opposition or attempt to overcome it by force. David, in like manner, showed that he disapproved of the murder of Abner and of Ishbaal (2 K 3:35–9; 4:9–12). He praised the people of Yabesh who had buried Saul with respect (2 K 2:4f). He wanted to be peaceable, friendly and generous towards everyone, and first of all to Saul's descendants, for whom he showed a courteous concern (2 K 9 and 10). Later, he refused to pursue Amnon for the affair of Tamar (2 K 13), and when Absalom carried out blood vengeance on Amnon, he simply banished the murderer, then, at Joab's request, agreed to his return on condition that he would not approach him, ended by consenting to see him, and embraced him. When this reconciled but always turbulent son compelled David to take flight—doubtless he could have resisted, but at what cost?—he preferred to give way and take refuge elsewhere (cf. Lk 9:56f; Mt 5:11f, 39f; 10:23; Ac 8:1). When Shimei had insulted him he refused to have him

---

[14] Cf. 1 K 24:13 and 16; 26:10, 23; 2 K 3:39. In the incident of Nabal and Abigail (2 K 25), David meant to do justice in the manner of the desert tribes, but he rejoiced that Abigail's action and Nabal's accidental death had spared him the necessity to do this (25:33), and he blessed Yahweh for having himself done justice (39). Cf. also the incident in the story of Joseph (Gn 50:19).

pursued and punished; in fact, when he had regained his capital and been restored to power, he forgave him as well as Mephibosheth of the house of Saul (2 K 19).

It is true that on his deathbed David left Samuel instructions to practise severe justice and to take revenge for injuries (3 K 2:1–9). We may interpret the passage in which this is recorded as evidence of the decided intention of the Books of Kings to bring out the continuity between Solomon and David. We may also regard it as of typological significance, in line with what we have described above: David and Solomon representing respectively two different stages in the single kingship of Christ—when he came in mercy, he put aside retribution and punishment until he should come again in justice. In St Luke's version of the parable of the pounds, the king allows his enemies to remain until his return, and only then does he ask for the accounts and has his enemies slain. For there is one régime for the journey and another at the journey's end. During the Exodus, Israel entered into relationship with the peoples it encountered; when it reached the Promised Land it received the order to exterminate them. David, the prefigurement of Christ in his coming in mercy, allows his enemies to live on; in fact, remarked Joab, he seemed determined to love precisely those who had done him wrong (2 K 19:6). David went so far as to have himself re-enthroned, after his flight from Absalom, by the very men who had betrayed him, thus giving them the status of his deserving followers (2 K 19:12f). Earlier, when he had been in flight from Saul and was staying with the priests of Nob, he knew that Doeg and Edomite had seen him and he suspected that that informer would betray him, but he resisted the impulse to kill him (1 K 22:22). Jesus, also, knew that one of his followers would betray him, but he made no attempt to get rid of him or even to expose him to public scorn. Such is the régime of the time of mercy.

It is impossible not to recall the Lord's instructions to leave the tares to grow with the wheat until the harvest (Mt 13:30). In the régime of Christ's coming in mercy, and while she is journeying, the Church is, in the traditional phrase, *mixta*; she is mixed like the field of wheat and tares that will not be separated until the harvest (Mt 13:25f), like the net after the catch of good and bad fish, only to be sorted when it reaches the bank, at the end of time

(13:47f). 'The moral of this is that we should make no hasty or premature judgements. When the Lord comes he will bring into the light of day all that at present is hidden in darkness, and he will expose the secret motives of men's hearts. Then shall God himself give each man his share of praise' (1 Co 4:5). While time lasts a certain tolerance is essential, for in this world we cannot wholly know who is loved by God and who is not, who works for him and who against him. 'God writes straight with crooked lines', says the Portuguese proverb, a favourite of M. Portal and the motto of Claudel's *Soulier de Satin*.

When Solomon came to the throne he established order with a firm hand, according to strict vindictive justice. He liquidated his possible competitor, Adonias, and dealt pitilessly with his followers, allowing them no time or chance to rally. He exiled Abiathar and removed him from the ranks of the priesthood. He had the valiant Joab, the commander of David's army, killed in hateful and even sacrilegious circumstances (3 K 3:15–35). He avenged the wrong done to David by Shimei (vv. 36–46). David had allowed his opponents to go on living; Solomon got rid of his (as well as those of David). It was the hour of strict judgement and of avenging retribution.

Even in the famous Judgement of Solomon, a testimony to his wisdom, we can see, if we consider it attentively, a characteristic reference to the eschatological sphere of judgement and justice. On this point we shall follow a suggestion made by M. W. Vischer.[15] He remarks that the question put to Solomon is not what was good and what was bad—obvious enough in this case— but *who* was the thief of the living child. It was thus an anticipation of the judgement that will be passed by the true and final Son of David, the king of glory, when he will reveal the hidden secret of men's hearts and will make known who, in secret, form the true Israel and who do not. To say what is true and what is false, what is good and what is evil, is within our power. But to say fully and conclusively *who* is good and *who* is bad, is a power belonging to the eschatological judgement of the Son of man, typified by Solomon.

We thus come back to the idea of the Lord's two comings, in mercy and in justice, represented respectively by David and

[15] *Das Christuszeugnis des Alten Testaments*, vol. 2, pp. 293f.

Solomon. This idea is so deeply present in the New Testament writings that it could not fail to become classical. The Fathers gave expression to it on more than one occasion,[16] St Augustine and St Bernard in particular. So that Pascal, who had been brought up on their works, was simply impressing his genius on a classical theme when he described it in these conclusive lines:

Had he wanted to have overcome the obstinacy of the most hardened, he could have done so by exhibiting himself to them so openly that they could not have doubted the truth of his nature, just as he will appear on the last day, amidst such a thunderclap and such an overthrowal of nature, that the dead will come to life and the blindest see.

It was not in this fashion that he wanted to appear when he came in gentleness; because so many were unworthy of his kindness, he decided to leave them deprived of the goodness they did not want. It would not therefore have been right for him to have appeared as obviously divine, and able absolutely to convince all men; but neither would it have been right for him to have come in so hidden a way that he could not have been recognised by those who were sincerely seeking him.[17]

In his first coming, Jesus came as a physician in order to call not the righteous, but sinners (Mt 9:12–13). He went down among the

[16] E.g. the Canon of Muratori, v. 200, 'ac de gemino eius adventu, primo in humilitate, quod fuit, secundo in potestate regali praeclaro, quod futurum est' (in Kirsch, *Enchir. Fontium Hist. eccl. ant.*, No. 157); Tertullian, *Adv. Marc*, 3. 7. St John Chrysostom: 'There are two comings of Christ, the first for the forgiveness of sins, the second in order to judge the world' (*Homil. 28 in Joann. 1. PG*, 59, 162, on v. 17 of ch. 3): 'For God did not send his Son into the world to judge the world, but that through him the world might be saved'. St Augustine, *De vera religione*, 50 (*PL*, 34, 144); *En. in Ps. 9, 1* and *95, 14* (*36, 109 and 37, 1235*); *Sermo 18, 1* (*38*, 128–9): 'primo adventi venit occultus, secundo adventu veniet manifestus (. . .). Tunc *non silebat*, quando vocem eius agnoscent et qui modo contemmunt . . .'.

St Leo 'He it is who will judge thee by the truth, who has redeemed thee by mercy' (*Serm. 21* x 1 *de Nativ.* c. 3, *PL*, 54, 193); St Peter Damien, *opusc. 37, dub. 10* (*PL*, 145, 628–30); St Bernard, *De adv. serm. 4* (*PL*, 183, 47–50); *De div. serm.*, *96* (184, 741) and his secretary Gebouin of Troyes (cf. J. Leclercq, in *Rev. sc. theol.*, *41, 1957*, p. 643, n. 13). Also Joachim of Flora, a Cistercian (*Concordia*, 5, c. 65, quoted at the trial at Anagni: cf. *Arch. f. Lit. u. K. G.*, vol. 1, p. 109).

[17] *Pensées*, ed. Brunschvicg, f. 430. Cf. the end of this quotation below, note 26.

publicans, personified by Zacchaeus; he went into their houses and, as St Teresa of Lisieux puts it, sat at the table of sinners. 'What did the Son of man come for but to seek and find the lost' (Lk 19:10). These words, in which our Lord explicitly defines the purpose of his first coming, and which summarise the gospel, are derived from the magnificent chapter 34 of Ezekiel (vv. 4 and 16) in which the prophet condemns the self-seeking and disloyal pastors and foretells the coming of a true and good pastor, a new David, who will pasture the flocks in the ways of God (cf. Jr 23:1–6). It is in continuity with this chapter of Ezekiel that the gospel theme of the good shepherd is delineated, the good shepherd who will give his life for the sheep (Jn 10:11). In the régime of grace, everything is a gift, everything is mercy; everything is due to Christ's gift and sacrifice; everything is grace. The Kingdom is offered and given gratuitously, as a fully constituted inheritance, a table prepared and provided with a meal; all that is needed is to accept the invitation and come in.

We have seen that the beneficiaries are the publicans, the sinners, the hungry, not the satiated (Lk 1:53). Of course the coming in mercy is not an idyll and God may test and correct his own, but in that case it is corrective mercy, whereby God is not so much concerned to display his anger, and to confound his creatures as to admonish and reform them.

At his second coming Jesus will come in order to judge and to assign rewards according to justice. The liturgy of Advent which, like the prophecies of the Old and New Testaments,[18] unites in one perspective the development of history and its eschatological conclusion, is concerned to characterise the awaited Messiah's reign as the coming of justice: 'I will raise up a righteous seed to David; he shall reign as king and he will be wise, and he will carry out righteousness and justice in the land' (Jr 23:5: liturgy of Advent, the scriptural verse for Lauds and Vespers). Evidently the Messiah is here proclaimed as the fruit of David, but also endowed with the characteristics of Solomon; he comes as judge and as the executor of justice. It is the liturgy also (the epistle and

[18] On this prophetic manner of bringing different perspectives within the unity of a single discourse, examples of which may be found in the preaching of John the Baptist and in the eschatological discourses of Jesus, cf. A. Lemonnyer, *Théologie du Nouveau Testament*, p. 21, and G. Thils, *Pour mieux comprendre saint Paul*, Bruges, 1942, pp. 101–8.

gospel for the first Monday in Lent), that relates Ezk 34, in which we have discovered the norm of the first coming, with the capital and decisive chapter 25 of Matthew (vv. 31–46) which declares the norm of the second: it is a norm of justice. 'When the Son of man comes in his glory, and all the angels with him, he will sit down on the throne of his glory. All the nations will be gathered before him, and he will sort out the people like a shepherd sorting out his sheep and goats. The sheep he will put on his right hand and the goats on his left' (31–3). Each is rewarded according to his works, i.e. according to what he has done during the time of patience and mercy. It would be impossible at the moment to mention all the relevant passages.[19] We shall return to the subject and show how it provides the biblical foundation for a theology of merit.

This point is of the greatest importance. It is clear that, from the biblical point of view, the conditions of the second coming and of the final judgement will be very different from those of the first which was characterised entirely by the gifts bestowed and the mercy manifested. But now it has become a matter of justice. The altar seen by St John in heaven (Rv 8:3–5) is no longer the altar of propitiation on which everything was obtained for us by the blood of Christ, appealing more eloquently than Abel's, but that of incense from which the prayer of all the saints ascends to God as an offering (cf. 19:8, their virtues or 'justifications').[20] In the first coming the Kingdom was freely offered; all that men had to do was to come in. Still, it did require that amount of initiative on their part, and it did impose certain conditions: they had to be on the watch so as not to miss God's visitation; they had to answer his call, to wear the wedding garment, to have a childlike soul, etc. At the final coming, however, entrance into the joy of the Kingdom is rigorously conditioned by how men have behaved, by the deeds done during the time of mercy: the Kingdom is now presented as a

---

[19] Confining ourselves to St Matthew and St Paul, the following passages may be noted: Mt 7:21–3; 10:15 and 32–3, 39, 41–2; 11:22–4; Rm 2:6f; 1 Co 3:8, 14–15; 2 Co 5:10; Ga 6:8; Ep 6:8; Col 3:24–5; 2 Tm 2:5f.

[20] Cf. the remarks of Dom Vonier, *Key to the Doctrine of the Eucharist*, 'The offerings placed on that heavenly altar are no longer the body and blood, but the prayers of the saints. That which comes from the altar of the Apocalypse is no longer mercy and pardon, but justice and judgement, "thunder, voices, lightning and a great earthquake". It is obviously the altar of the consummation, not that of propitiation.'

reward and the two keys that open it are faith *and* works, faith expressing itself in works as opportunity offers.[21]

The relation between judgement and mercy is, however, even more definite than this. It is not the mere fact that the one comes after the other; such a relationship would be simply extrinsic. It is, rather, a relationship between the *content* of each of them. The passage in Matthew 25 (vv. 31–46) brings this out strongly; judgement and its sentence will refer not only to the generality of the deeds done and to the attitude taken during the time of mercy, but, with the utmost definition, to the mercy—that mercy God first bestowed on us—which we have shown (or not shown) to our neighbour. 'I was hungry and you did not feed me' (cf. Mt 7:1f; Lk 6:37f; Mk 4:24; Mt 6:12; Lk 11:4). St Paul synthesises both points of view within the limits of a single passage in his epistle to the Galatians 6:2 and 4–5: 'Carry each others' burdens and so live out the law of Christ; Let every man learn to assess properly the value of his own work ... for every man must bear his own burden'. But this burden which each must bear and will have to carry to the judgement (St Paul is speaking of the future), consists of what we have been asked to do during the time of mercy, i.e. to bear the burden of others and to do as we would be done by (cf. Mt 18:23–5; 7:12; Lk 6:31). The Christ of judgement is the same as the Christ of mercy; the Son of man who will come on the clouds in power and glory is no other than the Son of Mary, the Christ of Christmas and the cross. And no doubt the presence of the Virgin Mary, whom tradition affirms will be with the Twelve who are to assist Christ when he does justice after his ministry of mercy is over (Mt 19: 28; Lk 22:30), is meant to indicate that the stern Judge of the *parousia* is also the Merciful One who came in weakness to save that which was lost.

At the same time, justice remains justice and the correction that God will administer at the end of time will no longer be the educative and fatherly correction of the time of mercy, whose moderate and pitying nature David had experienced (2 K 24:14), but the correction that vindicates and establishes justice, the

---

[21] Many passages in the Fathers with this meaning are given in G. W. H. Lampe, 'Some notes on the signification of *Basileia tou Theou, Basileia tou Christou*, in the Greek Fathers', in *JTS*, 44 (1948), pp. 58–73. cf. pp 67 f.

correction that belongs to the time of his anger. It is impossible to eliminate from the Bible, from the Old and New Testaments, the very many passages that confirm this. · · ·

The signs of the second coming will be startling and of a kind that will convince all men. Jesus himself described this coming in terms of majesty and power,[22] and spoke of his coming on the clouds with a company of angels.[23] 'Then all the peoples of the earth will beat their breasts; and they will see the Son of man coming on the clouds of heaven with great power and glory' (Mt 24:30). This, once again, was what Solomon had prefigured; princes had come from all parts to behold his majesty:[24] nothing of the sort is said of David. It is the time when the truth will become self-evident, as St Augustine remarks; those who had not wished to submit to God when he reigned in mercy will be constrained to do so when he reigns as judge.

Quite different are the circumstances when God comes in the régime of grace. Then 'watch as you may, you will not *see* the Kingdom of God come' (Lk 17:20). Happy the servant whom his master shall find watching,[25] on the look out for signs of God and for his initiatives, as was David in so remarkable a way. The signs of God's comings and visitations in the régime of grace, the ways in which he continues to make his presence felt, have something dim and ambiguous about them; as a rule they show no visible evidence. His approach may be recognised, or it may be ignored. For this choice, upon which man's whole spiritual destiny increasingly depends, there are no absolute and irrefutable external proofs. The light of decision is within; it comes from the grace of God and from the true disposition of the heart, as Pascal again realised and expressed in unforgettable words.[26]

[22] Mt 19:28; 24:30: 25:31; Lk 9:26; 21:27.
[23] Mt 24:30; 26:64; Mk 13:26; 14:62; cf. Mt 26:53.
[24] 2 Ch 9:23; cf. 4 K 5:14; 10:1f; 10:24, etc.
[25] Mt 24:26, 42f; 25:13; Mk 13:33f; Lk 12:36f, 43, etc.
[26] The passage quoted above (p. 16) concludes as follows: 'He wanted to make himself perfectly recognisable to these latter; and so, wanting to appear openly to those who seek him with all their heart and hidden to those who fly from him with all their heart, he so modified his knowability that it bears marks that are visible to those who seek him, but not to those who do not. There is sufficient light for those who only want to see, and sufficient darkness for those with a contrary disposition.'

CHAPTER TWELVE

The Holy Spirit in the Church[1]

'HE GAVE LIFE AND BREATH, INDEED EVERY-
thing. . . . In him we live and move and have our being': these
words spoken by St Paul to the Council of the Areopagus (Ac
17:25 and 28), might be applied to the Holy Spirit in order to express what he is and what he does for the Church. The study of
this theme, the subject of these pages, might be carried on in two
stages—that of the theology of the Church, the theology of the
effects produced by the Holy Spirit in the Church, or that of a
theology of the Holy Spirit himself, a theology that would consider his special position in the mystery of the Trinity that would
provide an explanation of the fact that the Holy Spirit functions in
the Church in exactly the way ascribed to him by Revelation.
Here I shall confine myself to the first stage, that of the Church.
Not without regret, for the second alone provides the foundation
and reveals the full depth of the remarks I shall make. But it would
involve an exposition of doctrine that from every point of view
cannot be envisaged now.

The present question therefore simply concerns the Holy
Spirit *in the Church*. I shall show: (1) that he is given to the Church
as such and enables her to have a stable existence in the world as
the body of Christ; (2) how he produces in that Church all the
activities of her life, and how he is the ultimate activating principle
of her unity.

The Holy Spirit was already at work in Israel before Christ: he
it was who, working through Moses, had led the people of God

[1] Article published in *Lumière et Vie* (Lyons), No. 10 (June 1953),
pp. 51–74.

148

out of Egypt and continued to guide them through the judges, the kings and the prophets (cf. Is 63:11f). And yet it is evident that he was sent in an absolutely new way as the result of the 'passover' of Jesus to his Father (his passion and resurrection; what our Lord, in St John, calls his 'glorification'). Jesus made this abundantly clear;[2] the apostles constantly describe the Spirit of Pentecost as the gift especially accompanying the messianic age;[3] the novelty of this coming was so radical that St John could write, 'For the Spirit was not yet in being, as Jesus had not yet been glorified' (7:39). Thus the same Spirit which led Israel and filled the world (cf. Ws 1:7) was communicated at Pentecost under new conditions and new modalities. What were these conditions and modalities?

Under the old dispensation God's Spirit worked through men who had been called to lead the people: priests, kings and especially prophets. In the messianic or Pentecostal régime he is given to each and all.[4] In the 14th to the 16th chapters of St John, Jesus, speaking to the Twelve who simultaneously represented both the tiny remnant and the first-fruits of the new people of God, said again and again: I will give *you*, I will send to *you*, he will teach *you*, he will guide *you*, he will tell *you*. . . . In this way he indicated that the Spirit was to be given both to individuals and to the community, to all men as one man, and creating that one man. This is why the Spirit came down upon the apostles and laity who were *assembled together*; he was given at the same time to all and each; he was given to the gathering, to the disciples as a whole—a fact made clear in Acts by the insistent use of the phrase *epi to auto*, all together: 1:15; 2:1, 44, 47. The Spirit requires a certain disposition of unanimity, and at the same time he brings unity into existence. He forms into a single body believers who have been baptised into a single spirit (1 Co 12:13); he builds up this body and out of the community of believers makes a temple which all construct together (Ep 2:18f).

[2] Jn 14:16; 15:26; 16:7. Cf. Lk 24:49; Ac 1:8.
[3] Ac 2:16f (Jl 3:1-5; Vulg 2:28-32; Is 43:3; Ezk 36:26-7; cf. Jr 3:33-4; and the passages in the New Testament on the baptism of the Spirit; Mt 3:11 (Mk 1:8; Lk 3:16)); Jn 1:33; 3:5; Ac 1:5; 2:33, 38; 11:16; 19:2-61 Ep 1:13.
[4] To all: cf. Ac 1:15; cf. Lk 24:33. To each: Ac 2:3. An analogous use of the plural pronoun *we* is to be found in St Paul (cf. e.g. Rm 5:1-11).

Under the old dispensation, God's Spirit entered into the leaders
of the people, but a new mode of his presence was foretold as the
characteristic of the messianic age. He was *to rest* upon the
Messiah: Is 11:2; 61:1. This was fulfilled in our Head, Jesus
Christ, as he himself affirmed (Lk 4:18–21) and as it was made
manifest at his baptism (Mk 1:9–11). The prophets had also foretold that, with the coming of the messianic age, the Spirit would
be widely diffused and given (*supra*, p. 3, n. 3).

It is this which Jesus promised to fulfil and did in fact fulfil:
'I will ask the Father and he will give you another to serve as
Advocate and be with you to the end of time' (Jn 14:16). The
terms used in this promise are remarkable. For the messianic
community, the Spirit will be a *gift*,[5] and a gift that will never
leave it: he *will be with* the disciples as Jesus had been with them,
in order to assist them, and this until the end of the present age,
eis ton aiôna.[6]

The Fathers had a predilection for these texts and were concerned to explain how the Spirit is the source of all the Church's
life, an idea which the Latin Fathers, St Augustine especially, expressed in the dictum: the Holy Spirit is *the soul of the Church*.[7]
Classical theology, papal encyclicals, contemporary theology of
the Church have adopted this idea and given it precision.[8] The
Holy Spirit, they affirm, does not enter into composition with the
Church in the way the human soul enters into composition with
the body; the words 'form' or formal cause may not be used in

[5] 4:10, 13–14; 14:16; Ac 2:38.
[6] He indwells: Jn 14:16–17, 23; Rm 8:9, 11; 1 Co 3:16; 1 Jn 3:24. The
word Paraclete, Advocate, itself, expresses the idea of 'being with'. *Eis
ton aiôna*: Jn 14:16; cf. Mt 28:20. These series of texts and ideas were
familiar to the Fathers: St Irenaeus, *Adv. Haer.* 3, 17, 1 (*PG*, 7, 929) is
an example.
[7] These passages from the Fathers are collected in S. Tromp, *De
Spiritu Sancto Anima Corporis mystici*. 1: *Testimonia selecta e Patribus
graecis*. 2: *Test. sel. e Patr. latinis*, Rome, Gregorian University, 1932;
2nd ed. 1948 and 1952.
[8] Classical theology: St Thomas Aquinas III. Sent. d. 13, q. 2, a. 2,
sol. 2, etc. Cf. E. Vauthier, *Le Saint-Esprit principe d'unité de l'Eglise
d'après St Thomas d'Aquin* in *Mél. de Sc. rélig.* 1948, pp. 175–196.
Encyc. *Divinum illud* 9th May 1897 (*AAS*, p. 650) and *Mystici Corporis*
29th June 1943 (*AAS*, 1943, pp. 219–220). Contemporary theology of the
Church: E. Mura *Le corps mystique du Christ*, 2nd ed. Paris, 1951. The
slight disagreement on nomenclature between these two theologians does
not concern us here.

this matter, at least not in their technical meaning. We must speak instead of a principle of life in the Church that is transcendent and yet active, dwelling in her, spiritually present in her, polarising and drawing to himself every element in the Church which is divine. This is indeed the function of a soul, but the expression avoids—and the greatest care must be taken to see that we do avoid—the disastrous error of imagining some physical connection to exist that would transform the Holy Spirit into a single reality with the Church.

We must not even speak of an incarnation, as Manning suggested we might—though, of course, he was careful to exclude a real hypostatic union.[9] The Holy Spirit was sent at Pentecost to a Church that was already endowed with her constitution and structure; he comes into her as a principle of life and movement, but the Church exists through being instituted by Jesus Christ. When we examine in the New Testament the special work of the Holy Spirit in relation to the work of salvation, we find that Christ gave to the Church in general and to individuals in particular, an existence in the realm of the new creation; the Holy Spirit was sent to give both of these life and movement, so that they may produce the activities and achievements that befit them.[10] As regards the individual soul, this is made very clear in passages such as Ga 4:4–6 and Rm 8:15. In like manner, the New Testament speaks of the Holy Spirit as *being given, received, remaining with, indwelling, witnessing, guiding, teaching* etc. He is a Person who dwells in the Church and acts in her, he is not a mere force or a mere activating principle that becomes a part of her reality.

This explains the fact that whereas the hypostatic union between the word of God and manhood in Jesus makes that manhood sinless and adorable, the coming of the Holy Spirit into the Church as an indwelling and active soul, allows what is human and therefore fallible in her to remain, as such, human and fallible. It leaves the Church conditioned by a genuine historical

[9] He suggested this at Vatican Council I. (*Mansi*, vol. 49, col. 171): cf. E. Mersch, *Le Corps mystique. . . . Et. de théol. histor.* 2nd ed., Brussels and Paris, 1936, vol. 2, pl 357 in n. No doubt the view here expressed by Manning lies at the root of certain exaggerations to be found in his ideas of the Church and the function of the hierarchy.

[10] Cf. my own study quoted in the bibliography: *RSPT*, 1952, pp. 6163; 1953, 33f; *Esquisses*, new edition, 1953, pp. 155, 158f.

development, a genuine dependence upon the conditions which space and time impose.[11]

What therefore is the nature of the bond that unites the Church with the Holy Spirit? It is, as we have shown elsewhere,[12] a union based upon an alliance, the grounds of which are the most stable, the most holy conceivable, because they are the products of God's will and faithfulness. If we are certain that God is in action in the Christian sacraments or in those deeds of the hierarchy which touch upon the very constitution of the Church, if, for example, wedded Christians can be sure that through the sacrament of marriage they are united in the sight of God and through an act of God himself, if baptism incorporates us with certainty in Jesus Christ, if the consecration in the Eucharist gives us his body, and sacramental absolution his forgiveness, if a solemn definition of a council or of the pope as supreme pastor accurately defines a point of divine revelation, this is because God is faithful to the promise he has personally given to his Church, whose essential constitution is involved to these various actions. It is because he is faithful to his alliance. It has been truly said that 'alliance is the Jewish [biblical?] category which corresponds to the Greek idea of "nature" as a permanent law of the realities which God has established'.[13]

This is why the Church through the gift of the Holy Spirit and through his indwelling in her—the supreme factor in the new and conclusive alliance—has a stability and a real infallibility in matters which concern her existence as the New Eve, the Bride of Christ, his helpmeet in the work of the second creation, which is that of the redemption and communion between men and God in Jesus Christ. Perhaps the strongest testimonies on this unfailing characteristic of the Church are those which we find in the Fathers or in the writers of the age of persecution: St Irenaeus, Tertullian, St Cyprian. We will quote only one passage—from Tertullian: 'Very well let us admit it; all of them have been deceived; the apostle was deceived when he bore witness (to this church or that); the Holy Spirit has not kept watch over any of them in order to

[11] Cf. *Le Christ, Marie et l'Église*, Paris, Desclée de Brouwer, 1952. (Eng. trans. *Christ, Our Lady and the Church*, London, 1957.)
[12] *Op. cit. suptra* (note 9), *RSPT*, 1953, pp. 33, or *Esquisses*, pp. 161f.
[13] J. Daniélou, in *Études*, March 1951, p. 365.

lead them into truth, that Spirit who had been sent by Christ and who he had asked the Father should be the teacher of truth, the steward of God, the vicar of Christ. He has neglected his duties and has allowed the Churches to take an altered view of the doctrine which he himself taught them through the apostles. But is it, in fact, likely to be true that so many Churches of such importance should have strayed and then finally come to agree in the same belief?'[14]

We must add, however, that although the Church is sure of the faithfulness of her Lord and of the Spirit given her as a dowry, she still remains the human aid of the most holy God; she has to imitate Jesus who in his manhood, knowing that his Father unfailingly heard him (Jn 11:42), prayed whenever he did anything that concerned the Church or involved her existence in the future: before he chose the apostles or when the wind buffeted their ship, before St Peter's confession of faith, and, with reference to that apostle, for the sending of the Spirit and the unity of believers....[15] In short, Jesus prayed for the Church. He also prayed during his baptism by John, when he was consecrated for his ministry (Lk 3:21). In her turn the Church must pray that the activity of the Spirit may accompany her preaching of the word, the celebration of the sacraments, the initiative and the decisions of the spiritual authority. She prays 'through Jesus Christ'. Or, to express this more profoundly: the body, united to its Head, prays with him with one voice, as the Fathers, St Augustine in particular, are keen to emphasise. Thus the Church must constantly be asking, through her Lord and Bridegroom that all this work of her self-development and her life may be accomplished, and this she does by accompanying all her actions with an *epiclesis*, i.e. an invocation of the Holy Spirit.

Do we, priests and preachers, think of this when we carry out, even (and especially . . .) with authority, the ministry of the word,

[14] *De praeser. 28.* In the French translation by De Labriolle the word *quibusdam*, which I have translated by the words in brackets, is simply omitted. Tertullian is referring to those Churches—the ones that elsewhere he specifically calls apostolic—to whose faith St Paul had borne witness: that of Rome (Rm, 1:8) or Corinth, (2 Co 8:1–16) in particular.

What we call, somewhat juridically, the indefectibility of the Church, the Fathers prefer to describe in terms of her virginity. The references are beyond counting.

[15] Lk 6:12; Mk 14:23–4; Lk 9:18, 22, 32; Jn 14:16; 17:9–24; etc.

F

the sacraments, or spiritual 'government'. Let us ask the Holy Spirit to add his witness to our own, as Scripture phrases it; to celebrate with us, in the magnificent words of the liturgy of St John Chrysostom.

As soon as the Spirit is given, he begins to act. This comes out with remarkable clarity with respect to Jesus: immediately he has been consecrated for his messianic ministry, through baptism and the descent of the Spirit, he was driven by the Spirit to perform its first act.[16] A similar activity is observable with regard to the Church: the summary given in a responsory of the liturgy of Pentecost: 'They were all filled with the Holy Spirit and (immediately) began to preach', is an accurate expression of the narrative recorded in Acts.[17] As soon as the Holy Spirit had come down the apostles began to speak, the Church took form, began to live and expand. It has been remarked with truth that the whole of this early history could be summarised in the following verse: 'The Church throughout Judaea, Galilee and Samaria enjoyed a period of peace . . . and it increased in numbers under the guidance of the Holy Spirit' (9:31). It is equally well summarised in another verse which precisely defines, although very briefly, the elements of the Church's internal life: 'They devoted themselves in close fellowship to instruction from the apostles, to regular Breaking of Bread and to prayer' (2:42).[18] In this verse we discover the three spheres of activity which form the norm and provide the means of the Church's self-development: teaching (the *magisterium*), the liturgy with its two elements, sacrifice and prayer (priesthood), community life regulated by pastoral authority (the rule of law). This is the framework within which the Church's life has developed from the beginning. It will serve to bring our thoughts on the way the Spirit acts in that life into order.

We would first point out an essential feature of that action that

[16] Mk 1:10–12: 'He had no sooner come up out o the water than he saw the heavens rent asunder and the Spirit descending like a dove. . . . Immediately after, the Spirit drove him into the desert'. Lk 4:1: 'Filled with the Holy Spirit, Jesus left the Jordan and for forty days was guided by the Spirit in the wilderness. . . .'

[17] Cf. 2:4; 4:31, 33.

[18] Cf. the first chapter of our *Esquisses du mystère de l'Église*, new edition, 1953. (Eng. trans, *The Mystery of the Church*, London and New York, 1960.)

is illustrated by the relationship between the two verses quoted above (remembering that there is other evidence): the Church develops through a combination of the external action of the Holy Spirit and the external action of the apostolic authority. This is also made clear by the teaching of the encyclical *Mystici Corporis* 29th June 1943: the Church, it affirms, is the product of two 'missions', both of them harmonious and both divine: a 'spiritual' mission and a 'juridical' mission, that of the apostolate which is continued in the various kinds of ministerial action that flow from apostolic authority. We shall not now discuss the research that has been carried out on the foundations of these ideas in Scripture (cf. the bibliography), but simply note the three conclusions that result from it: (1) Jesus employed and sent two agents to do *his* work; *his* Spirit and *his* apostles. (2) These two agents *act in unison* in their *mutual* work of building up the Body of Christ. (3) Nevertheless the Spirit retains a kind of *freedom* or autonomy.

The brief comments given below refer not so much to the origins of the Church as to her later, post-apostolic history. They presuppose these origins and are sanctioned by them, just as the apostolic period which in its essential elements has always been for her, *de jure* and *de facto*, a normative reference.

LIFE IN THE CHURCH. TEACHING

One of the activities most explicitly attributed to the Holy Spirit is that of *testifying*, or, in biblical phraseology, doing the work of God in the sphere of faith and knowledge.[19] Jesus himself also attributes to the Spirit the work of *teaching*.[20] His way of expressing this is most noteworthy: 'I have said these things to you while still with you. But the Advocate, the Holy Spirit, whom the Father will send in my name, will teach you everything and recall to your minds all that I have said to you'. 'I have much more to tell you, but you could not bear it now. But when he comes, the Spirit of truth, he will lead you into truth entire. For what he tells you will not be his own, but all that he has heard. And he will tell

[19] Chief texts: Jn 15:26; Ac 5:32; 1 Jn 5:8. Interior testimony to the believer: Rm 8:16; 1 Jn 3:19–24; 5–6.

[20] Lk 12:12; Jn 14:26; 16:13. And again, through interior testimony: 1 Jn 2:20, 27.

you of the things to come. He will enhance my glory; for he will be enriched from what is mine and pass it on to you (Jn 14:25–6; 16:12–14).

These words express, with great precision, two aspects of that activity of the Holy Spirit, two different but related and basically complementary aspects. On the one hand, the Paraclete (Assistant) only brings to mind what Jesus has said: he will be enriched by *that*. On the other, he is to teach 'everything'; he will lead men into 'truth entire'; he will declare it and even tell them 'of the things to come'. In short, he will unfold the truths of salvation more extensively than Jesus did. We are clearly confronted here by two functions of truth and of the Master who teaches it: a function related to its source that remains a constant norm, and a function related to its unfolding, which takes place in successive stages. All this, in my opinion, should be envisaged in the setting of the great biblical idea of Christ considered as simultaneously our Alpha and our Omega.[21] Jesus Christ is the source of all things, the originating principle of the new creation, the creation that comes into being through salvation and grace. But he must 'come to his fullness' in us (Ep 1:23), achieve his perfect stature through us, and develop until he is utterly complete (4:13, 15), and this not only as regards grace and charity, but also as regards knowledge.

This is basically what is meant by Tradition, of which, as the profoundest theology affirms, the originating principle is the Holy Spirit (Möhler: cf. Bibliography). For Tradition involves both continuity and development; in the here and now it involves a reference to both the beginning and the end. The sacraments involve this also, and theology analyses the threefold relationship of their symbolism with the salvation achieved by the Lord's passover, with grace at the present time and with that future glory whose initial stage they contain.

The facts, moreover, show that in the Church's tradition, from the beginning down to our days, there is both identity in trans-

[21] The first and last letters of the Greek alphabet, the beginning and the complete fulfilment. Cf. Rv 1:8; 21:6; 22:13. It will doubtless be agreed that light is shed on this aspect of the mystery of Christ in F. X. Durrwell, *La résurrection de Jésus, mystère de salut*, Le Puy and Paris, 1950 (Engl. transl., *The Resurrection*, London, 1960). Cf. also my *Jalons pour une théologie de laicat*, Ed. du Cerf, 1953 (*Lay People in the Church*, London, 1957).

mission and increase in knowledge. St John, who, in comparison with the earlier gospels, gives a more profound view of Christ, remarks several times that the apostles had not understood this or that saying or action of the Lord.[22] They realised their meaning later, thanks to the Spirit of Pentecost. What was thus accomplished within the space of a generation, and with the guarantee of God's grace of revelation, has been continued in a certain way throughout the ages and with the assistance of the Holy Spirit. And just as the apostolic body effected externally and visibly what the Holy Spirit effected internally and in a hidden manner, so these two aspects of testimony reappear in the teaching activity of the Church, of whom the first Vatican Council says that she has received the doctrine of faith 'as a deposit to be faithfully kept and infallibly declared'.[23]

We cannot, in these pages, even give an outline of a theory of Tradition or of dogmatic development; nor even a theology of the *magisterium*. But we must complete our brief comment with a remark of considerable importance. The Holy Spirit is not given to the Church exactly as he was given to the prophets and the apostles. To these he was given in order that the foundations of the Church might be established, to bestow her belief upon her through a special grace of revelation. But the foundations were established once for all time. O. Cullmann is right to affirm this, and it is not on account of this that we consider his position inadequate.[24] The grace given to the Church is not the grace of new revelation, but of permanency in the faith of the apostles and of exact definition of the faith which cannot remain in her inert and sterile. The accepted theological word is that of assistance, and the phrase used in our treatises in the infallibility of the Pope himself is that he is assisted *ne erret*, in such a way that when he makes a judgement that implicates the Church as a whole, in that supreme act he cannot be deceived. This does not dispose of his obligation (also incumbent on the Church as a whole) to seek by human endeavour, with the assistance of grace that must be asked for, to

---

[22] Cf. 2:19; 12:16; 13:7; 20:9; cf. 16:25. And cf. J. Guitton, *La pensée moderne et le catholicisme. 6. Le problème de Jésus et les fondements du témoignage chrétien*, Paris, Aubier, 1948, pp. 175, 175, 181f.

[23] Sess. 3, c. 4, Denz., n. 1800.

[24] Cf. 'Du nouveau sur la question de Pierre? Le Saint Pierre de M. O. Cullmann,' in *Vie Int.*, Feb. 1953, pp. 17–43.

ascertain what the truth, tradition, and the 'deposit', really are. It follows, therefore, that even in the case of dogmatic definitions, problems concerning the authentic relationship between their general statements and their details with their sources are not eliminated: it is not enough to make a general appeal to the assistance Christ promised to his Church, even though that promise and assistance are the real and objective foundation of the Church's infallibility.

What is meant here by 'the Church'? We have deliberately used this general word—incidentally, the word used by the Vatican Council—but we must now give it definition. We would, in any case, ask that whenever this word is encountered, its content, its coverage (in the scholastic phrase: *pro quo supponit?*) should be examined. Does it designate the hierarchy alone, or the laity alone, or does it include them both? The answer rings out clearly: it includes them both, organically united in a single body. This is undoubtedly the traditional position.[25] It may be expressed in the following way: the Holy Spirit is given to the entire body and he gives life to all the members of the body, to each member according to his nature and function. Some are simple living cells in the body, called into being in order to live; others have received a ministerial function, as St Paul explains: 'Some he (Christ) made apostles, some prophets, some evangelists, others he made pastors and teachers. His gifts were made for the perfecting of the saints, for the work of the ministry, for the building up of the body of Christ' (Ep 4:11-12). These latter are assisted and led by the Holy Spirit so that they may not be simply members (it will be evident in what sense we take this word), but pastors and teachers, overseers (bishops: Ac 20:28), and, finally, a supreme overseer or pastor, with respect to which the capital words recorded by St John were spoken (Jn 21:15-17; Lk 22:32; Mt 16:17-19).

In this organic setting which is, we repeat, that of Tradition (and of the encyclical *Mystici Corporis*), it can easily be seen that *the whole Church* co-operates in guarding and unfolding the

---

[25] Without prejudice to later studies, I show this in *Jalons pour une théologie du laïcat* (*Lay People in the Church*) (cf, in particular, for what follows, ch. 6, on the laity and the prophetic function of the Church), and in the vol. of *Études* intended to complete this work.

deposit of faith, in bearing apostolic witness to it) in intellectual reflection upon it, and, of course, in living from it in prayer and holiness. The entire history of the Church as well as her present circumstances illustrate this truth. It was the pope, the supreme spokesman and pastor of the Church who defined the dogma of Mary's bodily assumption, but he did not do so without first consulting the bishops and through them their clergy and people.[26] Nor was his action without recognition of the fact that for centuries Christian devotion has understood that Mary, 'the eschatological icon of the Church', joined to the incarnate word as his immaculate Mother, had already personally received what is promised as a gift to all Christians at the end. In fact a host of examples could be given in illustration of this truth of the organic quickening of the whole body and of every member in the degree of his membership (cf. our chapter referred to in note 25).

SACRAMENTAL LIFE AND SANCTIFICATION

We shall simply note the following points, without developing them:

It is the Holy Spirit who operates in the Christian sacraments. No means of sanctification begins to work in the Church without his presence and activity.[27]

The Spirit of Pentecost is always a Spirit of Catholicity, one of the most striking features of Christian holiness is the infinite variety of the type. The Fathers had a predilection for comparing the Holy Spirit's action with that of the rain or the sun from which every created being benefits according to its nature, or to that of the mind and nervous system which effects each part of the body according to its function and needs.

The action of the Spirit might also be considered in the different stages of the movement by which he endeavours to lead us from sin to purity of life and perfect communion with God and, in him, with all good things. We might consider the way in which he first makes us realise that we are sinners and moves us to seek forgive-

[26] Cf. on this subject: H. Holstein 'L'infaillibilité pontificale et le dogme de l' Assomption,' in *Études*, November 1952, pp. 145–56.
[27] Cf. St John Chrysostom, *De S. Pentec. hom.*, 1, 4 (*PG*, 50, 548 and 549).

ness (cf. Jn 16:8), then to desire the good and to do penance, then gives us the conviction that the faith is true, and the sense that we are the children of God. We could examine how he enables us to call upon our Father in prayer, and bestows the calm and powerful certainty that we are indeed God's children, and his unruffled and potent guidance of our lives, and all the consequences of grace in joy and peace.[28] These are realities whose hallowing experience those who pray with faith have undergone and continually undergo.

Now the work done by the Holy Spirit in an individual soul, as though it were the only one in the world, is also done by him in countless souls, harmonising each and all in the development of a history which amidst the history of the world in general, is a history of holiness in that world and of the world's salvation. Whilst bringing to each man his daily bread of grace, he carries on the construction of a single work: Scripture, speaking of this, not only mentions a city (Jerusalem), but also a temple and a body: metaphors which all imply the ideas of a unity formed from diversity and of a reality which grows by the addition of new elements in accordance with a total plan fixed beforehand. In the New Testament the Holy Spirit is explicitly connected with the descriptions of the temple and the body.[29] Moreover the body and the temple are the same thing, since in the messianic régime of the temple now at last existing, there is no other real temple than the spiritual body of Christ (Jn 2:19–21). When Jesus gives us his Spirit he sanctifies us and makes us the members of his body; and doing this he fulfils God's purpose—to dwell in his creation that has at last achieved its unity, as in a temple of absolute holiness, *not made by the hand of man*,[30] in the image and like an extension of that body, absolutely holy and pure, which the Holy Spirit, and no human eros, formed in the womb of the Virgin Mary: cf. Lk 1:35.

---

[28] Cf. among others, these texts in the following order: Rm 8:4, 9f; 1 Co 12:3; Rm 8:16, 26–7; 1 Jn 3:19–24; Rm 8:14. The fruits of the Spirit: Ga 5:22.

[29] Body: 1 Co 6:11–18; 12:4–11 and 13; 15:45; Ep 4:4; cf. Rm 8:9; 1 Jn 4:13. Temple: 1 Co 6:19; Ep 2:18–22. Cf. 1 P 2:5. Many of these texts speak of *the Spirit*, but this latter always presupposes the action of the Holy Spirit.

[30] Cf. Mk 14:58; Ac 7:48; 17:24; Heb 9:11 and 24; 2 Co 5:1.

THE LIFE OF THE CHURCH AS A SOCIETY
AND ITS SPIRITUAL GOVERNMENT

We shall be dealing here not with the intimate life of the Church, not with the holiness that belongs to her inner and personal reality, but with what is externally observable in her structure and historical development.

This also concerns the body as a whole. The Church does not exist solely for the clergy, and the laity do not exist as an inactive and inert mass within her. The teaching of the apostles is that the spiritual gifts distributed to all Christians and with which each man 'should serve with the particular gift God has given him, as faithful dispensers of the magnificently varied grace of God' (1 P 4:10). 'Men have different gifts, but it is the same Spirit who gives them. There are different ways of serving God, but it is the same Lord who is served. God works through different men in different ways, but it is the same God who achieves his purposes through them all. Each man is given his gift by the Spirit in order that he may serve the common good. One man's gift by the Spirit is to speak with wisdom, another's to speak with knowledge. The same Spirit gives to another man faith. . . . Behind all these gifts is the operation of the same Spirit, who distributes to each individual man, as he wills' (1 Co 12:4–11).

But, as we have already shown, if the whole body is quickened, it is quickened organically and in such a manner that some members exercise a regulating power with the precise purpose of serving unity. Chapters 12–14 of the 1st epistle to the Corinthians show how St Paul understood these matters; the pastoral epistles and several passages of the Acts show that in the Church there exist functions of pastoral authority derived from those of the apostles, whose permanent responsibility it is, among other things, to regulate the activity of the laity with reference to the unity that must be maintained. Consequently, under the action of one and the same Spirit the life of the Church always exhibits itself as involving a kind of polarity between an abundance of individual initiative and moderating control, between a great variety of gifts or contributions and firm declarations of the requirements of unity.

The diversity of gifts is the reason for the diversity of vocations and tasks. For, from a Christian point of view, all men, and more especially all believers, form a single body in which ability and potentiality of a given individual represents, as such, a vocation and a service. Within the body all activity is the expression of tasks being done and responsibility accepted in view of a collective work whose main lines we know, but whose details form part of that 'daily bread' which we ask God each day to give us and make known to us.[31] The particular task of a given individual becomes his vocation from the fact that he receives it from God as his special work within his general vocation as a member of Christ. This task is determined by his gifts, and among these the attractions or the idea of some reality is not the least significant. It is determined also by circumstances or events, these masters whom God appoints (Pascal). Thus the slightest initiative suggested to us by the Holy Spirit,[32] the services to others to which he prompts us, the tasks he moves us to accept, count not only as a means of fulfilling our own destiny (cf. Ep 2:10), but also for the building up of the body of Christ and for the coming of his kingdom.

When an attraction to some work or to some service has been unmistakably felt to concern the body of Christ and his kingdom, and instead of remaining exclusively inward and personal seeks expression in some corporate body or activity of the Church and receives the sanction of the spiritual authority, then we may speak of a vocation in a stronger and more definite sense; vocation to the priesthood, to the monastic life (with its many spheres of charity), and including the vocation to the lay apostolate in authorised Catholic Action. It is always the Holy Spirit who directs matters to the extent in which the fidelity of some or the fervour of others permits him. He aims at making the laity realise the nature of their work of service and enables them to carry it out; and he inspires the pastors who are responsible for harmonising the general development of the body and for the factors necessary for its unity.

[31] Cf. *Jalons pour une théologie du laïcat* (*Lay People in the Church*): ch. 3 (The Kingdom, the Church and the world); ch. 8 (The laity and the Church's apostolic function; Catholic Action and Christian temporal commitment); ch. 9 (In the world, but not of it. Lay 'Spirituality').

[32] Significant examples of this may be found in Scripture; e.g. the story of Philip, Ac 8:26f, that can easily be transposed to the scale of our own lives and to the most common circumstances.

Such is the law of the Spirit's action in the ordinary course of our lives and in the environment of the humblest parish. Transposed, it is equally applicable to the history and development of the Church as a whole. For the Church does develop; although she is not of the world she is in it and has a mission to it. She cannot disregard the world's development and its needs, first because she must herself exist in its midst, and secondly because she must supply an answer to its needs and thereby fulfil the commission given to her to proclaim the Good News to all creation (Mk 16:15). But the world is not inert, it does not stay motionless, waiting for a word to drop out of eternity. The centuries advance, mankind increases, new fields of activity are endlessly opened up or disclosed. If the Church is alive and fruitful, if she is to have a message and a special love for everything which comes into existence throughout space and time, if the Spirit is that living water in her that was promised by Jesus,[33] and which, as it streams along, endlessly renews the foliage of the living trees whose leaves, according to the Apocalypse (22:1-2), serve for the healing of the nations, then just as the sap rises up into the branches, producing a constant succession of leaves, flowers and fruit, so the Spirit is constantly creating initiatives of every kind, every sort of activity and movement. At this point we must inevitably refer to the famous passage from St Irenaeus (c. 180) on the faith which always remains identical with that of the Apostles, and yet is always alive, and 'which always, under the action of the Spirit is like a precious liquid kept in a vessel of good quality that rejuvenates itself and even rejuvenates the vessel that contains it. . . . For where the Church is, there also is the Spirit of God, and where the Spirit of God is, there the Church is and every grace'.[34]

These noble themes, whose realism should not be obscured by their metaphorical expression, have been constantly verified in the history of the Church, especially in missionary enterprises and those of the apostolate. When, for example, I read the scrolls that flanked the altar of the Missionary Pavilion in the colonial Exhibition of 1931 I was almost physically affected; nothing could have

---

[33] Cf. Jn 3:5; 4:10f; 7:37f; 19:34 and F. M. Braun, Le baptême d'après le IVe Evangile, in *Rev. thomiste*, 48 (1948), pp. 347–93; *L'eau et l'esprit, ibid.*, 49 (1949), pp. 5–30.

[34] *Adv. Haer.*, 3, 24, 1 (*PG*, 7, 966).

been more eloquent than that sober list of new races evangelised, of martyrs, of the religious orders devoted to missions. If we take a closer look at this question and study, for example, the missionary endeavour of the nineteenth century, the Spirit's activity becomes obvious; in the words of Pius XI, we are taking part in a continuation of Pentecost and of the Acts of the Apostles.[35] We constantly come across inner callings as definite as those heard by St Paul. ('I hear the Chinese calling me', said the child, Just de Bretenières, with his ear pressed to the ground); we observe providential creations like the *Oeuvre de la Propagation de la foi*, by Pauline Jaricot, or that of the Holy Childhood by Mgr Forbin-Janson assisted by Pauline Jaricot. We see almost every year new missionary orders coming into existence, often in improbable circumstances and marked by the suffering of the cross. The active participation of women in this movement took place a century before that of our own time when women have come to take their part in university, professional and political life (the foundation of the Sisters of St Joseph of Cluny by Mother Javouhey dates from 1806).

The foundation or restoration of religious orders should also be mentioned, and the creation of the Catholic social movement, as well as countless charitable institutions, thanks to which the Church can say, with St Paul: 'Do you think anyone is weak without my feeling his weakness? Does anone have his faith upset without my longing to restore him?' (2 Co 11:29). Or, again, we ought to note the entirely new and vigorous creations such as the Y.C.W.,[36] or the *Mission de Paris*. In all this two elements are especially noteworthy with regard to the action of the Spirit in the Church.

First, we note the fact of an adaptation of which no one, at the start, had any idea, or of an astonishing concurrence of men and circumstances that had been neither expected nor foreseen. When St Paul on the road to Damascus suddenly received the manifestation of the Lord Jesus, a disciple, Ananias, who had never seen

[35] Cf. our chapter in *Hist. illustrée de l'Église*, published under the direction of G. de Plinval and R. Pittet: *La Catholicité en marche. Réalisations et espoirs de l'Église* (nineteenth–twentieth centuries) (fasc: 18, or vol. 2, c. 7) Geneva and Paris, 1948.

[36] Y. C. W.—Young Christian Workers (French: J. O. C. *Jeunesse Ouvrière Catholique*).

Paul and only knew that he had done considerable harm to believers in Jerusalem, received a mysterious command to welcome
him (Ac 9:10f). In all the enterprises which God promotes, he
causes similar things to happen: the unfailing sign that the Holy
Spirit is at work is that people who had not previously known
each other, disparate circumstances which no one had pre-
arranged, finally come together in some common activity for the
building up of the body of Christ.[37] When, for example, Fr
Cardijn, a priest in a Brussels suburb formed the idea that was
soon to find expression in the creation of the Y.C.W., Pius XI, on
his part, was 'not without a divine inspiration', forming the idea of
Catholic Action, 'the participation of the laity in the apostolate of
the hierarchy'. The two men were to meet, and what each had
created was made more perfect by the contribution of the other.

This fact also provides an illustration of the second feature,
connected with what we have said about the organic nature of the
Church. The Church's life is symphonic; in it every member has
his own theme to contribute, corresponding to his nature, his gifts
and his position in the Church. Or, he is like one of the strings
whose combined sound the musical instrument expresses.[38] To
take an example nearer to present-day experience, Fr Godin,
describing the creation of the *Mission de Paris* and of episcopal
reactions to it, remarked, 'They have their hand on the brake, we
are in the driving seat; both of us are needed'.[39] This admirably
expresses a characteristic aspect of the way things happen.

The Holy Spirit is a spirit that finds new ways that bring about
renewal and adaptation. He is constantly stimulating movements
of this kind within the Church; I have discussed it at length in
Vraie et fausse réforme (Édit. du Cerf, 1950). Now in order that
these movements of adaptation, renewal or reform may be a
genuine movement of *the Church*, they must be harmonised with
unity and they must issue from the heart of tradition and not from
innovations that are foreign to it. The concrete and practical
criterion of concordance with the Church is the approval of the
spiritual authority who is the guardian of both tradition and unity.

[37] This is what we have shown to be in fact happening now in the
present time, cf. *L'appel oecuménique* (*Vie Sp.*, Jan. 1950, pp. 5–12).

[38] This comparison is patristic: cf. St Ignatius of Antioch, Ep 4:1 (cf.
Ph 1:2); St John Chrysostom, *In Lazar.* 1, 1 (*PG*, 48, 963).

[39] Cf. Fr Glorieux, *Un homme providentiel, l'abbé Godin*, p. 317.

That is why the different movements we have been considering must be developed in a kind of a dialogue between the elements of initiative, which are often on the periphery, with the elements a1 the centre. In reality both these elements fuse into a common work in obedience to the same spirit. It is the same spirit who moves some to seek new ways and others to ensure that there is no straying from tradition and unity, for 'if these are lacking, the new way is a mere deviation'.[40]

From all this we can see how the Holy Spirit is the conductor of the full orchestra of the Church's life, and the invisible controller of her communion.

Nothing less than the Spirit of God could have the power to bring so many different realities into unity and yet to respect their differences, and this, in fact, is the Spirit's special work.[41] We have seen that he is given to the whole and to every part with regard to that part's function in the whole (for the building up of the body). He is intrinsically a Spirit of Communion. The daily, normal actions of the members, as they mutually show forth Christ, help and fulfil each other, is inspired by him. He also inspires the harmonisation of the elements contributed by individuals into the unity and utility of the whole. Thus, as Spirit, he is the inner law of the mystical Body, as a whole and in its parts. It is not surprising that St Thomas considered that the grace of the Spirit is the essential element in the new law,[42] and that tradition has often perceived in the Christian Pentecost, the successor of the Jewish Pentecost, the feast of the gift of the law, the coming of the new law, the communion of the most widely differing members in the same unity. This indeed is the Holy Spirit's special work: to bring plurality and diversity into unity—without violence, and by an interior stimulation that acts as a spontaneous and joyful initiative in the individual.

This corresponds with especial truth to the personal nature of the Holy Spirit—if 'personal nature' is a phrase applicable to him. He is not only love (cf. St Augustine, n. 41), but as the Third Person in the divine Trinitarian reality, the final moment of the

---

[40] A. D. Sertillanges, Saint Thomas d'Aquin (Les grands Coeurs), p. 8.
[41] 'Societas unitatis Ecclesiae Dei . . . tamquam proprium est opus Spiritus Sancti', St Augustine, Sermo 71, 20, 23 (PL, 38, 463).
[42] Sum. Theol. Ia–IIae, 9, 106, a. 1.

fertility, it is his work to continue and in some sort to extend to creation God's fertility, the communication of his inmost being. By his nature he is the communication of a unity to many, who retain their manifold distinction, a unity which these many discover to be their fulfilment and joy. He is essentially Communion. That is why the most profound and comprehensive remark about him is that which concludes the 1st Epistle to the Corinthians: 'The grace that comes through our Lord Jesus Christ, the love that is God, and the fellowship (i.e. the communion, the communication) that is ours in the Holy Spirit be with you all!'

BIBLIOGRAPHY

J. A. Möhler, *Unity in the Church* (cf. the book, *L'Église est une. Hommage à Möhler*, published under the direction of Fr Chaillet, Paris, Blond, 1939).

Dom A. Vonier, *The Spirit and the Bride*.

E. Baroy, *Le Saint-Esprit en nous et dans l'Église d'après le N. T.* Albi. Press of the Orphelins-apprentis, 1950.

Yves Congar, *Le Saint Esprit et le Corps apostolique, réalisateurs de l'oeuvre du Christ*, in RSPET 1952, pp. 613–25, 1953, pp. 24–48 (produced in the new ed. of *Esquisses du mystère de l'Église*, Édit. du Cerf. 1953) *Idem. La Pentecôte*, Paris, Cerf. 1956. English transl., *The Mystery of the Church* (London, 1960; new revised edn., 1965).

CHAPTER THIRTEEN

The Eucharist and the Church of the New Alliance[1]

THE THEOLOGICAL SUBJECTS OF THIS CON-
gress were chosen in order to harmonise with the main teaching of
the encyclicals *Mystici Corporis* and *Mediator Dei*, so that they
will be both ecclesiological and liturgical. This combination is so
natural and corresponds so well with the trend of my own work
that I feel very much at home. I must express my thanks to His
Excellency the Bishop of Nancy, who has conferred on me the
honour and indeed the joy of discussing this central issue with my
brothers in the priesthood, ministers of Jesus Christ for the
building up of his body the Church: the Eucharist, and the nature
of the Church, the people of God under the new and eternal
alliance, or, to express it differently, the function of the Eucharist
in effecting the transition from the Church of the Old Testament
to that of the New.

It may seem surprising to some of you that I should begin with
the Old Testament and go back if not to the Flood—for the
alliance contracted with Noah was concerned with the natural
order of the world and not with the specific destiny of the people
of God—at least to Moses, the Exodus and ultimately to Abraham.
And yet, if there is one thing that emerges with certainty from the
research of recent years it is this: the Church must be understood
as existing midway between the foretelling or preparation which
filled the period of the old dispensation and that consummation

[1] A paper read to a gathering of priests at the Eucharistic Congress of
Nancy, 9 July 1949, published in *Vie Sp.*, April 1950, pp. 347–72.

for which we are still waiting. Several years work have convinced me that this idea of an interim position is what is most lacking in the doctrine of the Church as set forth in the Counter-Reformation period, and in most contemporary manuals. That doctrine was most concerned with controversy; its main purpose was to establish the Church's credentials and it discussed the Church as an isolated phenomenon unrelated to the development of the historical movement, that movement whose progress permeates the Scriptures and indeed defines their purpose. They move from an initial promise to its complete fulfilment. The first stage is one of foretelling and prefigurement; the second is that of realities, but realities still incomplete, still waiting for their completion. The twofold rediscovery—of the eschatological point of view on the one hand (events moving in series to a consummation yet to come), and of the organic bond between the Old and New Testaments— would appear to be the most assured result of contemporary biblical studies, and it involves a doctrine of the Church, with all the consequences for her ministry that follow from it.

God's purpose, originating at the moment of creation, declared to Abraham, brought into effective action through the mediation of Moses, is to construct a people from the human race that shall be *his* people; to bring mankind into communion with his own life, into the enjoyment of his fatherly heritage—his presence, life, glory, peace and joy. From the start, all this was contained in the promises made to Abraham. It was a twofold promise; Abraham was to have an heir, Isaac, the child of promise and of grace, but also, more than this, his heirs were to be 'all the nations of the earth', and the inheritance was to be the land of Canaan, the 'promised land', given by God for the enjoyment of Abraham and his descendants. This twofold promise thus contains the whole mystery of the people of God who were to become the Church, and, in its ultimate and perfect stage, the Kingdom, the heavenly Jerusalem, of which the Apocalypse speaks. This mystery of God's people which moves steadily onwards to its consummation, receives particular definition in the work of Moses and the decisive history of the Exodus.

The events of that time prefigure the essential happenings in the Church; these exemplify, with respect to God's work, what has now come about, not figuratively but in its fulfilled reality in the

Church. The people of God are a people constantly being called out of Egypt, i.e. out of the world, that they may 'pass over' into the promised land. They are a people who having been spared through the blood of the Lamb, quit Egypt, when their numbers have increased, and begin to live as pilgrims *en route* to their true native land, the land given them by God, flowing with milk and honey, in which, freed from the world and its idols, from Pharaoh and Baal, they will live as the people *of God*, serving him in his presence. What was a hint to Abraham, what was foretold to him, has acquired definition. Abraham was called to leave his own land and his relations in order to serve in the land God was to show him and manifest himself to him. As yet it is not all mankind who is summoned in Abraham (*Ekklesia*—convocation), but neither is it a single man; it is a people who testify, the prefigurative and prophetic people, the people of Israel. Ultimately, there is only one mystery and one action: the *passover* from Egypt to the Holy Land, from the world to the Kingdom of God. And the Church is essentially the proclamation (the convocation or summoning), the ministry, the reality of this passover, leading to the full enjoyment of what she has introduced.

For Israel, the reference was to the real Egypt, the real desert, the real Palestine. Israel experienced an historical development which, although prophetic, figurative and promissory, was none the less real and of this earth. *Omnia in figuris contingebant illis* (1 Co 10:11). Israel's history was real and earthly; it was also holy, a 'metahistory', to use a modern expression, a history that is a prefigurement of future spiritual realities, a history that is sacramental, at least inasmuch as it foretells and is a sign of things to come. But I need scarcely remind you of the way in which the apostles described the events they had been called to witness; they said that the messianic age had come, that the people of God had entered into the last days. This conviction, in spite of the views of some eccentrics, in no way implied that the world was about to end; it meant that we have now entered into the final order of things, after which nothing really new will occur. 'God,' says the epistle to the Hebrews, 'who gave to our forefathers many different glimpses of the truth in the words of the prophets, has now, at the end of the present age given us the Truth in the Son. Through the Son God made the whole universe, and to the Son he has ordained that all creation shall ultimately belong' (1:1-2). The Church of the apostles was still Israel, was still the people of God. But the régime had changed, the people of God are assembled and now live under a new dispensation, a new and eternal alliance, that will have no successor, a new and final dispensation that can be followed by nothing newer or more perfect. For the people of God have passed from the régime of the prophets to that of the Son, to that of God's own and only Son. What more could God communicate than his own life, given once for all and perfectly in his Son? The people of God has crossed from a régime of promises, foreshadowing and prefiguration, or, at most, of anticipation, to a régime of reality. In the régime of the Messiah who has really come, what is communicated is not earthly and prefigurative, but the ultimate realities, the life of Sonship, the realities of God's own life. These are God's own endowments: his life, communion, joy, glory and his Spirit.

It is clear that such realities could not have been communicated by a Messiah of ordinary stature, one who would simply have been 'the prophet', the greatest of prophets, but only a prophet, i.e. a man of this world, born of a woman, like the others. If heavenly realities were not only to be revealed, but also bestowed, then a heavenly being was needed to do this; and if these realities involved access to an enjoyment of the fatherly heritage *of God* himself, who but the Son could bestow them? From the fact that the inheritance promised to Abraham and his descendants, i.e. to the people of God, is nothing else and nothing less than the patrimony *of God himself*; from the fact that the inheritance promised to our ancestral father is eternal life, that *lucem sanctam*, that *transire ad vitam*, referred to in the offertory antiphon in the requiem mass, it follows that it cannot be Abraham who is the true heir, it is not through sharing *his* life and *his* rights that we become heirs; *that* can only be possible through the Son, the Son who through a common nature is God's Son, and who came down from heaven.

God's purpose, envisaged from the beginning, from the moment he made man in his own image, inaugurated as a collective reality by the promise made to Abraham, and then through the alliance contracted in the time of Moses, now emerges with sufficient clarity: his purpose is to bring mankind into fellowship with his life and glory, to enable men to share in the life and possessions of the divine community, and lead them to the enjoymen of his heavenly inheritance, a life in fellowship with the Father. We can see that this purpose could not have been effective without both a descent and an ascent; the coming down of God to us, his self-abasement to our own condition, and an ascent by us to God, an extension of ourselves—the phrase sounds presumptuous—an extension that culminates in a divine condition. It is a human ascent and extension that depends upon a descent, an act of condescension, a self-abasement of God. This statement is so traditional as to be almost a platitude; Irenaeus and Athanasius already use it. 'He made himself what we are in order that we might become what he is'. But it should be seen in a setting that refers more explicitly to the Church, and that will lead us directly to the central *mysterium fidei* of the Eucharist.

In the ancient economy, foreshadowing and figurative, there are two central issues: with Abraham we have the promise of an inheritance and of an heir who would become the people of God; with Moses, the passover from Egypt into the promised land. In the new and final economy, the economy of realities, we have these same two issues, but now in their fulfilled truth; the inheritance is eternal life; the heir is the Son, by nature Son of God, but who has become our head and leader; the passover, made possible by the condescension of the only Son who took human flesh, is the transition from the ordinary human condition into the reality of sons, *filii in Filio*, members of the only Son become incarnate, members of that filial organism which is the (mystical) Body of the Son of God made man. In short, it is now not our crossing from Egypt into Palestine, under the leadership of Joshua, but from enslavement to this world to the life of heaven, from the disintegrated nature of the first Adam to the spiritual or mystical nature of the second. It is the literal fulfilment of our Lord's words to Nicodemus, 'No one has gone up to heaven, but he that came down from heaven, the Son of man who is in heaven' (Jn 3:13). But we ascend there with him provided we are, in St Paul's words, 'found in him', provided we exist in him, being members of his body, mystically identified with him, so as to form with him only one filial organism, one single son, the God-man, and hence one single heir: *Si filii heredes*. This is the point where the mystery of the mystical Body can be seen in its full significance. It is evidently central to God's purpose, and hence central to the mystery of the Church which is precisely the fulfilment of that purpose. The Church is the people of God, the true Israel. But in the new and final dispensation the people of God only acquire their proper status through becoming the body of Christ; for they only enter into the promised land and into the possession of their inheritance when they become participants of that true heavenly and filial life which is in Christ Jesus. This is why in the Church there are always two irreducible aspects to which there correspond two different characteristics, that of a social institution and that of communion, organisation and organism. This is why the treatise on the Church which I envisaged exactly twenty years ago would be entitled: the Church, the people of God and the Body of Christ. But this does not mean that there are two Churches, and the fundamental teaching of the encyclical *Mystici Corporis* consists in reminding us of the union of these two aspects in the Church: an organised society and the mystical Body of Christ, or the mystical, that is, spiritual identity with Christ.

This mystical identity with Christ is essentially achieved through faith and the sacraments of faith to which there corresponds two main powers or activities of the ministry: the ministry of faith or the word, and the ministry of the sacraments of the faith, and pre-eminently of the Eucharist. For it is through these two means that our head who lives in glory at the right hand of the Father, draws us and assimilates us to himself. Through faith he substitutes, in a sense, his mind for ours. I say 'in a sense', because —and this is amazing—he makes no encroachment upon our own personality. It is true that Christ comes to live in me: 'My present life is not that of the old "I", but the living Christ within me. The bodily life I now live, I live believing in the Son of God . . .' (Ga 2:20). And yet it is I myself who lives this life of Christ. The fact that many, whilst remaining many, whilst retaining their distinct personality, yet live from a single life, the life of the Son of God made man, is precisely what is meant by the mystery of the mystical Body, *unum corpus multi sumus*, we, though many, form one body. It was this that was envisaged from the start; it is implied in that comparison with a marriage which goes back beyond St Paul, beyond the prophet Hosea and finally comes to rest in the first

verses of Genesis: 'We will make man in our own image'. Its
momentum carried it to the vision of the marriage of the Lamb in
the last Book of Revelation. It really is 'in our image', for the
mystery of God himself essentially involves the same fact: a single
life shared by several persons; one life communicated to many....

But if faith itself changes our outlook and gives us the mind of
Christ and inserts us into this mystery of unity, what light this
sheds upon the Eucharist! My brothers, here is the core of our
subject, and you will realise it not only from my paper tonight, but
from all the discussions in this congress. It is at the heart of our
ministry, of the Church, of our very life. See to it that this heart is
not on the surface, but deep seated and sublime.

How does Christ, our head, now in the glory of heaven, draw us
to himself, assimilate us to himself and form us into his body
through the Eucharist? The best approach to this mystery would
seem to be by way of the equally mysterious fact of assimilation in
the natural order where it is easily observable. Are we not, in fact,
confronted by an extraordinary mystery—one of Du Bois-
Reymond's 'enigmas'—in this happening which is yet an everyday
affair? We eat animals and plants, and they sustain our life;
animals are sustained by plants or other animals, plants are sustained by minerals which we cannot directly assimilate. What, in
fact, does assimilation mean? It means nothing less than the conversion of an alien substance into our own. I eat animals and plants;
it is I who am alive, the assimilation takes place in me; foreign
bodies literally enter into my substance and become myself. . . .
Feeding means precisely this: the assimilation of other things into
my own substance.

There is another way in which I receive sustenance from the
world; it is that of knowledge. Through knowledge things outside
me come into me and they also become myself. They really sustain
me, but the circumstances are different. For, on the one hand—
and this is the special mystery of knowledge on which St Thomas
and his commentator Cajetan so profoundly reflected—things
enter into me, become me, without ceasing to be themselves, and
retaining, if not their own mode of existence, at least their character
and what may be called their 'personality'. On the other hand,
with respect to them and myself, the strength lies with them,
whereas I am passive when confronted by them. In the relation-

ship between truth and the mind, it is the mind that receives sustenance, but it is truth that assimilates the mind to itself because it is truth that is the active principle. This is expressed in St Augustine's well-known phrase: *Cibus sum grandium, cresce et manducabis me.* 'I am the nourishment of great souls (it is truth speaking). Grow up and you shall eat me. But, unlike the food your body consumes, you will not change me into yourself; I shall change you into me'.[2]

St Augustine wrote this with reference to truth, but he was probably thinking of Jesus Christ and his words have more than once been applied to the Eucharist.[3] Through the Eucharist we eat the Lord's body given to us as food. But, in comparison with us, it is the Lord who is alive; his is the greater strength, his activity is predominant. It is we who eat, we who receive the sustenance, but it is he who assimilates us to himself, so intimately that we become with him, mystically, one single living being. This means that it is through the Eucharist that our own transition from the first to the second Adam, from an earthly to a heavenly status and, in a sense, divine status, is supremely achieved. Through the Eucharist we obtain our mystical identity with Jesus Christ, the only person who has come down from heaven and returned and who is by nature heir to his Father's patrimony.

We can now acquire a little more insight into the mystery of transubstantiation and into that of communion. Eucharistic transsubstantiation should be invisaged as the supereme expression of the most definite aspect of God's purpose as revealed to us in the Bible. Protestants who take their stand on Scripture (I am thinking of the Calvinists) seem to me to misconstrue, on this point, the way in which the biblical revelation did in fact develop and also the fulfilled 'realism' of our era which is that of 'the last days', the

---

[2] *Confess.*, Bk. 7, ch. 10, n. 16 (*PL*, 32, 742), cf. *In Joannem* (*PL*, 35, 1353). In Ps 33, serm. 2 (*PL*, 36, 310).

[3] E.g. in the Middle Ages, William of Auxerre (cf. the Quarrachi edition of the works of St Bonaventure, 4, 187, n. 6); St Bonaventure (*IV Sent.*, d. 11, q. 2, a. 1, q. 1, ad 6; vol. 4, p. 225). St Thomas (*Sum. Theol.*, IIIa, 73, 3, ad 2; *Com. in Joan.*, C. 6, lect. 7), etc. Cf. H. de Lubac, *Corpus mysticum*, p. 205, n. 53.

The general idea developed in this chapter has been frequently discussed by the Fathers and theologians: St John Damascene, St Leo, St Bonaventure, Albert the Great, St Thomas, etc. Cf. E. Mersch, *Théol. du Corps mystique*, Paris, 1944, vol. 2, p. 328.

messianic era, the era of the new and final dispensation. For what is in fact involved is God's especial plan, his call to us to enter 'his kingdom and his glory'.[4] This plan involves the fact that our movement towards God, a movement really from below to above, is, at a given moment, one may say, taken over by God, and brought to its conclusion by a gift, a heavenly gift, from above. If we look at the series of Abraham's descendants or at what was promised as his inheritance, or at the perpetuity promised to David's line, we see that God fulfils his plan and his promise by substituting a heavenly for an earthly reality and, in the end, by the donation of himself, as Abraham's descendant, as the inheritance, as the everlasting David. He comes to incorporate and graft a reality from *his* world—which is finally nothing else and nothing less than himself. Instead of an earthly Adam, an earthly head—by head we mean an activating principle of life—it is a head, an Adam, from heaven that has been given to us. 'The first man came out of the earth, a material creature; the second man came from heaven and was the Lord himself. . . . And just as we have been made like the material pattern, so we shall be made like the heavenly pattern' (1 Co 15:47-9). God had given manna to his people for their sustenance in their journey from Egypt to the promised land, but our Lord said, 'It was not Moses who gave you that bread from heaven; but it *is* my Father who offers you the bread from heaven. For the bread of God is the bread that comes down from heaven and gives life to the world. . . . I am the bread of life. He that comes to me shall not be hungry and he that has faith in me shall never thirst [this illustrates how a man is sustained by Christ and assimilated to him through faiths and the Eucharist]. . . . I am the bread that comes down from heaven. If any one eats this bread he shall live for ever. He that has faith has eternal life. I am the bread of life, your fathers ate the manna in the wilderness, and died. But here is the bread that comes down from heaven—eat it and you shall not die. I am the bread, the living bread that came down from heaven. If anyone eats this bread he shall live for ever. Know too, that the bread which I will give, to bring the world to

---

[4] 1 Th 2:12: there are other words that denote this 'calling' which characterises the Church (*Ekklesia*—summoning, convocation): his light (1 P 2:9); his glory (*idem* 5:10). fellowship in God's Son (1 Co 1:9); the peace of Christ (Col 3:15); the glory (2 Th 2:14); eternal life (1 Tm 6:12).

life, is my flesh' (Jn 6:32–3; 35:41, 47–51). We should not fail to recognise the realism that these words imply; it is a realism involved in the concrete development of God's plan, in what it really signifies. God's ultimate purpose is to communicate *himself* to us; himself, in his own life, and not through a substitute for himself, a similitude. He began by foretelling this, he will conclude with its perfected reality. But between the two—characterised respectively by the Synagogue and the Kingdom, the time before John the Baptist and the time after him (cf. Lk 7:76; Mt 11:12–13)—there is the time of the Church in which the reality has been given, although only in part and still veiled. This successive unfolding is most evident in the two forms of the bread of life in which God communicates himself to us: the word and the sacraments. In the Old Testament, a word truly came from above (cf. Heb 12:25); and men were already being told that their nourishment did not depend on bread alone, but on every word that proceeds from the mouth of God. Nevertheless it did not come down from above in the way it was to come down in Jesus Christ, that is, substantially, it was a sign of the word, and not yet the word itself. Similarly, the bread given from above was a sign; it was not the substance of the heavenly, the living bread (Jn 6:51), not that super-substantial bread of which our Lord spoke. In this transitory life we are sustained by earthly bread, produced by the soil; it supports that life which we receive from the earth and that will return to the earth. But in order that we may have eternal life we need the sustenance of bread that really has come down from heaven, and is by nature heavenly. That bread alone has the power to enable us to live a life that will be in the image of God, and therefore a life lived for God, a life that is the supernatural life of our native land.

Thus, in the Eucharist, and precisely, in transubstantiation, it is the essential point of God's purpose that is fulfilled; our approach to him suddenly concludes because it has been met with a gift from above. We were on the right road, but by our own effort we could not reach its end. And yet that end is also our way: God in Jesus becomes our way, our door;[5] we shall enter into intimacy with God because God comes to us. We do our best to regain that intimacy, and in order to express our effort we make use of these

[5] Jn 10:7, 9; Heb 10:20, and the entire theme of our entry into the Holy of holies, through our High Priest.

humble offerings of bread and wine. Then, through transubstantiation, these humble signs of our return become the operative signs of the work accomplished, once for all time, for our benefit, by the beloved Son. The expression, the sacrament, of our 'return' (sacrament-sign, originating from below, like those of the Old Testament) is changed through the eucharistic consecration, into the expression of his own return, the sacrament of his own passover. Our humble offerings will prove acceptable because God himself, in Jesus Christ, becomes our offering, transubstantiating our offering into himself, himself becoming our means of transition, our essential passover.[6] This is so literally true that the most decisive way of 'passing over' to God, of gaining possession of our inheritance will not be merely to commit ourselves to Joshua's (Jesus') leadership, but to absorb him, to assimilate him, to identify ourselves mystically with his absolute passover, the passover mystically commemorated by the ministry of sacramental priesthood.

From this point of view we can also understand that the same word, *body*, denotes both the reality of the Eucharist and that of the Church. Another word, *communion* expresses both the eating or assimilation of the Lord's body and also our corporate life in the Church, the Catholic communion. Before the days of competent modern exegetes, Albert the Great, a scholastic theologian, had observed that the description of the Church as the body of Christ is based on its essential relationship with the Lord's body sacramentally present and active amongst us.[7] It is supremely through the sacrament of the body of Christ that we become, mystically, the body of Jesus Christ; it is by assimilating us all to the one who, from heaven, draws us to himself that we become incorporated in his (mystical) Body.

[6] This point of view is developed in the fine book by Canon E. Masure, *Le sacrifice du chef* (Beauchesne). (Engl. transl., *The Christian Sacrifice*, London, 1945).

[7] Cf the great passage in Albert the Great, *De Eucharista*, d. 3, tract 1, c. 5, n. 5 (Borgnet, 38, 257). From present-day exegetes I prefer to quote non-Catholics, and especially Anglicans whose exegesis is often memorable: A. Ed. J. Rawlinson, *Corpus Christi* in *Mysterium Christi*, edited by Bell and Deissmann, London, 1930, pp. 225–44: Bishop Palmer in *The 1930 meeting of the Continuation Committee of Faith and Order*, p. 71; L. S. Thornton, *The Common life in the Body of Christ*, Westminster, p. 330, n. 5.

When I expound these truths—elementary Christian truths—I have the same feeling that comes to me whenever I discuss the theology of one of our mysteries: I have a sense of things that are too sublime for the human mind. *Durus est hic sermo*: not merely because the ideas are difficult or their expression obscure, but on account of their sheer loftiness. How can we *dare* to put forward ideas and to express such things?

Like everything related to God's purpose and the life of his people these things can only be attained and held 'in faith', to use the expression reiterated throughout the eleventh chapter of the epistle to the Hebrews. Faith alone enables us to hold on to the things for which we hope, with certainty that they are true. It provides the reason why, says the epistle, we can affirm that these invisible realities exist. 'It was because of his faith that Abel . . . it was because of his faith that Noah . . . it was because of his faith that Abraham . . . Sarah, Isaac, Moses, etc. . . .' 'Surrounded then as we are by these serried ranks of witnesses . . . let us run the race that we have to run with patience, our eyes fixed on Jesus the source and goal of our faith' (12:1–2). What takes place here is infinitely beyond anything we can personally experience. It is something we believe and are glad to believe; and that sums up the matter. *Mysterium fidei*.

In conclusions I shall draw some of the consequences that flow from this brief survey. After summarising the data that will enable precision to be given to what was said above on the nature of the Church's existence, I shall outline three applications that more directly concern our approach to the ministry and the spiritual life.

1. As regard the nature of the Church's existence. As I said at the beginning this can only be understood as occupying a midway position between the Synagogue and the Kingdom. But she is still 'to some extent "away" from the Lord' (2 Co 5:6), and this fact relates her to the Synagogue and involves the activity of a complete structure, of a diversity of functions, all the means that are necessary in order to reach her end. She certainly obtains her life from the realities of the last days, and they are already hers in a deeper way than that of expectation and hope, and yet she only partly possesses them—she has the first-fruits, says St Paul (1 Co 13:9–12; 2 Co 1:22; 5:5; Ep 1:14)—and these are veiled, not yet

clearly evident. It is the literal truth, and not a symbol from senti-
mental 'religious' poetry, that the Eucharist is the bread of angels,
because it gives Jesus, the true bread from heaven, as food. But it
gives that bread in a hidden way, obscurely without enabling us to
experience its real taste, and in a manner wholly inadequate to its
reality. We have already set foot in the land where milk and honey
flows—the versicle in the Dominican Breviary *ante laudes* on the
feast of Corpus Christi assures us that this is so—and yet we are
still distinctly foreigners in this territory of the Father to which
we have been transported by our Head who is the King. Even
though present it all seems very remote. These, then, are the two
aspects of the Church and, this, if the phrase is acceptable, is the
expression of the tension, the inner dialectic of her present
existence. She is on a journey, a journey that is in continuity with
the Old Testament; she is the people of God constantly getting
ready to leave Egypt and to journey through the wilderness to the
Promised Land ('Happy are the gentle, for they shall inherit the
earth!'). Nevertheless, although *ex parte, in speculo et aenigmate*,
she does, in fact, now possess the reality towards which she is
moving. What is precisely new in the new dispensation in relation
to the old, in the new Israel in comparison with the old, is that
the passover really has taken place; not the prefigurative passover
from Egypt into Palestine, across the Red Sea and the Jordan, but
the true passover, to *the true* Promised Land, that which has effected a transfer from this world to the next, from existence as
children of wrath to that of beloved sons. The passover has been
accomplished for our sake, once for all time in Christ, our Joshua.
Jesus died as the descendants of the first Adam died, died as a
man, 'born of human mother and born under the jurisdiction of
the Law' (Ga 4:4), but he rose again with a life received *from
above*, its activating principle being God's Spirit. The whole function of the Church consists in making this passover accomplished
for us, practically available to us; to enable us to make the crossing,
in our own turn, from this world to God, by passing into Jesus
Christ, through faith and the sacraments of faith whose ministry is
entrusted to us. The Church in her entirety, and in both her
aspects, consists in being, as an institution (an institution for a
journey, and therefore transitory), the minister, the sacrament of
our crossing to the Father in Jesus Christ, and, as the mystical

Body, forming the actual reality of the human race that has thus 'passed over' into Jesus Christ.

It is true, indeed, that the Church is founded on Christ's death, his passover; but his death is inseparable from his resurrection. The phrase used by St John to describe the events that began in the evening of Holy Thursday—he speaks of Christ's 'passing to the Father'—only became completely true when, through the resurrection and ascension, he had finally returned to the Father, henceforth drawing all things and incorporating them in himself: 'all things', and not only all men. It is most true that the new dispensation, which no longer has to do with prefigurations but with the ultimate régime of realities, was sealed 'in his blood'. It is this —nothing less and nothing other than this—that we celebrate, that we handle, every day. . . . Every day, at Mass, we celebrate, we renew the alliance in his blood; we celebrate the memorial of the new and eternal alliance concluded in his blood. In the faith and worship of the Church this 'memorial' is something much more than a commemoration or a mere memory; it is the actual reality of what is celebrated that is made sacramentally present and active.

2. It follows that the Church is in no sense a terminus, but a means. She is herself a sacrament, that is an external, physical reality whose effect is inward and invisible. In fact, it would be both accurate and rewarding to apply to the Church St Augustine's well-known analysis that makes a distinction between *sacramentum* and *res*. All the things that are done ministerially in the Church have their existence in her as an external and physical activity intended to produce an inward and invisible reality of communion with God in Jesus Christ. For us priests it will not be without profit to look beyond the apparent banality of this statement and consider for a moment what it concretely represents.

In every sphere of life there is a temptation to allow means to become ends or to obscure the end. The danger is magnified by the fact that in practice all our work consists in the production of *means*. I study for the sake of God's glory and the salvation of souls, but in practice my time and labour are wholly occupied not with static contemplation of God's glory, but by intellectual work. That work is hard and demanding, but also of extreme interest. The temptation lurks that would make me lose sight of the primary end of my work, and transform that work which should be a means into the end of my activity. Something similar can occur in the sphere of the apostolate and the ministry. Our good works, our religious services are done for God's glory and the salvation of souls, or, to express it more concretely, in order to lead souls to an encounter and union with God, in Jesus Christ. But how great a danger lurks of making these things the real end of our activity, for they are interesting, absorbing and sometimes even flattering. How great the danger that we may in practice forget the ultimate union with God that all this is meant to secure, and only be really concerned with having a crowded church, a faultless service, an impressive parade of parish athletes, a group of the Y.C.W. with a large membership that draws attention to itself, etc. Sometimes, after being sincerely impressed by the labour expended by priests and laymen and by the outward success of their undertakings, one wonders what is their real worth in terms of prayer and of the union with God they obtain. This very congress, gentlemen, this splendid congress will only make a genuine contribution to the work of the Church through the increase in prayer, obedience, faith, union with God, and ultimately charity of which it has been the occasion or the means. On the other hand, apparent, obvious, overwhelming setbacks may conceal the emergence of a most authentic spiritual work. It is not only our personal life that is hidden with Christ in God; it is our apostolic life also. Its true reality is not visible to bodily eyes that can only grasp appearances; its existence is evident only beyond the veil where our Head reigns.

But I want to be even more precise. The reason for all the work of the ministry and its goal is not simply the formation of spiritual realities within the human consciousness; these spiritual realities arise not from this creation but from the heavenly world. Our ministry is wholly relative to Christ who sits at the right hand of the Father. He himself is the sole priest upon whom every valid action that takes place in the sphere of reconciled existence which constitutes the very essence of the Church *directly* depends. We do not sufficiently reflect upon this. We carry out the acts of our ministry as though they were the results of powers inherent or rooted in ourselves and not perpetually in need of our divine Head. We do not sufficiently reflect that it is he who personally intervenes in order to bring into effect the realities with which we are only associated by a visible ministry, that, so to say, represents their earthly stage. It is he who sanctifies, it is he who operates in all our sacraments, it is he who draws and incorporates all things into himself. The one real priest is in heaven. Gentlemen, let us regain a spirituality that is based on Christ in glory in heaven, omnipresent and universally active in the Church. The liturgy is full of a spirituality of this kind. We should rejoice that our Head is in heaven and is gradually drawing his body to him there. We should realise that the Church is being built not on earth but in heaven, built from the atoms which, through our ministry, are transferred from the scattered elements of the first Adam into the mystical reality of the second.

From the point of view of a spirituality of this kind which penetrates St Paul's epistles and is at the heart of Christianity, even the external aspects of eucharistic worship are not a matter of indifference. I am thinking, for example, of the structure of the altar, of the way of representing Christ on the cross, of certain forms of eucharistic worship. The encyclical *Mediator Dei* rightly censured certain exaggerations which are only explicable as an excessive reaction to exaggerations in the opposite direction. But the encyclical had no intention of criticising ways of thinking and acting that spring from the most unsullied, most ancient and unquestionable tradition of the Church. The Christ of our crucifixes should not make us forget that our Lord is now in glory, and that when we pray it is to this glorious Lord, the High Priest and King of whom the Epistle ot the Hebrews speaks.

In eucharistic worship we should avoid as far as possible everything which tends to treat the Eucharist as a *terminus* or *object*, for in reality it is the means of relating, uniting and incorporating us with our Head in heaven, reigning there, praising his Father and summoning us. Some altars with monumental reredosses that arrest the mind's attention and progress, as well as some forms of devotion, have the disadvantage of becoming ends in themselves for us and unfailingly block the sacramental movement which is wholly relative to the realities of heaven. You will draw your own conclusions in your own time. I will simply remark that history as well as theology shows that a connection exists between a loss of a full understanding of the Mass and the Church, on the one hand, and consideration of the Eucharist and of the institution of the

Church as things existing entirely for their own sake, as terminal realities and objects, on the other.

We have seen that Eucharist is the sacrament of Christ's passover to his Father, which is the real passover from Egypt to the Promised Land and which, since Jesus is our head, was accomplished for our sakes. The new dispensation is wholly founded on this passover which, through Christ's death and resurrection, is a passover to the true Promised Land, that of eternal life. It is this that we celebrate at Mass: *Unde et memores*, we his servants and his holy people, being mindful of his blessed Passion, his resurrections from the dead and of his glorious ascension, that is, of his passover to his Father, made once for all time for our sakes, *uper êmôn*, but which we, in turn, and through the power of what it has achieved for us, must carry out day after day in our lives until it reaches the moment of consummation in our own supreme 'passover'.

You will realise that this point of view, which is the main, the one central point of view of Christianity, comprises a complete spiritual doctrine of the Mass. The Eucharist is the sacrament of Jesus' passover to his Father, accomplished for our sakes and in which we must accomplish our own. What has been done for us, we have also to do for ourselves, making it effective in our own lives. If we had been totally saved without any initiative on our part, without there being anything for us to do, it is difficult to see why there should be a sacramental celebration of the sacrifice of the cross in the Church daily, 'until he returns'. But on the supposition that we ourselves have to make effective that passover which Jesus opened up once for all times in his body, we can understand that Christ's sacrifice must be applied to us and that, for this to be done, it must be 'celebrated', made sacramentally present and active. But this passover of Jesus to his Father is inseparably both death *and* resurrection. 'Was it not fated that the Christ should suffer thus, and then should come into his glory?' So Jesus explained the matter to his disciples on the evening of Easter day. He could only enter a new heavenly life and bring us into it through the death of what was mortal in him. The Eucharist, the sacrament of the passover of Jesus and of our own passover, only brings about deification and resurrection by traversing a death (Jn 6:39–40).

In the light of what was first effected in Jesus the meaning of our celebrations of the Mass and of our communions becomes clear. What we must insert in them, or rather, what we must seek in them, is our own 'passover': our death, truly our death, but also and first of all, that *quotidie morior*, of which St Paul speaks, every means by which every day we leave Egypt in order to cross over to God, that love, that service, those self-denying actions by which the life of the risen Christ who henceforward dies no more, but 'lives for God', takes the place in us that is occupied by the carnal life received from Adam—carnal meaning not only what is terrestrial but also what is sinful. You will see that everything implied in what is commonly call St Paul's 'mysticism' is included here. *Licet is qui foris est noster homo corrumpatur, is tamen qui intus est renovetur de die in diem, contemplantibus nobis quae videntur, sed quae non videntur . . .* (2 Co 3:16). It is also the mystical teaching of the French School of the seventeenth century, of M. Olier in particular, that continued to develop the great Pauline ideas on Christian men who die and rise again and live 'for God' in Jesus Christ.

4. Our fourth and final application will lead us to theological considerations that concern the ministry, and which will enable us to illustrate one of the points made in the encyclical *Mediator Dei*. I referred above to two aspects of the Church. The Church is the people of God who are seeking God, moving towards him, setting themselves to serve him and to secure the inheritance he offers. This, in short, is a movement from below. From this point of view the Church is a continuation of the people of God of the Old Testament, the people who were chosen, set apart, consecrated as God's servant and his witness to the world: 'You have seen what I did to Egypt and how I carried you on eagles' wings and brought you unto myself. Now therefore, if you will obey my voice, and hold to my alliance, then you shall be to me a peculiar people above all people, for all the earth is mine. And you shall be for me a kingdom of priests, and a holy nation' (Ex 19:4–6). These words describe the nature of God's faithful people; the whole Church as the community of believers is precisely this. 'You come to him, as living stones, to the immensely valuable Living Stone . . . to be built up into a spiritual house of God, in which you, like holy priests, can offer those spiritual sacrifices which are acceptable to

G

God by Jesus Christ . . . you are God's 'chosen generation', his 'royal priesthood', his 'holy nation'. . . . It is for you now to demonstrate the goodness of him who has called you out of darkness into his amazing light. . . . In the past you were not 'a people' at all: now you are the people of God. In the past you had no experience of his mercy, but now it is intimately yours' (1 P 2:4–5; 9–10). Inherent in God's people is a universal priesthood, a priesthood that offers itself, its life, its testimony, and a priesthood in which every believer is a priest on account of his baptism and his faith.

But there is something else in the Church and this other thing is the special attribute that belongs to her as the people of God in the new dispensation in this messianic age of the last days. The Church is not simply the people of Israel who have at last received and accepted their Messiah. She is much more than that. Since, as we have seen, God's purpose involves the fact that in the fullness of time when every preparation had been made, that which all the prefigurations collectively signified was bestowed from above, once for all time, in a single action. The Kingdom, eternal life, the inheritance of God's family, the real fulfilment of the promises made to Abraham and the working out of the alliance, are heavenly realities given in Jesus Christ in which we now participate in him. Consequently, a new priesthood came into existence in the Church; and this is not the priesthood immanent in the whole body, common to all its members, whose work is praise, service, witnessing to God, but a ministerial priesthood, apostolic, hierarchical, coming from above, whose function is to communicate the good things of truth and grace given once for all time in Jesus Christ.

The mediation in this case will not be that of prayer, of the *sacrificium laudis*, but that of the sacraments which transmit the grace of the cross, and especially of that sacrament which not only transmits grace, but contains Christ himself in his passover to the Father which he accomplished for our sakes: the sacrament of the Last Supper. The priests in this case are not merely the ministers of the community (of believers), they are the ministers *of Jesus Christ*, ministers of that which comes from above and is given from above. This is the meaning and high significance of the hierarchy in the Church. It signifies and ensures that the life lived under the régime of the New Alliance shall not only be the life of the people of God journeying to its inheritance but the life of Jesus Christ, Son of God by nature who came down from heaven, the sole heir of the Father's heritage, and who became the Son of Man and our living bread that we might have the life of the children of God. Thus the régime of a sacramental and hierarchic priesthood, distinct from the spiritual priesthood immanent in the body of the faithful, is bound up with the special and essential attribute of the new and definitive dispensation, inaugurated for the people of God, in the 'passover' of Christ.

This, I believe, supplies the soundest theological basis for the traditional teaching, recalled in the encyclical *Mediator Dei*, on the distinction between the hierarchic priesthood and the spiritual priesthood of believers. It supplies an explanation of the fact that the structure of the Church is essentially hierarchical. The whole body is alive, *the life* of the Church, pervades her through and through, but her *structure* is hierarchic. The whole body thinks and actively uses its mind with regard to religious truth, but the structure of belief is hierarchic, because it does not originate in ideas in the minds of the faithful, but is a treasure of truth apostolically communicated from above, originating in Jesus Christ. The whole body receives the grace of the sacraments, but the structure of sacramental action is hierarchic because sacramental grace is a reality very different from the collective seal of believers or from its result; it is the treasure of grace communicated from above and originating in Jesus Christ. It is true that the priest is a delegate of the community inasmuch as he simply presides when the community assembles for prayer (although even here important qualifications are necessary). But when he consecrates or absolves he is something other and something more than a minister of the community; he is the minister of Jesus Christ.[8] Neither of the two aspects should be forgotten, either with regard to the Church or the Mass. There is a communal aspect, that of the community's prayer and praise. It is an aspect that may in a sense

[8] For this reason I do not consider some of the expressions used nowadays to be entirely correct and acceptable. I am thinking, for example of those used by J. A. Jungmann and E. Walter in their contribution to the interesting volume *Volks liturgie und Seelsorge*, von K. Borgmann (ed.), Colmar, 1942, pp. 28 and 41, respectively. On this point, cf. *Mediator Dei*.

be said to be the product of the Church on earth, and it is regrettable that the liturgy of the Mass should be restricted to forms in which such prayer, the *sacrificium laudis*, the communal expression of the people of God, finds little outlet. It has consequently sought an outlet in various kinds of 'paraliturgies'; the rosary, benediction, prayers after Mass, etc. These are good, but one may hope for a better state of things.

There is, however, in the Church, an hierarchic aspect, an institutional aspect bestowed from above. At present this aspect is not so much questioned as inadequately understood; it is not denied, it is even strongly emphasised. But its wonder and its meaning is not always appreciated. I shall be happy if I have helped you towards a better understanding of both these aspects.

CHAPTER FOURTEEN

The Eucharist and the Fulfilment of the World in God[1]

THE DOGMA OF THE EUCHARIST AFFIRMS THAT the 'substance' of the bread is 'converted' into the 'substance' of the body of Christ and that of the wine into the 'substance' of his blood. *Quod in carnem transit panis et vinum in sanguinem*—as St Thomas Aquinas expresses it in his hymn *Lauda Sion*.

The theology of St Thomas cannot be equated with dogma, but it holds such a position of authority in the Church, and its teaching on the Eucharist in particular has so few competitors, that it is on a different level from the work of an individual theologian and has almost become the common teaching of the Church. Now, one of the points of his teaching is that as regards the 'substance' of the bread, it neither remains together with the body of Christ, nor is it annihilated and its place taken by the body of Christ. 'God', he says, 'conjoins his divinity, that is his divine power, to the bread and wine not in such a way that the bread and wine remain, but that *thence* he may produce his body and blood (*ut faciat* inde *corpus et sanguinem suum*)'.[2] It follows that we cannot say that at one moment there is bread and wine, and then a moment when their 'substance' completely ceases to exist, and then a third moment when the 'substance' of the body and blood replaces the natural 'substance' of the elements, even though their outward appearance remains unaltered. In the

---

[1] An article published in *Bible et Terre Sainte*, no. 12, June 1958, pp. 2–4.
[2] *Sum. Theol.*, III, 75, 2, ad 1.

Eucharist there is no annihilation; there is a change or conversion of the bread into the body and of the wine into the blood.

I believe that the importance of this point of doctrine, its religious significance, is very significant. It is an explanation that seems to harmonise remarkably with two very important aspects of the Eucharist to which they are related, not perhaps to such an extent that without this connection these aspects would lack foundation, but as providing them with a very definite and felicitous support.

I shall not dwell for long on the first of these aspects; it really needs independent treatment, and, moreover, it is the better known. Excellent historical or theological explanations of the Mass[3] have shown how its celebration begins by men offering themselves to God under the sign of bread and wine. Humble offerings indeed, and it is difficult to see how they could be acceptable to the most holy God. And, in any case, how can man, earthbound and sinful as he is, succeed in reaching the throne of God?

And then the miracle occurs, God himself takes our place and fulfils the sacrifice. Even before this happened we could offer him only what we had already received from him, somewhat in the way that children can only celebrate their parents' birthdays by offering flowers gathered from their father's garden, or a present bought with money from their mother's purse. But what we are now considering is something much greater than this. Through transubstantiation, our humble offering is transformed into that of Christ, whilst still remaining our own, or rather that of the Church; this is why after the consecration, the liturgy continues to speak of the elements on the altar as *our* gifts and also as the offered body and blood of Christ. Ultimately it is always a question of that *admirabile commercium*, that wonderful exchange and intercourse, hymned in the Christmas liturgy, and of that principle in which the Fathers sum up God's whole purpose: He became man in order that we might become God! Our offering, and ourselves in and through it, can travel all the distance to God, because it has

[3] I am thinking particularly of Dom Gregory Dix, 'The idea of "the Church' in the primitive liturgies, in *The Parish Communion*, London, 1937, pp. 95–143, and *The Shape of the liturgy*, London, 1945; E. Masure, *Le Sacrifice du chef* (Engl. transl., *The Christian Sacrifice*, London, 1945), Paris, 1932.

been transformed into the supremely holy and effective offering of
Jesus Christ, which, in this way, retains its autonomy and yet is
extended to his mystical Body.

I intend to dwell at greater length on the second aspect.

Only a few of the early liturgical documents have come down to
us. But there is sufficient evidence to show that in those days the
Eucharist was in fact celebrated as an act of thanksgiving and that
this thanksgiving concerned two points: the benefaction of
creation and that of redemption (including the sanctification of
the people of God which flows from it). In some very early works
—the Didache, Hippolytus—as also in some more recent ones,
thanksgiving for the redemption would seem to be primary. But
the truth is that the thanksgiving refers to everything which God
has done for us. The first of his benefactions is creation which in
the great 'eucharistic' prayer, as in the Genesis narrative and in
the ancient Jewish liturgy, is presented as the first chapter of
sacred history or of the *Mirabilia Dei*.

This explains the way in which St Justin, in his *First Apology*
written about 152 in Rome, describes the Christian Eucharist.
The worship they give to God, he tells the emperor, consists in
making use of his gifts to them and to the poor 'by giving thanks
to him and addressing our hymns of praise to him for having
created us and provided us with the necessities for our welfare,
for the diversity of created things and the succession of the
seasons'.[4] A few lines later, in describing the actual celebration—
apart from the Didache, this is the earliest description we possess—
he writes: 'Then bread and a cup of wine mingled with water is
presented to him who presides over the brethren. He takes them
and gives praise and glory to the Father of the universe in the name
of the Son and the Holy Spirit, and expresses heartfelt thanksgiving for the fact that God has given us these things'.[5]

Thirty years after Justin, St Irenaeus, the greatest theologian
and the most important witness to Tradition in the second century, has a phrase, rich in meaning, that is even closer to our subject: *in the Eucharist, we offer to God the first-fruits of creation.*
The context shows that he is here referring not to Christ but
definitely to the first-fruits of the created world. We shall, there-

[4] *I Apol.* 13 (*PG* 6, 345).
[5] *Ibid.*, 65 (Col. 428).

fore, set aside other evidence—some of it slightly later than Irenaeus,[6] and also a considerable amount in the fourth century[7]—and confine ourselves to the context and the precise idea which Irenaeus himself had in mind: in the Eucharist we offer the first-fruits of the created world, as a gesture of thanksgiving for God's gift.

For what in reality are the bread and wine that make up our offering? They are products of the soil that are both lowly and magnificent, common and noble. They are comparatively natural products, but these have been developed,[8] and this in two stages: the first is the actual cultivation both of wheat and the vine—the latter being a matter of considerable difficulty; the second is the work that transforms the wheat into bread and grapes into wine. Thus what we offer is not only the first-fruits of the created world but the sign and first-fruits of the work through which man completes that world and ennobles it by raising it to the level of a human culture and human usage.[9]

Moreover, the position occupied by bread and wine in human usage is no ordinary one; their value as signs is of special significance, and is explicitly in the Scriptures. Bread nourishes the worker and renews his strength;[10] it is ordained to the activities of life. And bread is essentially something that is shared. In the New Testament when bread is mentioned, the image is evoked of a father who takes a loaf, pronounces a thanksgiving over it, breaks it and divides it among those at table with him.[11] Bread is essen-

[6] For St Irenaeus, cf. *Adv. Haeres*, 4, 18, 1 (*PG*, 7, 10245); cf. 4, 17, 5 (Col. 10235) and E. Scharl, *Recapitulatio mundi*, Freiburg, 1941. After Irenaeus, cf. Tertullian, *Adv. Marc.* 1, 14; Clement of Alexandria, *Strom*, 7, 3, 6.

[7] Cf. *The Anaphora of Serapion* (5, 339–60), and especially the *Apostolic constitutions*, *Anaphora*, 8, 12, 5f, quoted below. In the liturgies of St Basil and of St John Chrysostom, between the words of institution and the epiclesis, note the phrase '*In everything and for everything*, we offer to you what is yours and what we have received from you.'

[8] Cf. Ps 104, 14–15: 'He bringeth forth grass for the cattle: and green herb for the service of men; that he may bring food out of the earth, and wine that maketh glad the heart of men.'

[9] This aspect of the eucharistic mystery has been well expounded by Fr H. M. Féret, 'La messe, rassemblement de la communauté' in *La messe et sa catéchèse* (*Lex Orandi*, 7), Paris, 1947, pp. 205f; cf J. Mouroux, *Le sens chrétien de l'homme*, Paris, 1945, pp. 38f.

[10] Cf. Mt 6:11, parallel; 2 Th 3:12; Jg 19:5.

[11] Cf. *Strack-Billerbeck*, vol. 4, pp. 620f; *TWB*, 2 *NT* by Kittel, vol. p. 475.

tially something which sustains life, but also something that one shares (cf. Jn 13:18), and thanks to which life can be enjoyed in common.

This note of joy is even more dominant when the Bible mentions wine.[12] Its abundance is a sign of God's blessing. In our Lord's thought and sayings wine is also connected with the idea of newness, it foretells a new, kindly and joyful order of things, beyond the sorrows of the present. It has the significance of a promise.[13]

Clearly it was not without deliberate intent and not without result that Jesus chose these signs of his Eucharist which, as celebrated by the Church in memory of him until his return, are first of all signs of our own humble offering. Bread and wine are symbolic; in our offering or our thanksgiving, they stand for the created world, launched into existence by God and then, as it were, left by him to be completed through human industry.[14] These signs are truly the first-fruits of the created world, but developed by man and implying the hope of a renewal by God: that fresh start or culmination or renewal for which creation yearns (Rm 8:20).

Now throughout the New Testament this fresh start, completion or renewal, with man as its living centre, is shown as necessarily accomplished in and through Christ. When St Paul speaks of being 'in Christ', he means first of all 'through Christ'. The texts are well known, and we shall only consider the foremost of them, those whose theology is most developed. It has been clearly shown, however, that the gospels, even the Synoptics, contain many statements or references which presuppose and support the same doctrine.[15] This doctrine is that Christ is the origin and con-

[12] Cf. Ps 104:15 (*supra* note 8); Jg 9:13; Si 31:27; Zh 10:9.
[13] Cf. Mk 2:22 and par.; 14:25 and par.; and Jn 2, the marriage at Cana.
[14] After he had created the world and man, God in a sense withdrew and left man to develop his creation: Cf. Gn 1:26f; 2, 2, 5, 15.
[15] Cf. J. Jeremias, *Jesus als Welt vollender*, Gütersloh, 1930—on the cosmic outlook of the New Testament, cf. E. Drinkwelder, *Vollendung in Christus*, Paderborn, 1934; Fr Meister, *Die Vollendung der Welt im Opfer des Gottmenschen*, Freiburg, 1938; H. Biedermann, *Die Erlösung der Schöpfung beim Apostel Paulus*, Würzburg, 1940; A. Frank-Duguesne, *Cosmos et gloire* . . ., Paris 1947 (Catholic); M. Goguel, 'Le caractère et le rôle de l'élément cosmologique dans le sotériologie de S. Paul,' in *RHPR*, 1935, pp. 335-59. A. D. Galloway, *The Cosmic Christ*, London, 1951. (The last two are Protestant.)

clusion of everything God has made, because, in his own being, in a manner beyond anything we could have imagined, he *constitutes* the union between God and his creation. 'All things were created by him and for him (Col 1:16; cf. 1 Co 8:6, and the theme of Christ the Alpha and Omega in Rv 1:8; 21:6; 22:13)'.

It follows from this that God's purpose, in its concluding (eschatological) phase, entails the fact that all things shall be drawn to him. In them he will reign and in his reign they will find their fulfilment. And this is to be brought about by the establishment of Jesus Christ as the Head, the unifying principle, the completely comprehensive reality that includes and brings to perfection all things, not mankind only but the world itself. 'He purposes . . . that everything that exists in heaven or earth shall find its perfection and fulfilment in him (Christ)' (Ep 1:10.) 'It was in him that the full nature of God chose to live, and through him God planned to reconcile, in his own person, as it were, everything on earth and everything in heaven by virtue of the sacrifice of the cross' (Col 1:19–20).

It is thus foretold and promised, not, doubtless, that all men individually will be saved, but that creation as a whole, with mankind as its living and conscious centre, will be brought back to God in Christ (through Christ) with Christ as its Head.

It is certainly easier to gain an insight into this amazing plan if, with the abundant help provided by Scripture,[16] we express it in terms of the Temple. (1) In the messianic régime, that of the new and eternal alliance, there is no other Temple of God than the body of Christ who died and rose again (cf. Jn 2:19f). (2) Eschatologically, that is, in that concluding phase referred to by St Paul, the whole world will again become the Temple of God; this will be accomplished in and through Jesus Christ.[17] (3) The last stage of this work of God in and through Christ is indicated in those passages which provide an inexhaustible subject matter for our religious meditation and theological development.

Then, and not till then, comes the End, when Christ having

[16] For what follows cf. our *Mystère du Temple* (Engl. transl., *Mystery of the Temple*. London & Westminster, Md, 1962), (*Lectio divina* 22), Paris, 1958.

[17] Hence the words with such depth of meaning in the Martyrology at Christmas and in the great Preface at the ordination of deacons.

abolished all other rule, authority and power, hands over the Kingdom to God the Father. Christ's reign will and must continue until every enemy has been conquered (Ps 110:1). And when everything created has been made obedient to God, then shall the Son acknowledge himself subject to him who gave him power over all things. Thus God shall be all in all. (1 Co 15:24–5, 28).

I saw the Holy City, the New Jerusalem, descending from God out of heaven . . . I heard a great voice from the throne crying, 'See! The home of God is with men, and *he will live among them*; *they shall be his people*, and *God himself shall be with them*' (Ex 37:27; Is 8:8). . . . Then he who is seated upon the throne said, 'See, I am making all things new. . . . He pointed out to me the City, the Holy Jerusalem, descending from God out of heaven, *radiant with the glory of God* . . . I could see no Temple in the City, for the Lord, the Almighty God, and the Lamb, are themselves its Temple' (Rv 21:2a, 3, 5a, 10b, 11a, 22).

The culmination of the world's development is thus clearly stated as a condition of inner relationship as perfect as is possible without involving the contradiction of pantheism. God, perfectly present in all things, and the world existing in Jesus Christ and, through him, in God—this will be the final Temple: the Temple of perfect mutual Presence, of an existence lived perfectly, each for the other.

Now the Eucharist is the pledge that all this will come about. It is in very truth the sacrament of the *new* and *eternal* alliance. For this bread and wine which represent the first fruits of the created world, and also, at the same time, our own humble offering, the sign of our approach to God in search of communion with him, is now changed by Jesus into his body and blood. Moreover, he does this, we repeat, through a 'conversion' which means that the bread and wine are not annihilated, but form the starting point from which Jesus gives us, as our sustenance for eternal life, the sacred reality of his body and blood, his manhood and his godhead. Thus an element that represents both him and us together, our common lowliness and our common nobility, is, at the very moment when we are using it as a means of thanksgiving for all things, changed into the perfect praise and the Temple of the living body of Jesus Christ. And thus transubstantiated, it returns to us as food, not to be assimilated into our mortal and transitory bodies, like ordinary food, but for us to be assimilated to him in his incorruptible existence: the eschatological bread, the living bread of everlasting life.

I find particular pleasure in quoting here a difficult but instructive passage from Maurice Blondel, written in 1893. It shows the depth and catholicity of mind of a man who was for long suspect, but whose influence is now becoming important in many spheres of Catholic thought:

> Transubstantiation, by substituting the *Vinculum ipsius Christi* for the natural reality of the bread and wine, is seen to be the prelude, the mysteriously veiled prelude of the ultimate assimilation, the supreme incorporation of all things in the incarnate Word: *Verbum caro factum ut caro omnia assimilarentur Deo per Incarnatum* . . . (In this way preparation is being made for that) spiritual configuration which, without confusion and without identification of substance, is completed in the transforming union which is the normal conclusion of the spiritual life and of sacramental communion. For if the things of earth are destined to be transposed into a new earth and a new heaven where the Word, *Alpha Omega, primogenitus omnis creaturae*, will be the sole light, the only food and the universal bond, *in quo omnia constant*, then for spiritual beings the *vinculum* is not a suffocating destruction of identity, but an embrace which unites and yet respects their nature; it has a certain analogical resemblance to that *osculum* of the Spirit which consummates the unity of the Trinity itself.[18]

What more can I say? Is it not better to leave the matter for personal reflection? I shall simply conclude not with any further difficulty, but with a scene from a novel, *Lord of the World*, by R. H. Benson, published some years ago (1908). It is more than and different from a novel about the future—more than a mere novel about the 'end of the world'. It is an eschatological novel.

[18] *Une énigme historique, le 'vinculum substantiale' d'après Leibnitz et l'ébauche d'un réalisme supérieur*, Paris, 1930, pp. 1930, pp. 105–6. (French adaptation of a Latin thesis written in 1893.)

It is a description not only of the end of the world, but of the consummation of all things. The last pope has fled to Bethlehem. There he celebrates not Mass or the Eucharist—we should have preferred that he had—but benediction of the Blessed Sacrament. The end of the world occurs during the singing of the *Tantum ergo*. The transubstantiated bread of the earth is absorbed into the supreme reality of Christ who is about to make all things new. The harvest is following the first-fruits, the world is completing the development signified, during the Church's existence on earth, by the destiny of the bread and wine, cultivated, processed and offered in memory of what Christ had done and in the expectation of what he will do one day—*when he returns*.

APPENDIX

Text of the 'Preface' in the Apostolic Constitutions. (Fourth century)

It is truly right and fitting that we should glorify thee, first of all, God truly existing before all created things, and from whom all fatherhood in heaven and on earth is named. Thou art the uncaused knowledge, the eternal vision, the unbegotten wisdom.

Thou has brought all things from nothingness to existence through thine only Son, whom thou has spiritually begotten before all ages, the Word of God, the living Wisdom, the First-Born of every creature, the Angel of Great Counsel, the high priest and king of all spiritual and material reality.

Through him thou hast made before all things the cherubim and seraphim, the aeons and the heavenly hosts, the archangels and the angels, the principalities and thrones; and after them, this visible cosmos itself and all things in it.

It is thou who hast established the sky as a dome and extended it as a tent, and hast set the earth over the abyss by thy will alone. It is thou who hast created the firmament and established night and day. It is thou who hast called forth the light from its hiding-place and then made it cover the darkness as with a garment, for the joy of all living beings who move about the world.

It is thou who hast established the sun to rule over the day and the moon to rule over the night and hast made the order of the stars as a choir to praise thy majesty. It is thou who hast filled and adorned the world with sweet-smelling and health-giving plants.

And thou hast not only created the cosmos, but hast made man as a citizen in the cosmos and like a cosmos within the cosmos. For thou didst say to thy Wisdom: let us make man in our image and likeness. And let him rule over the fish of the sea and the birds of the sky.

Thou didst bring him into the Paradise of delight, and when he ate the forbidden fruit, thou didst rightly drive him from

Paradise, but in thy goodness thou didst not abandon him who was completely lost, for he was thy creature.

And not only that, but among all his countless descendants, thou hast punished those who turned from thee and glorified those who remained with thee.

Thou didst receive Abel's offering because he was a devout man, and didst reject Cain's because it came from a man stained with sin. And later thou didst accept Enos and Seth and took Enoch to heaven.

Thou art indeed the creator of men, the guide of life, the benefactor of the poor. Thou art the lawgiver, and dost reward those who keep thy laws and punish those who break them.

It is thou who brought the great flood upon the world because of the host of sinners. . . . It is thou who sent the terrible fire upon the five cities of the plain. . . . It is thou who didst ordain Melchisedech. . . .

For all things, glory be to thee, O Lord, the Almighty.

Addendum, 1961

Recent German works that deal with the subject discussed above: W. Dürig, *Die Eucharistie ale Sinn-Bilder der Consecratio-Mundi*, in *München. Theol. Zeitsch.* 10 (1959), pp. 283–8. A. Auer, *Die Eucharistie als Weg der Welt in der Erfüllung*, in *Geist and Leben*, 33 (1960), pp. 192–206. L. Scneffczyk, *Die materielle Welt in lichte der Eucharistie* in *Aktuelle Fragen zur Eucharistie*, hrsg. V. M. Schmaus, Munich, 1960, pp. 156–79 and 190–94. Ad. W. Ziegler, *Das Brot von unseren Feldern* in *Pro Mundi Vita, Festschrift der Theolog. Fakultät München*, 1960, Munich, 1960, pp. 21–43.